Amateur Images and Global News

For Alma, Emma and Stella, our best works

Amateur Images and Global News

Edited by Kari Andén-Papadopoulos and Mervi Pantti

intellect Bristol, UK / Chicago, USA

First published in the UK in 2011 by
Intellect, The Mill, Parnall Road, Fishponds, Bristol, BS16 3JG, UK

First published in the USA in 2011 by
Intellect, The University of Chicago Press, 1427 E. 60th Street,
Chicago, IL 60637, USA

A catalogue record for this book is available from the
British Library.

Cover designer: Holly Rose
Copy-editor: Macmillan
Typesetting: Mac Style, Beverley, E. Yorkshire

ISBN 978-1-84150-420-9

Printed and bound by Hobbs, UK.

Contents

Acknowledgements

The editors would like to thank all colleagues who contributed to this book. Our thanks also go to the Swedish Research Council and to the Helsingin Sanomat Foundation for their financial support.

Introduction

Kari Andén-Papadopoulos and Mervi Pantti

In recent years, amateur photography and video have become a powerful – and problematic – new source for professional news organizations. The rapid rise of digital communication technologies, and with it the widespread take-up of camcorders and camera-equipped telephones, has encouraged 'ordinary' citizens to participate in the making of news. As this book sets out to demonstrate, amateur images have come to have cultural significance and shape public perceptions of world events mainly because of their dissemination and publication in the mainstream news media. While the news industry has used amateur film and photography in the past, some of the most memorable examples being the film of the Kennedy assassination and the videotape of the Rodney King beating, there has been an explosion of imagery from non-professionals over the past years. In addition to these images having become more common, they are today circulated with an unprecedented speed in a complex, global media environment. The starting point of this book is that the rapid rise of amateur photography as a new resource for journalism's representation of reality raises important questions that call for careful analysis and critique. Such images warrant close attention in their own right (e.g. their production, their evidential status and their aesthetics), but also with regard to their significance for journalism and its capacity to relay events of central importance to public life.

In this book, the terms 'non-professional images' and 'private images' are often used as synonyms for amateur images, but they all refer to images, both still and moving, that originate from *outside* the professional media. The fundamental characteristic of amateur imagery is that it is not governed by the same standards of ethics, or aesthetics, as professional photojournalism. When these 'outsider' images are pulled into the coverage of mainstream news, their often personal point of view, their aesthetic quality or their 'untamed' (graphic) content, may clash with the standards and values of professional journalism. In the context of journalism, however, the very phenomenon of the 'amateur image' is not a simple one; rather it entails many forms, including breaking news images, photographs from the family album that are used to illustrate, for example, crime stories, and audience members' pictures of their holidays, pets or weather that are often published in news organizations' online photo albums. Accordingly, amateur images are perceived and used in the mainstream organizations, on the one hand, as sources of information, and, on the other hand, as entertainment and as a means of bonding with the audience (Pantti and Bakker 2009). In this book, we focus on amateur images as news sources since it is in this function that they evoke crucial ethical issues, for example what is deemed acceptable to show? How to confirm the reliability of imagery originating from external and oftentimes anonymous sources? And how to deal with the blurring of the boundaries between an 'objective' observer of events and a participant with an interested perspective?

The significance of the study of amateur news images hinges on the rising importance of photography as an all-pervading social practice and mode of public communication in the digital era. Theorists of visual culture have stressed the centrality of visual images to how we represent, make meaning and communicate in today's world. Over the course of the last two centuries, western culture has come to be dominated by visual and sound-based media (i.e. cinema, television, the computer) that play the central role in daily life once occupied by oral or textual media. As W. J. T. Mitchell (1994: 15) points out, 'the era of video and cybernetic technology, the age of electronic reproduction, has developed new forms of visual simulation and illusionism with unprecedented powers'. In the early twenty-first century, we live in cultures that are increasingly permeated by digital images and imaging technologies that allow for the global circulation of ideas and information in visual forms. We are thus at a moment in history in which images are at the forefront of efforts to negotiate, interrogate, memorialize and create the individual and collective experiences of social realities.

In the context of journalism, the power of visual images to inflame emotions, to iconize global events and to shape our knowledge and memory of international conflict and crisis has been considered by numerous media scholars (e.g. Andén-Papadopoulos 2008; Hariman and Lucaites 2007; Perlmutter 1998; Roeder 1993; Taylor 1991, 1998; Zelizer 1998, 2002, 2004). It has been proposed that visualness is one of the most dominant news values of our times, that is the availability of compelling images determines whether an event is selected as news or not. As John Corner (1995: 59) states, '[T]he offer of "seeing", is absolutely central to the project of television journalism, to its impact, memorability, and public power as well as to its commodity value'. Photographic realism has helped journalism prove its own on-site presence, so crucial in marking the credibility and authenticity of journalistic reports. Because of their perceived status as transparent records of the real, still and moving images have served the key function of guaranteeing the objectivity and truth-value of news reporting (Zelizer 1998, 2007; Taylor 1991, 1998). The rise of 24/7 news and the increasing centrality of live coverage – as a means of projecting the sense that the news organization is in fact *there* – has made the value of compelling visuals evermore central to professional journalism. Traditional newspapers have also become more dependent on visuals, not only because they are increasingly design-driven in order to attract viewers but also because of having online platforms for displaying (an unlimited number of) images (Bridge and Sjøvaag 2009).

The Proliferation of Audience Content

In the emerging 'participatory media culture' (Jenkins 2006), members of the public are more likely to be regarded as active participants, rather than as passive consumers. The term 'web 2.0' describes a new generation of web-based services that emphasize social networking, collaboration and participation, evidently heralding a new digital era in which control seems to be shifting from established institutions to ad hoc groupings of users. Public trust in the 'old' 'media appears to be eroding, with 'new' media alternatives gaining in popularity. It would seem, therefore, that this is a crucial moment in the history of journalism. The need to develop strategies for addressing the challenges ushered in by an increasingly global, networked media environment is a pressing priority for mainstream news organizations, and the development of participatory forms of content production is becoming key to legitimacy, revenue and competitive force (e.g. Domingo et al. 2008; Paulussen et al. 2007). Established media across the world are experimenting with the involvement of citizens in the production of news. This is linked with both the practical need for low-cost news and the normative-theoretical ideal of citizens as 'collaborators' with professional journalists – rather than providers of raw material – in the processes of newsgathering, selection and publication.

In contrast to 'citizen journalism' where the news-making process is removed from the hands of journalists and controlled by citizens, in so-called participatory journalism the citizen involvement takes place within the framework and control of professional journalism. In journalism studies, a large body of literature has examined how the new forms of audience participation have affected the professional culture of journalism. Previous studies have examined professional journalists' attitudes towards participatory practices and mapped the range of formats used by news organizations to enable contributions from the public (e.g. Allan and Thorsen 2009; Cedersjö and Gustavsson 2009; Chung 2007; Deuze et al. 2007; Domingo et al. 2008; Hermida and Thurman 2008; Paulussen et al. 2004; Singer 2005; Thurman 2008; Örnebring 2008; Williams, Wardle and Wahl-Jorgensen 2010). These studies, mainly focusing on textual contributions from the public (blogs, comments and conversations), typically conclude that while news organizations are opening their doors to citizen contributions, traditional gatekeeping and editing are still features of participatory journalism. Most news organizations appear to be incorporating audience material by 'normalizing' it to fit traditional journalistic norms and practices (Singer 2005).

Today, nearly all news organizations actively solicit digital photography and video from their audience members, especially when a major news story is breaking, which they then process before considering its possible deployment in cross-media platforms: online news websites, newspapers and television newscasts. Moreover, news organizations are also quick to tap into distribution channels for amateur material, such as personal blogs and social networking sites, such as YouTube, Flickr, Facebook and Twitter. The enthusiasm with which mainstream news organizations have included amateur photography in their coverage testifies to the value of such material to the news agenda and news narratives. It used to be that most dramatic news events had typically already taken place by the time the journalists arrived at the scene. As Corner (1995: 59) points out, 'in these cases news typically recounts *what happened* against images which show spaces and places *after* the event'. In order to provide items with visual 'presence', news teams normally turn to tricks such as reconstructions, staging and the use of previously shot material.

The most important characteristic of amateur news images, then, is that they provide content that the news organizations cannot produce themselves, that is, eyewitness recordings of events as they unfold. Accordingly, as recent studies have shown, amateur photography is appreciated by professional journalists first and foremost because of its capacity to provide visual coverage from locations where professional journalists either do not have access or are simply not present in time (Pantti and Bakker 2009; Williams, Wardle and Wahl-Jorgensen 2010). Journalists – as well as audiences – value amateur visuals for their perceived immediacy, authenticity and proximity. Amateur images are judged to be more 'authentic' because they typically are dim, grainy and shaky, but more importantly, because they constitute first-hand recordings by individuals who witnessed or experienced an event as it was actually happening. In this regard, amateur imagery is contrasted with the impersonal, detached approach of professional journalists who, besides being expected to provide an objective perspective on events, often have a formulaic, pre-selected point of view (Williams, Wardle and Wahl-Jorgensen 2010).

Not surprisingly, then, the visuals of breaking news by amateur photographers, such as the first images from the London bombings showing people making their way out of smoke-filled carriages or the dramatic video footage showing Japan's tsunami waves carrying cars, ships and houses inland, constitute the most embraced type of user-generated content (UGC) in the mainstream news media. Owing to their supreme news value, they often lead broadcast news and the front pages of newspapers around the world. Some of them also become iconic images of the events and even media events in themselves, such as the cell phone video of the killing of Neda Aghan-Soltan during the 2009 post-election protests in Iran. While a great majority of the amateur images that are offered to news organizations are characterized by their *lack* of news value (Pantti and Bakker 2009), such exceptional cases of breaking news amateur visuals are in return highly visible. They typically enter public circulation with an extraordinary force and become key referents for subsequent public debate about 'what really happened' and often for political, emotional and humanitarian responses to the event too (see Corner 1995: 61). Especially in the contexts of war and conflict, amateur photographers are playing an ever more significant role in providing imagery of a strongly evidential and affective character, which at times challenge or even disrupt the official framings of the events (e.g. Andén-Papadopoulos 2008, 2009). A case in point is the amateur photographs of Iraqi prisoners being tortured and humiliated by US soldiers in the notorious Abu Ghraib prison that, due to their worldwide circulation, grew into a major threat to the legitimacy of the US occupation of Iraq.

Amateur Images and Global Journalism

While still largely dominated by western news corporations and news flows from the 'West to the rest', today's global media landscape also, as Cottle (2009a: xi) points out, 'incorporates established and emergent non-Western news formations and a plethora of alternative news forms and outlets generating news contra-flows and/or circulating oppositional views and voices – from the "rest to the West", the local to the global'. The fast-developing rise of citizen photography, then, can be seen to challenge or recast traditional hierarchies and relations of communicative power, thereby posing new questions about how the 'local' is rendered 'global' via processes of journalistic mediation. For the typically hyper-local and modest amateur snapshot to be transformed into a global media event, it must do so through today's more 'complex news media ecology' with its circulating communication flows as well as various local and regional counterflows, oppositional contraflows and alternative forms of citizen and online journalism (Cottle 2009b: 17). However, as Cottle (2009b) shows, for local crises to register as issues of global importance, concern and possible action, they continue to depend principally on prominent exposure in the established mainstream news media. And contemporary news organizations are, as we have seen, certainly tuned in to the added value that first-hand recordings by ordinary citizens can now bring when incorporated into their own news frames and narratives – especially when reporting crises and catastrophes.

Amateur imagery is often credited with providing global journalism with a new kind of closeness, that is, a 'raw', immediate, intensely subjective perspective on crisis events through the eyes of ordinary people struggling to bear witness to the scene around them. Images taken by involved citizens promise to eradicate former barriers of physical and social distance between spectators and sufferers seen in the media. In some cases, then, the presumption may be that amateur recordings will afford a heightened sense of emotional identification (see Chouliaraki 2008), and yet there can be no guarantee that they will necessarily narrow the distance between the structural interests of 'people like us' and the suffering of strangers. Critics have indeed used the derisive term 'snapparazzi' (Allan 2006: 155) to characterize the actions of citizens snapping pictures of breaking news events, indicating that such imagery might play into sensationalism and voyeurism and even be fraught with the risk of dehumanization. As Roger Silverstone (2006) points out in his seminal discussion on 'proper distance', closeness and intimacy do not guarantee commitment and responsibility. Rather, audiences' moral engagement with the lives and misfortunes of distant others is contingent on the specific parameters of how the sufferer is depicted in a particular image and on how the scene of suffering is narrated in a particular news discourse.

Commentators recurrently identify the aftermath of the South Asian tsunami of December 2004 as the decisive moment when eyewitness accounts and imagery by ordinary citizens became a prominent feature of mainstream media's breaking news coverage (Allan 2006, 2009). Virtually all of the most newsworthy images of the catastrophe were taken not by professionals, but by victims and witnesses who happened to be at the scene of the tragic events. 'Never before has there been a major international story where television news crews have been so emphatically trounced in their coverage by amateurs wielding their own cameras', noted one British newspaper. 'Producers and professional news cameramen often found themselves being sent not to the scenes of disaster to capture footage of its aftermath, but to the airports where holidaymakers were returning home with footage of the catastrophe as it happened' (*The Independent*, 3 January 2005; cit. in Allan 2009: 7).

The two crises that unfolded in the summer of 2005, the 7 July bombings in London and the devastation created by Hurricane Katrina the following month, seemed to consolidate the transformation of the news-gathering process brought about by the rapidly spreading phenomenon of citizen reporting. In both cases, citizen eyewitness imagery and stories made vital contributions to the reporting of unfolding events, giving striking evidence of the extent to which mainstream news organizations were now relying on citizens to provide them with information and images of what was happening on the scene. On 7 July, journalists were denied access to London Underground stations due to tight security, which meant that they were prevented from recording the aftermath of the explosions. Instead, the images that defined the media coverage of the terrorist bombings came from ordinary Londoners caught in the attacks. Commuters trapped underground used their camera phones to capture the perspective of people making their way out of smoke and soot-filled carriages, while other citizen footage documented the rescue efforts that took place above ground. Within minutes after the attacks, the grainy still and video images made their way to blogs, photo-sharing websites, online news websites and TV news. The personal, immediate feel of these blurry amateur images apparently made them all the more compelling, proving a powerful way to improve reporting by providing a human perspective directly through the eyes of those involved in the tragic events. Later in the summer of 2005, in the immediate aftermath of the wreck caused by Hurricane Katrina along the Gulf Coast in the United States, citizen news-gathering again took centre stage. People caught up in the disaster were posting poignant eyewitness texts, images and videos online, thereby helping to narrow the information gap arising in the absence of reporters and photographers on the scene of breaking events. According to Mitch Gelman, executive vice president of CNN.com, more than 3000 files with hundreds of images and video were e-mailed to CNN.com over the first three days, many of which included heartrending scenes. Gelman, like many other representatives of major news organizations, readily acknowledged the important ways in which this amateur material was augmenting professional news coverage, testifying to its extraordinary capacity to take 'our online audience into the heart and soul of the story' (*TechWeb News*, 1 September 2005; cit. in Allan 2006: 161).

In the case of events such as the September 11 attacks in 2001, the South Asian tsunami in 2004 and the London bombings in 2005, amongst others, the availability of eyewitness record from individuals who simply happened to be at the scene afforded vital perspectives and, arguably, enriched the quality of journalistic reporting. The public sharing of amateur images of the Mumbai attacks in November 2008, the post-election protests in Iran in June 2009 or eyewitness imagery in the early hours of the earthquake in Haiti in January 2010 and of the Japan earthquake and tsunami in March 2011 can be seen as further turning points in this regard, effectively demonstrating how citizens may have an increasingly important role to play in crisis coverage by bringing events to international prominence. However, it should also be noted that while new user-friendly technology has no doubt empowered people to make their voices heard, we should keep in mind that the 'digital divide' still exists and that access to this technology and the skills in handling it are not democratically distributed. A crucial question in this respect is whether the availability of dramatic amateur images shapes what is considered a newsworthy story.

Hence, insofar as amateur images are becoming an increasingly important component in the news media's reporting on distant crisis events, then they play a recurrently decisive role in shaping how audiences collectively recognize and respond to such events. For researchers concerned with communication in the digital age, and specifically with the ethical status of global mediated culture, it is of central importance to consider how amateur images represent distant people and events, how they are embedded into particular news texts and what their significance is in developing audiences' moral and political engagement with international crisis events.

The Contribution of Chapters in this Volume

Amateur Images and Global News aims at providing a more nuanced and empirically based understanding of the contexts and uses of amateur imagery in the mainstream media and of how it is perceived and valued by journalists and audiences. The collection strives to shed critical light on the ways in which the evolving trend of citizen camera-reporting is recasting the traditional practices and standards of journalism. In so doing, it engages with several of the most significant topics for this important area of inquiry from a range of critical perspectives. The chapters discuss different aspects, contexts and types of non-professional images, with a special focus on their role and impact vis-à-vis crisis events such as armed conflict and school shootings. Calling upon the expertise of scholars from numerous countries, each with an interest in the ethics and practices of amateur images in the context of global news media, the book is divided into three sections. Part I sets the scene for the book's discussion by considering, from varied historical and theoretical perspectives, the changing relationship between professional journalism and its amateur alternatives, that is images from private cameras. Part II examines the specific ways in which amateur images have been appropriated and used by established news media in a contemporary global context. Part III looks at the circulation of amateur images within an expanded and fragmented new media landscape and explores how actual audiences perceive the value and truthfulness of amateur images.

Part I: Histories

Drawing on historical examples and various journalistic genres, Karin Becker (Chapter 1) identifies specific strategies that professional journalism has employed in order to make the amateur photograph fit the constraints of an ethical journalism. She makes the case that each of these strategies takes as their point of departure the need to add distance to the emotional excess and sensational closeness of the 'outsider' image. Visual, audio and textual means are shown to be employed in order to 'tame' the non-professional image and reframe it within a journalistic discourse characterized by proper distance.

Stuart Allan (Chapter 2) adopts a historical perspective in order to explore the contributions made by the 'amateur' to the emergence and evolution of war photography. He identifies and critiques examples of amateur combat photography across several conflicts, ranging from the 1840s to the close of World War I. Such an approach, Allan demonstrates, casts new light on the challenges facing citizen photojournalism today, not least with regard to the amateur photographer's moral responsibilities where visual truth-telling in the warzone is concerned.

The moral implications of the new centrality of the citizen eyewitness as recorder of current news events is also the focus of Mette Mortensen's contribution (Chapter 3). She argues that the contemporary citizen photojournalist should be conceptualized as a 'web 2.0 incarnation of the eyewitness', that is, as a successor to the historical figure of the witness with its perceived moral, cultural and political authority. Mortensen draws on the rich theoretical literature on the witness – by literary, psychoanalytic, philosophical and media scholars – in order to provide a framework for defining the non-professional producer of images arising over the past decade. Subjective and involved, the private citizens now increasingly filling in as photographic eyewitnesses render the space of media witnessing more contested than ever before.

Part II: Practices

Helle Sjøvaag (Chapter 4) discusses to what extent journalistic authority is threatened by the substitution of amateur images of breaking news events for professionally produced images. She analyses how the two main Norwegian television news organizations, NRK and TV 2, incorporated amateur images into their coverage of the London bombings in 2005 and the assassination of Benazir Bhutto on 27 December 2007. The case studies show that mainstream television news is able to maintain editorial authority by using narrative strategies to incorporate amateur images into the journalistic product, thereby retaining narrative authority over user-generated visual material.

Mervi Pantti and Kari Andén-Papadopoulos (Chapter 5) consider another breaking news event, the Iranian street protests in the wake of the disputed presidential elections in June 2009. Their focus is on how mainstream news organizations handle the challenges that eyewitness amateur imagery raises for professional ethics, specifically for the standards of accuracy and the use of graphic images. The authors explore how the eyewitness footage captured by 'ordinary' Iranians was integrated to the news coverage of the transnational channel CNN and three national public service news channels, YLE in Finland, SVT in Sweden and BBC in the United Kingdom. Addressing the question of whether these news organizations adhere to the rising ethical norm of transparency – deemed crucial in the networked media environment – the authors make the case that the use of amateur imagery of the Iran post-election crisis also became a test case for traditional journalistic standards of accuracy and responsibility.

Ray Niekamp (Chapter 6) examines amateur videos of the Hurricane Ike story in the US media and the different standards applied to video shot by non-professionals compared to professional shooting and editing standards. He singles out for special attention amateur video submitted to the CNN's iReport website, examining the aesthetic quality of this imagery in terms of its photography and editing. Niekamp shows that the aesthetic quality of amateur video is far below the standards of professional photojournalism; Images that would not have been broadcast in the past, he argues, are passing muster now because of their immediacy and authenticity.

Johanna Sumiala and Marguerite Moritz, respectively, consider what the latter terms 'a macabre form of participatory journalism', namely the ways in which mass murderers' own homemade videos are gaining visibility over national and international news networks. Sumiala (Chapter 7) explores how the killers' self-portraits in the case of the two Finnish school shootings (Jokela in 2007 and Kauhajoki in 2008) were incorporated into the news media. She makes the case that the excessive circulation and massive visibility of the Jokela and Kauhajoki shooter imagery in the Finnish media made the killers 'celebrities of the dark', in particular since the victims were all but invisible in the news coverage. The issue of how contemporary journalism deals with photographic materials that allow the school shooters themselves to shape their own public images and circulate their heroic self-portraits is also the focus of Moritz' contribution (Chapter 8). She singles out for special attention how journalists reflect on their own standards and practices in reporting such crimes. Taking the Jokela and Kauhajoki shootings as a case in point, her chapter is based on interviews with Finnish journalists, all of whom played prominent roles in the coverage of the shootings. The interviews reveal journalists expressing deep concern over being manipulated by the killers into glorifying their acts by showing their videos, being especially fearful that these would spark copycat killings. Moritz points out that the Finnish school shooting cases suggest that reader and viewer concerns do have a significant impact, forcing journalists to examine their choices and to acknowledge that they have a variety of options in their choice, framing and repetition of images.

Part III: Circulations

Liam Kennedy (Chapter 9) explores the flourishing phenomenon of serving US soldiers who are photographing their experiences in Afghanistan and Iraq and posting them on the Internet. In considering the distinctive visual language and the functions of this 'amateur' soldier imagery, he makes the case that it is disruptive of the conventional flows of news and has become a major issue of concern for both military and media elites. This photography offers compelling, real-time perspectives on the American soldier at war that suggestively supplement if not challenge other forms of visual knowledge about the conflicts in Iraq and Afghanistan. In different ways, Kennedy shows, this imagery illuminates aspects of American military culture that are officially disavowed and only rarely documented, and has thus introduced a fascinating uncertainty into the documentation of warfare that military and media elites are struggling to contain.

While a significant body of scholarly work has been devoted to the production practices and journalistic cultures surrounding audience material, less attention has been paid to the audiences who produce and consume the content. Chapters 10 and 11 seek to fill this gap by examining how audiences value the use of amateur audio-visual material in mainstream news coverage. Drawing on interviews with Finnish newspaper readers, Liina Puustinen and Janne Seppänen (Chapter 10) investigate whether or not, and for what reasons, readers place trust in images taken by non-professionals. The authors show that amateur images are perceived as equally trustworthy or even more trustworthy than photos taken by professional photographers, mainly because they are believed to bear immediate and authentic evidence of the photographer 'having-been-there' where the actual news scene took place. Andrew Williams, Karin Wahl-Jorgensen and Claire Wardle (Chapter 11) take this discussion further. They also detect high levels of audience approval for the inclusion of amateur audio-visual material, deriving from a perception that amateur contributions are more 'real and less packaged' than news produced solely by journalists. A key factor in contributing to this sense of authenticity is the emotional impact of viewing news events from the perspective of those affected. In considering the ideological implications of these audience discourses on amateur content, the authors suggest that the emphasis on the realism and emotional value of user-generated visuals can be seen to cement many of the power relations which have traditionally informed journalistic practice. Indeed, they conclude, rather than advancing the potentially democratizing interventions of citizens into the processes of journalism, these ways of understanding the (limited) role of the audience allow journalists to recuperate the participatory potential of the audience in the process of journalistic production.

References

Allan, S. (2006), *Online News: Journalism and the Internet*, Maidenhead and New York: Open University Press.

Allan, S. (2009), 'Histories of Citizen Journalism', in S. Allan and E. Thorsen (eds), *Citizen Journalism: Global Perspectives*, New York and Oxford: Peter Lang.

Allan, S. and Thorsen, E. (2009), *Citizen Journalism: Global Perspectives*, New York and Oxford: Peter Lang.

Andén-Papadopoulos, K. (2008), 'The Abu Ghraib Torture Photographs: News Frames, Visual Culture, and the Power of Images', *Journalism: Theory, Practice and Criticism*, 9: 1, pp. 5–30.

Andén-Papadopoulos, K. (2009), 'Body Horror on the Internet: US Soldiers Recording the War in Iraq and Afghanistan', *Media, Culture & Society*, 31: 6, pp. 921–38.

Bridge, J. and Sjøvaag, H. (2009), 'Amateur Images in the Professional News Stream', in ICA, *Keywords in Communication, 59th Annual Conference of the International Communication Association*, Chicago, United States, 20–25 May.

Cedersjö, J. and Gustavsson, R. (2009), *Hot eller möjlighet? En kvantitativ studie av svenska landsortsbaserade dagspressjournalisters inställning till användarskapat innehåll*, Göteborgs Universitet, IMG: Arbetsrapport nr 58.

Chouliaraki, L. (2008), 'The Symbolic Power of Transnational Media: Managing the Visibility of Suffering', *Global Media and Communication*, 4: 3, pp. 329–51.

Chung, D. S. (2007), 'Profits and Perils: Online News Producers' Perceptions of Interactivity and Uses of Interactive Features', *Convergence*, 13: 1, pp. 43–61.

Corner, J. (1995), *Television Form and Public Address*, London: Edward Arnold.

Cottle, S. (2009a), 'Series Editor's Preface', in S. Allan and E. Thorsen (eds), *Citizen Journalism: Global Perspectives*, New York and Oxford: Peter Lang.

Cottle, S. (2009b), *Global Crisis Reporting: Journalism in the Global Age*, McGraw Hill: Open University Press.

Deuze, M., Bruns, A. and Neuberger, C. (2007), 'Preparing for an Age of Participatory News', *Journalism Practise*, 1: 3, pp. 322–38.

Domingo, D., Quandt, T., Heinonen, A., Paulussen, S., Singer, J. B. and Vujnovic, M. (2008), 'Participatory Journalism Practices in the Media and Beyond', *Journalism Practice*, 2: 3, pp. 326–42.

Hariman, R. and Lucaites, J. L. (2007), *No Caption Needed: Iconic Photographs, Public Culture, and Liberal Democracy*, Chicago: The University of Chicago Press.

Hermida, A. and Thurman, N. (2008), 'A Clash of Cultures: The Integration of User-Generated Content within Professional Journalistic Frameworks at British Newspaper Websites', *Journalism Practice* 2: 3, pp. 343–56.

Jenkins, H. (2006), *Convergence Culture: Where Old and New Media Collide*, New York: New York University Press.

Mitchell, W. J. T. (1994), *Picture Theory: Essays on Verbal and Visual Representation*, Chicago: University of Chicago Press.

Örnebring, H. (2008), 'The Consumer as Producer – of What? User-Generated Tabloid Content in the Sun (UK) and Aftonbladet (Sweden)', *Journalism Studies*, 9: 5, pp. 771–85.

Pantti, M. and Bakker, P. (2009), 'Misfortunes, Sunsets and Memories: Non-Professional Images in Dutch News Media', *International Journal of Cultural Studies*, 12: 5, pp. 1–19.

Paulussen, S., Heinonen, A., Domingo, D. and Quandt, T. (2007), 'Doing It Together: Citizen Participation in the Professional News making Process', *Observatorio (OBS*) Journal*, 1: 3, pp. 131–54.

Perlmutter, D. D. (1998), *Photojournalism and Foreign Policy. Icons of Outrage in International Crisis*, London: Praeger.

Roeder, G. H. (1993), *The Censored War. American Visual Experience during World War Two*, New Haven and London: Yale University Press.

Silverstone, R. (2006), *Media and Morality. On the Rise of the Mediapolis*, Cambridge: Polity.

Singer, J. (2005), 'The Political J-Blogger: "Normalizing" A New Media Form To Fit Old Norms and Practices', *Journalism: Theory, Practice and Criticism*, 6: 2, pp. 173–98.

Taylor, J. (1991), *War Photography. Realism in the British Press*, London: Routledge.

Taylor, J. (1998), *Body Horror. Photojournalism, Catastrophe and War*, New York: New York University Press.

Thurman, N. (2008), 'Forums for Citizen Journalists? Adoption of User Generated Content Initiatives by Online News Media', *New Media & Society*, 10: 1, pp. 139–57.

Williams, A., Wardle, C. and Wahl-Jorgensen, K. (2010), 'Have They Got News for Us? Audience Revolution or Business as Usual at the BBC?', *Journalism Practice*, iFirst: http://www.informaworld.com/smpp/content~content=a921303452~db=all~jumptype=rss. Accessed 4 September 2010.

Zelizer, B. (1998), *Remembering to Forget: Holocaust Memory through the Camera's Eye*, Chicago and London: Chicago University Press.

Zelizer, B. (2002), 'Photography, Journalism, and Trauma', in B. Zelizer and S. Allan (eds), *Journalism After September 11*, London: Routledge.

Zelizer, B. (2004), 'When War Is Reduced to a Photograph', in S. Allan and B. Zelizer (eds), *Reporting War: Journalism in Wartime*, London and New York: Routledge.

Zelizer, B. (2007), 'On "Having Been There": "Eyewitnessing" as a Journalistic Key Word', *Critical Studies in Media Communication*, 24: 5, pp. 408–28.

Part I

Histories

Chapter 1

Looking Back: Ethics and Aesthetics of Non-Professional Photography

Karin Becker

T his chapter explores, from several historical and cultural perspectives, the changing relationship between professional journalism and its amateur alternatives, that is images from private cameras. Drawing on historical examples and various journalistic genres, I examine how the border between professional and non-professional photography in the press has been continually challenged and redrawn, and discuss the ethical dilemmas that arise in this uneasy borderland. Journalism's ambivalence over using pictures from outside its professional domain has a long history, which I trace here, focusing particularly on the aesthetic and documentary character and appeal of the private photograph, and what happens when this appeal coincides with the interests of news. I consider, further, some of the routines and strategies that journalism has used to pull in these 'outsider' images, explaining or 'taming' them to fit within the news frame.

The Private Photograph as News

I begin with 1912 and the major news event of that year, the sinking of the passenger ship the *Titanic*. No photographs were available of the tragedy itself; and in the aftermath, a portrait of the captain's widow, Eleanor Sarah Smith, holding their daughter, began circulating widely in the press. The newspapers that carried the picture on their front pages include *L'Echo du Nord*, in Quebec, and the *London Daily Mirror*, both well-established newspapers, but with a tendency towards sensational journalism. Strictly speaking, this is not an amateur photograph, but a studio portrait made by a professional photographer. Yet it does have similarities to the amateur's photograph, even today, that make it relevant for unravelling questions about the ways in which journalism handles pictures that come from outside the press. Like the amateur photograph, it was made for use within a private, domestic setting. It was not intended to be a press photograph but *became* one when it was taken out of its intended context, and reinserted into the news, whereby it raised several ethical issues. First, it was not a current photograph, but had been taken six years earlier. Although conveniently dressed in black, the woman in the picture was not yet a grieving widow, and the three-year-old child on her lap had reached the age of nine. Yet the desire to publish a photograph of people affected by the tragedy overrode any questions about its lack of currency. Secondly, this was apparently the only photograph available of the widow Smith, which enhanced its value to the press: it was an exclusive picture. Whereas today one could expect many public pictures of a woman with the social standing of a captain's wife, at the time a different standard of privacy prevailed. Women who exposed themselves to the public's gaze (actresses, singers, entertainers) were viewed as of questionable character, so it was no accident that pictures of this woman were hard to come by. Mrs Smith should have been allowed her privacy, not because she was in mourning, but because according to the social norms of the time a woman of her standing should have remained out of the public eye. By exposing her to the public (and a global public, at that), the press was degrading her to the status of a 'common' woman. The photograph became a benchmark of the excesses of visual journalism and was seen as the first example of 'presenting private grief as a breakfast-table spectacle' (Baynes 1971: 48).

There are several things we can learn from this example. First, the photograph that gets close to its subject runs the risk of transgressing the boundary of what is seen as ethical journalism. The line may be drawn differently at different times, and for different kinds of events. Yet, ethical questions are raised and the boundary is invoked whenever a photograph promises an exclusive look at a subject that, although it may be public knowledge, has not previously been visually exposed to the public eye. Second, there is a long history of incorporating pictures into the press from external, freestanding sources that lie outside

Figure 1.1: This private photograph of Captain Smith's wife, Eleanor, holding their daughter was on the front page of tabloid newspapers on both sides of the Atlantic the week after the Titanic sank. Photo: (London) *Daily Mirror*, 22 April 1912.

strict editorial control. In these cases, we find that the desire for pictures has taken the upper hand in the decision to publish.

Another aspect that this example illustrates is that the desire for photographs was particularly evident in the tabloid press, which from its early days actively sought and used images to sensationalize the news. Large photographs were widely used, with violence, sex, accidents and society scandals as major themes. The *Daily News*, for example, with its front-page photograph in 1928 showing the murderess Ruth Snyder at the moment of her execution, was offering what a later photojournalism textbook described as 'daily erotica for the masses' (Kobre 1980: 17). US press historians continue to point to the period as a low point for journalism, an expression of what they consider the loose morals and loss of ethical standards that threatened public and private life. In the United Kingdom, *Daily Mirror* had established 'a genre of making public the grief of private individuals,' and was among the newspapers influenced by the US tabloids' early use of photographs (Baynes 1971: 46, 51). In the meantime, many broadsheet newspapers remained dominated by text long into the inter-war period, with the *New York Times* as a prime example. Their restrictive use of photography can be seen as a response to the visual excesses of the tabloid press (Becker 1992), grounded in an ethical position embedded in evolving standards of a professional journalism.

The Emotional Baggage of Sensational Journalism

Why is the polarization of photography in daily journalism relevant to a discussion of amateur photography in the press? With photography as a central feature of sensational journalism, in its turn characterized by emotional excess and unethical practices, it became increasingly difficult to conceive of a journalistic photography outside the boundaries of this genre (Becker 1992: 133). Central to the legacy of the yellow press of the 1890s and still evident in the circulation wars that raged in New York's tabloid press of the 1920s, was the power of the image, and in particular the photograph as non-mediated, speaking directly to the reader. In its directness and immediacy, the photograph carries an emotional power that undermines the possibility of rational reflection. The sensational image – and by extension any photograph – was seen as impeding the public's ability to maintain a reasoned response to the event it represented. The reader is pulled into the event, getting 'too close,' thereby losing the capacity to weigh its significance. The photograph had come to represent a potential threat to the 'proper distance' that was a cornerstone of ethical, professional journalism (Silverstone 2007). Issues of emotional and ethical excess in visual journalism had bracketed photography as suspect within the profession as a whole.

With the rise of a professional photojournalism, as newspapers and news agencies employed photographers and the wire services began sending photographs, journalism grew less dependent on photographs from other sources. Yet there would continue to be events where photographs from outside journalism would be needed for full and adequate coverage of the news. In these circumstances, the ways the photograph is understood, how it represents, including its power and its appeal, raise ethical issues for the profession.

In an oft-repeated quotation the iconic war photographer Robert Capa claimed that if the photograph is not 'good enough' it is because the photographer is not close enough. Closeness is therefore an admirable quality or attribute, conflating physical and emotional distance into a visual representation of what is it is like to be present, witnessing the event as it happens. Obviously, this is mined territory, not only for war photography. The border between getting too close and maintaining a proper distance must be negotiated each time it arises. What does this closeness look like? In order to identify when the photograph signifies that it violates the 'proper distance' of professional journalism, I now turn to the specific visual attributes of photographs that appear *too* close. My argument is not confined to the amateur or non-professional photograph, but includes references to ways ethical distance is constructed, maintained and violated in the practices of professionals. As I hope to show, the framework of professional practice is necessary for understanding when a news organization allows the amateur photograph to cross the border and enter the news. This includes identifying specific strategies that journalism employs to make the outsider image fit the constraints of an ethical journalism. Each of these strategies stems from the need to insert distance between the image and the viewer. Visual, audio and textual means are employed to defuse the emotional power of the photograph and reframe it within a journalistic discourse characterized by proper distance.

The Look of the Family Photograph

The private portrait has a long history in the press, and continues to be a staple of a certain kind of news story. When people who are not public figures suddenly become newsworthy, the usual way of picturing them is with a private picture, usually a school photograph or a snapshot from a family collection. Examples include news events such as the disappearance of a child, a murder or other violent crime or tragedies or catastrophes where many people are missing or dead. In these news situations photographs – either of the victims or the perpetrators – gain currency within journalism, and the most sought after images do not exist in press or public archives. The iconography of these images is easily recognized. Both the school portrait and the family picture from a private setting carry connotations of the presumed warmth and intimacy of the private, domestic sphere (Hirsch 1981; Kuhn 1995). Inserting them into the public display of the newscast or newspaper page creates a radical disjuncture. The closeness, the visual connotation of emotional and physical proximity, is ruptured. The reader knows immediately that something is not as it appears in the image; the altered context signifies differently, as tragedy. The closeness established through the familiar look of the picture is thereby intensified. Re-framing the private image within a discourse of journalism zooms in even closer to what the reader now reinterprets as only a visual semblance of normalcy.

The private picture in the press also collapses time. The viewer is presented with an image from the past simultaneously with a current event that is news. Inserting the past into the present creates a special form of temporal immediacy. Looking at the people in the photograph we see how they were, at the same time that we are witnessing the tragedy in their future. The privacy of the past moment is fused with knowledge of the tragic event that brought them into the public eye. The temporal closeness created when the private photograph is re-situated in a journalistic frame closes the gap between the private past and its future made public.

The photograph from the family collection is frequently posed, with the subject looking into the camera. This effect of direct eye contact presents the person in the picture as a subject, engaged with the photographer, and in turn with the viewer. This 'look' implies complicity between the photographer and the subject, acknowledging that a photograph is being made. The subject position established through eye-to-eye contact is an important way the private photograph signifies closeness, suggesting a personal bond with the person holding the camera and with the intended audience of family and friends. The family photograph is one of the few cases when the direct gaze appears in photographs in the press. It occasionally occurs in the local press, where even front-page news photographs may show their subjects looking directly into the camera. The local newspaper's editorial policies typically include a responsibility to represent the local community, underscoring the close bond it enjoys with its readers, an exception that supports the rule of unposed photography as the norm (Becker, Ekecrantz and Olsson 2000). Other exceptions include portraits of well-known social figures and celebrities in private settings, where the direct gaze with its sense of intimacy establishes the photograph as privileged and exclusive (Becker 1992). More generally, photojournalists develop strategies to avoid the gaze in order to make their photograph appear unposed. Waiting for an unguarded moment, or simply directing subjects not to look at the camera are examples. The distance that is constructed through such strategies presents the event 'as if' it were not being observed or documented. By looking away from the camera, the person is being asked to behave 'naturally', that is, as if the photographer were not present. The fictive absence of the journalist that these strategies construct is one form of proper distance.

The amateur picture violates this distance, particularly when it is pulled into coverage of mainstream news. Publishing private pictures of victims of crime and tragedy are frequently seen as particularly invasive. They avoid the intrusion of the professional's camera, but substitute the more intimate view from the victim's daily life with its cruel appearance of normalcy. Claire Wardle (2007) shows an increase in the visual coverage of child murders during the 1990s, where emotionally charged personal photographs of the victims and their families 'suggest to readers that this is no longer a personal affair; it is one which affects us all' (p. 279). Private photographs of perpetrators of crimes, far less common in Wardle's material, can raise additional issues. A childhood photograph or school portrait of the offender presents a mask of normalcy, inviting the viewer to look for signs of deviance to come. Publishing a photograph where the perpetrator of a crime looks directly into the camera establishes the person as a subject, which may not be the desired effect. Before discussing the ways the press controls this dangerous proximity, I consider the other familiar look of the amateur photograph, the snapshot aesthetic.

Beyond Control: The Amateur as Paparazzi

Even when posed, the amateur photograph can have a rather haphazard look to it. The composition may be a bit off, crooked or awkwardly framed. People may squint into the camera or their faces appear contorted by the harsh light of an unexpected flash. Objects close to the camera can look amorphous and out-of-focus, while other objects may appear too far away to clearly identify. Although the amateur photograph is typically taken during highly predictable moments, during family gatherings and celebrations, trips and holidays, it nevertheless looks unplanned as if people are caught off guard by the camera. Although these visual features do not characterize all family or amateur photographs, they nevertheless cohere around a type of image that is generally understood to be made by a non-professional. The look of the amateur photograph, as an iconic form, has been part of visual culture in the West since the first hand-held cameras entered the market in Europe and North America. With its long history and traditions, it also evokes a complex emotional response among viewers who identify its visual form with the private and domestic spheres. This includes an expectation that the photographer is familiar with the people in the picture and may even belong to the group. The haphazard look of the amateur snapshot signifies intimacy and closeness. These qualities adhere to the image, regardless of the photographer's actual relationship with the people and events pictured. The visual form of the snapshot is read as an insider's view.

These visual characteristics are not confined to amateur photography, and they also signify in other ways. The 'candid' photograph that catches its subjects at unguarded moments also has a long history in the press. Celebrity journalism, including paparazzi photography, and crime reporting offer many examples of press photographs that follow the snapshot aesthetic. The people and events are not the same as those found in the family collection, but the visual form is similar: awkward composition, harsh contrasts and uncertain focus that appear to be the result of simply pointing the camera at a subject that might 'make a picture'. The frozen moment captured in the candid photograph suggests that neither the photographer nor the subject had time to 'compose' themselves for the picture. Like the amateur's photograph, this style of press photography appears raw and immediate. In his discussion of the paparazzi, Alan Sekula (1984) argues that these photographs follow a different order of truth than the carefully composed image. The photograph that catches its subject off guard 'is thought to manifest more of the "inner being" of the subject than is the calculated gestalt of immobilized gesture, expression and stance' (p. 29). Standards of good composition and technical control are sacrificed in favour of getting the subject on film. The raw appearance of the image signifies that the subject's public facade has been ripped away, revealing the inner character, what the subject is 'really' like. News photograph taken of people responding to tragedy and loss follows a similar logic; in such situations people are exposed, revealing human nature at its most basic level. Photographs of such moments, when the comfortable facade of daily life has crumbled, provide a psychological closeness to the experience. The moment of trauma becomes the moment of revelation.

The press is generally wary of publishing such photographs, regardless of the source. There is first the ethical issue of the camera as intruder, where photographs get 'too close' to the suffering subject, violating them by exposing their grief and trauma to a world of strangers. There is also a different way of understanding closeness, one that turns on the photographer's emotional distance to the events and people in the picture, and that carries different ethical considerations. As mentioned above, photographs that follow the snapshot aesthetic signify a close relationship between the photographer and subject, at least in the realm of the family snapshot. However, lack of control over the image may also mean that the photographer has been pulled into the event, stripped of the composure necessary to make a 'good' picture. In the heat of the moment, unable to adhere to professional standards of technical mastery and journalistic distance, the photographer 'reverts' to making pictures that resemble the amateur's.

Yet the raw quality of the unposed photograph also signifies authenticity, a quality that the press certainly wants to maintain, particularly in coverage of breaking news. In such cases, the professional photograph that resembles an amateur snapshot presents a dilemma. The immediacy that makes the photograph a strong visual account of the rescue effort could well have been made by anyone who happened to be there with a camera. Picture editors discuss the visual quality of news photographs of victims being rescued from accidents and fires in these terms. In a press photography contest a number of years ago, a candidate for the prestigious spot news award was a chaotic image of an accident scene, taken at night. A heated discussion arose among jury members: Was the photographer making a conscious compositional selection, or simply taking the kind of picture anyone on the scene might have taken? One member argued that the photograph looked 'amateurish' and was 'probably just a matter of luck'. Asking whether a photograph is accidental or intentional is ultimately a question of source credibility; it turns on the photographer's ability to provide an authoritative account of the event. The grab shot *looks* authentic, but until it can be established that the person holding the camera was making reasoned decisions in the heat of the moment, the picture remains in doubt. In such cases, the line is difficult to detect.

Journalists use the word 'raw' repeatedly when describing these problematic pictures, suggesting that they must be reworked and prepared before they can fit into the frame of the news story. Looking more closely, we find that the word is used to refer to two distinct characteristics. It can mean, first, that the pictures are 'raw' in the sense that they are unedited; they show a chain of events that is confusing, multi-dimensional and must be packaged, clarified, explained and condensed if they are to follow the narrative structure of news. The second characteristic refers to image content, what it portrays. In this sense 'raw' refers to material that is 'too graphic' to show to a general public: it is explicit, often with obvious violence or its bloody effects. Victims may in some cases be identifiable. The images cannot be presented in their 'raw' form, if at all, but must be first be sanitized, removing the offensive or shocking content, in order to make them more tasteful or palatable for the general public. These two senses of raw are conflated when journalists describe the amateur's pictures, motivating both the need to edit and condense the raw footage, but also to tame its offensive or grisly content – in order to protect the public.

Taming the Unruly Photograph

Journalism generally handles photographs that look accidental, have 'graphic' content or in other ways appear too close to their subject by adding text that explains them. Often embedded in a caption or a headline, the text suggests the conditions that led to publishing the image, framing it as an exclusive perspective on the event. The text serves as a disclaimer, acknowledging that the event (and therefore the picture) is unusual, even unique. It suggests that ordinarily the press would refrain from publishing such a photograph, but the extraordinary event demands extraordinary coverage. It is important to recognize this framing (or reframing in the case of the family snapshot or portrait) as double-sided: the provocative power of the image is encapsulated and tamed by the text, at the same time that the news story itself (with the images as an integral part) is presented as exclusive or even sensational. This is accomplished in different ways, but similar techniques are used to textually frame and contain unruly images whether from professionals or amateurs.

One strategy is to frame the news story as a first-person account. A breaking news event that is violent or tragic is often reported in the voice of the journalist as eyewitness. The subjective voice tells the reader that even the seasoned reporter or photojournalist could not maintain a professional distance, but was pulled into the dramatic event. In the Swedish tabloid *Expressen's* 1989 coverage from Beijing, for example, the main article on events in Tiananmen Square included large, stark black-and-white flash photographs of youthful victims of the Chinese soldiers' gunfire, under the headline 'He dies as I take the picture' (Kadhammar and Andersson 1989). The present tense adds immediacy to the photographs, and quotation marks provide an additional frame for the statement, converting the images into 'metapictures' of the photographer's experience of the unfolding drama. In this meta-context, the rawness of the photographs signifies qualities of immediacy and being-there, adding to rather than detracting from their authenticity.

Amateur photographs of such dramatic events have been rare in the press, even after the rise of digital photography and its links to the Internet. First-person visual accounts by amateurs appear on websites frequented by citizen journalists and their audiences, but seldom appear as such in newspaper and television news. More common are examples where the photographs themselves are visually dramatic, giving an alternative view on an event that is being covered by professional news media. The 'insider' perspective of the amateur is not presented in the first person, but is instead framed by a text that adds distance between the picture and the event it depicts. Often this is done by calling on a unique news value to justify publishing a non-professional photograph. Photographs taken by British football hooligans, published in *Expressen* in 1995, can serve as an example. British supporters' pictures from violent confrontations with police were published on the front page with the headline 'The hooligans' own pictures', and a subhead explaining, 'This is how foreign vandals spread football violence in Sweden' (*Expressen* 1995). Framing them as exclusive news(worthy) photographs did not stave off controversy. *Expressen* was criticized on grounds that publishing the amateur pictures gave hooligans public legitimacy, and further, that obtaining them third-hand, through the police, represented a threat to press autonomy.

As suggested by these examples, the tabloid press continues to be the journalistic genre where photographs from non-professionals most often appear, and that is especially true for the family portrait. In the evening papers where the border between private and public life is most frequently challenged and transgressed, family pictures are the ideal illustration for news events involving personal tragedy and loss. On 21 September 2010, the German tabloid *Bild* published a photograph of a smiling woman standing next to a Christmas tree, holding her young son. Two days earlier the woman had 'gone amok' in the little town of Lörrach, killing the boy and his father in an explosion, and killing or wounding several other people before the police finally shot her. The picture of a family Christmas celebration is one of the amateur pictures that *Bild* included in the stream of 41 photographs in its net edition that day (Bachner et al. 2010). Above the picture was the text, 'The bloodbath in Lörrach. Here is the woman who ran amok.' Beneath it, the article led with the question 'Who was the woman who wiped out her family, killing three?' Following Sekula (1984), the question suggests that the snapshot may contain the 'truth', revealing a human nature that could explain the tragedy. Presenting the photograph as (possible) visual evidence works as a frame to justify the ethically questionable practice of publishing a private photograph. Although *Bild* is an extreme example, this way of framing family pictures is not unusual for the tabloid press, while morning papers are more likely to refrain from publishing them at all. That same day, the net edition of the conservative *Süddeutsche Zeitung* published 14 pictures from Lörrach, many from places where people had placed flowers and candles, but with no photographs of the victims or the woman herself (Beitzer 2010). Nevertheless, *Süddeutsche Zeitung* describes the Christmas picture, embedding it in a longer analysis that draws on a range of experts and other news sources to explain the tragedy. In both newspapers the picture of family Christmas is framed as having news value, offering keys to understanding the event, but in ways consistent with the respective news genre, and following different ethical standards for what may be pictured.

When Pictures are News

Occasionally amateur photographs themselves make news, when the mere fact of their existence becomes the news event. The pictures taken of US soldiers torturing prisoners in the Abu Ghraib facility are a case in point, shocking the public when they surfaced in

2004. The shock of these photographs was not only due to the acts of abuse and torture they portrayed, but also because the soldiers themselves had taken and circulated the pictures. Despite active attempts by the US government to deny or minimize the brutality they revealed, and then to limit their spread, these amateur photographs stood as stark visual evidence of the abusive acts that had taken place at Abu Ghraib. The fact that the pictures had obviously been made by someone who was an insider and participant and that their form and composition followed the accepted conventions of amateur family photography – the lighting, posing, camera distance and angle – heightened both their authenticity and their news value (Andén-Papadopoulos 2008).

How were these provocative and ethically problematic photographs framed within journalism? A common strategy is to include an obvious source attribution in the image itself, signalling the accountability of that other source for the content. Since the Abu Ghraib photographs had first appeared on the CBS programme *60 Minutes*, the network's logo often appeared in the frame when those photographs were subsequently published elsewhere. This afforded CBS credit for its scoop, at the same time that it shifted responsibility for the image away from the newspaper or newscast that was showing it. Retaining the CBS logo showed their path into the discourse of news and, backed by this respected news source, legitimated publishing photographs that included violent actions and nudity, in some cases with identifiable participants.

During the weeks and months that followed, the debates over these photographs revealed the problems of including them within a journalistic frame. Circulating through broadening arenas of culture and influence, they were adapted into other genres, including street art and protest posters around the world. The photographs from Abu Ghraib refused to be contained within the dominant newsframe, but worked instead as 'critical prisms' through which perspectives on US foreign policy were refracted (Andén-Papadopoulos 2008). Within journalism they were discussed *as pictures*, including why they had been made, the positions and states of mind of those who had made them, on what authority they were acting and the effect of these degrading forms of representation on the prisoners themselves. The Abu-Ghraib photographs thus became metapictures, always presented as second-order representations of what had taken place in the prison, which signified as 'other' than a journalistic account of what was portrayed.

Consistently pointing to them as representations became in itself a strategy of containment, a way for journalism to treat these photographs that had become their own news story, including the ethical issues they raised about showing both the prisoners and the perpetrators. This is not uncommon when visual representations become news, as seen for example in the ongoing story of the Mohammed caricatures that were first published in a Danish newspaper, with repercussions across the globe (Becker 2008). Within journalistic discourses *about* such specific and problematic kinds of images, they continually are used, in W. J. T. Mitchell's terms, to 'depict themselves'. Even when the pictures themselves are not present in their visual form, they remain in the discourse as 'second-order reflections on the practices of pictorial representation' (Mitchell 1995: 9).

Drawing attention to the photograph *as a visual representation* removes the viewer one step further from the event the picture represents. Shifting the photograph to the status of a metapicture creates distance, necessary in order to contain the raw and dangerous image within the discourse of journalism. In the meantime, the images themselves may continue to circulate in parallel spheres as part of the larger discourse in which they operate. The possibility of images circulating more or less freely is a relatively new phenomenon, the result of rapid technological change in both personal photography and the transnational image-bearing networks that are used to circulate them. In this sense, the examples from Abu Ghraib and the Mohammed caricatures must be seen as part of a larger phenomenon, where forms of vernacular expression are being re-evaluated and the amateur photograph has gained a new status.

Participant Photographers in the Digital Era

There has been a decided shift in the value of the amateur photograph, paradoxically related to the omnipresence of picture-taking devices in everyday life and the escalating numbers of photographs being taken at any given moment. This means that the chances of someone, amateur or professional, being on site with a camera at the moment the newsworthy event takes place are decidedly greater than a decade ago. The ease and immediacy of transferring images has also vastly increased the flow of non-professional photographs. In 1989, the digital transfer of photographs from Tiananmen Square was from western photojournalists using a then new technology to supersede Chinese authorities' attempts to block film leaving the country. By the turn of the twenty-first century, digital technology had sufficiently expanded to provide this kind of access to the amateur. As became vividly apparent in the aftermath of the attack on the World Trade Center in New York in 2001, a turning point had occurred. Despite efforts to keep the area around the WTC 'camera free' out of respect for the victims, people flocked to the now-historic location with their digital cameras. In the meantime, the project 'Here is New York' began gathering photographs by both amateurs and professionals (including many world-renowned photojournalists) to document and commemorate what was taking place. The 'democracy of photographs' as it was called, became an ongoing exhibition, both online and eventually moving to other cities (Here is New York 2001). Any image in the project could be purchased, but without information about the photographer until the picture was delivered. 'Here is New York' flattened the hierarchy of photography, placing the amateur on an equal par with the professional. It also recognized the vernacular aesthetic of the amateur photograph as a valuable, participant perspective on a historic event.

Professional news coverage of the aftermath of 9/11 included many photographs of ordinary people taking pictures, as well as the many ways amateur photographs were used during the search for victims. Photographs *of* amateurs themselves were becoming common in the press. Today photojournalists often document news events by including in their pictures ordinary people, non-professionals, taking pictures. On some occasions these photographic subjects are motivated by their news value, such as a teenage immigrant boy photographing a burnt-out school in a Paris suburb during the riots in 2005, or a demonstrator in Gothenburg turning the camera towards the police in the confrontations during the 2001 EU summit meetings. In other cases these metapictures provide an alternative or feature angle on a news event, showing, for example, a head of state using his own digital camera, or members of the public taking pictures. In August 2010, the Swedish newspaper *Svenska dagbladet* ran a series of photographs by tourists under the headline 'Stockholm in my camera'. The front-page photograph was a self-portrait taken by a woman as she watched the Crown Princess' wedding celebration on television (*Svenska dagbladet* 2010). Presented as news, the photograph showed a participant's perspective on this historic event.

Alongside amateur photographs, we now meet their photographers in the visual discourse of journalism. Journalism is presenting a visual representation of a shift in society, as photography becomes easier and more integrated into daily life. Publishing pictures of amateurs is in this sense a reflexive move, perhaps mirroring the challenge these omnipresent participant photographers represent to professional journalism. The 'first version of history' is no longer monopolized by the press, but is also captured through the eyes and cameras of ordinary people documenting their versions of their own place in the flow of history. The reflexivity supported in these many metapictures highlights the perspectives of 'ordinary' people, as they observe and document events, large and small, that they find noteworthy.

Covering the Gaps

The omnipresence of the amateur photographer vastly increases the possibility that pictures exist of newsworthy events. When journalists miss a major event, a search begins for amateur pictures that can fill the gap. Looking back in time, we find precedents that predate the digital era showing how journalism handles situations when key moments in history are missing from its own visual repertoire. The Kennedy assassination in 1963 provides a case, examined in Barbie Zelizer's (1992) analysis of the event and the gaps in media coverage. The press had missed this journalistic 'scoop', and most of the pictures of the presidential motorcade through Dallas were by amateurs. The TV cameras trained on the motorcade 'didn't get usable pictures', so the main film of the event was by amateurs, including the notorious footage by Abraham Zapruder. With the single exception of an AP photograph of a Secret Service agent jumping onto the back of the Kennedy car, the only still photographs of the shooting was from bystanders with Polaroid cameras. Trade publications described them as 'distanced, unprofessional and unfocused images' (Friedman 1963: 16; cit. in Zelizer 1992: 68). In the face of this amateur challenge to journalistic professionalism, the press minimized the importance of the 'scoop', and shifted the focus of their competition to acquiring amateur accounts of the event which in turn became the 'exclusive' material journalists used to maintain their position as professionals. As Zelizer notes, 'journalists adjusted "missing the scoop" into a second-order practice, in which they bought, took or borrowed the records generated by others'. (1992: 69) The journalistic task of locating these exclusive records took precedence over the threat they represented to the profession. The re-framing of this critical documentation from amateurs' cameras involved reasserting its value as journalism.

The amateur's 'exclusive' and often dramatic pictures, the first or only ones from a breaking news event, raise specific issues that the press must deal with before it can publish or broadcast them. The problems that arise for the news organization involve first, the difficulty of substantiating their credibility; and second, a visual content that may include violence or graphic images of people who are wounded or dying. Add to this the amateur photographer's own interest – political, personal or economic – in the unfolding events and commitment to seeing the pictures reach a larger, even global public.

Although the dilemma has arisen throughout history whenever pictures have been missing from breaking news stories, it is compounded in the contemporary media landscape. Amateur footage becomes commodified in the spiralling competition to be the first to present this exclusive material and journalism shifts its focus to re-establishing its authority over the narrative. Following what Zelizer (1992: 87) calls 'reconstructive work', journalism finds ways to claim the look of the amateur's footage as its own, in a discourse that points out the dangers of the images, at the same time that it grounds them in journalistic professional judgement that demands that they be revealed. On the surface, the discourse appears reflexive and transparent, leaving it open to viewers to weigh and decide on the ethics of exposing the pictures to the general public. At the same time it is a strategy that reconstructs these compelling visual reports as part of journalism itself, bearing its responsibility to inform the public, whatever the ethical consequences. The proper distance is as close as it gets, from inside the event, embedded in journalism's authority to bring us the news.

Conclusion

This chapter has examined the relationship between professional journalism and amateur pictures, considering under what conditions they enter the news and the problems they present for the profession. Throughout history we find a continuing interest and fascination for the private picture and what it brings to the news agenda. Initially, journalism's interest arises from a lack of visual material from established, professional sources for coverage of an important news event. On a closer examination, however, we find a fascination with the look of the private picture and what it can introduce into the news narrative. The portrait from the family collection with its connotations of domestic intimacy can bring the reader closer to the rupture of tragedy and loss. The haphazard snapshot or film suggests an authentic eyewitness account by someone in the midst of the event. In both these forms, the private image brings the public closer to the event, both emotionally and proxemically, at the same time that it violates the distance demanded by professional standards of journalism. In order to include the aura of 'truth' embedded in the private picture's apparent closeness and lack of control, journalism must frame the picture within its own agenda of news, including the ethical considerations that entail. As we have seen, the tabloid press is the genre where this boundary is most often transgressed with sensationalized publication of private pictures.

Regardless of the genre, however, the 'raw' non-professional picture has to be incorporated into a news frame. On ethical grounds, this requires introducing distance between the viewer and what the image represents, while at the same time retaining the power of the image. As seen in the examples above, this is most often accomplished by a text that supports and legitimates the photograph as a news image. The private source in the by-line, the explanatory caption, the first-person text, each refer to the photograph in ways that establish a second order of interpretation, outside the picture, distancing the image and what it represents from its viewer. The relationship is ambiguous, however, for the framing simultaneously marks the image as unusual, unique, providing evidence not available through professional sources, and pulling in the viewer for a closer look. The challenge is particularly acute in major breaking news events, where the demand for immediate, eyewitness testimony reaches its peak. The omnipresence of photography in daily life has made this testimony more readily available, offering the 'first draft of history' as seen through the eyes of its participants. This continues to have consequences for the ethical, aesthetic and technical constraints of the profession as journalists struggle to re-establish their authority as the primary narrators of history.

Acknowledgements

I thank Solveig Hoppe for drawing my attention to the example from Lörrach, and for her analysis of the coverage of the event.

References

Andén-Papadopoulos, K. (2008), 'The Abu Ghraib Torture Photographs', *Journalism*, 9: 5, pp. 5–30.

Bachner, A. et al. (2010), 'Das Blutbad in Lörrach. Das ist die Amok-Läuferin', *Bild*, 22 September, http://www.bild.de/BILD/news/2010/09/22/amoklauf-blutbad-loerrach-so-toetete-sie/vater-und-sohn-lagen-auf-dem-bett.html. Accessed 22 October 2010.

Baynes, K. (ed) (1971), *Scoop Scandal and Strife. Study of Photography in Newspapers*, London: Lund Humphries.

Becker, K. (1992), 'Photojournalism and the Tabloid Press', in P. Dahlgren and C. Sparks (eds), *Journalism and Popular Culture*, London: Sage.

Becker, K. (2008), 'The Power of Pictures in Journalistic Discourse. As News, as Commentary, as Art', in E. Eide, R. Kunelius and A. Phillips (eds), *Transnational Media Events: The Mohammed Cartoons and the Imagined Clash of Civilizations*, Gothenburg: Nordicom.

Becker, K., Ekecrantz, J. and Olsson, T. (eds) (2000), *Picturing Politics, Visual and Textual Formations of Modernity in the Swedish Press*, Stockholm: JMK, Stockholm University.

Beitzer, H. (2010), 'Amoklauf in Lörrach. Sabine R., Mutter und Mörderin', *Süddeutsche Zeitung*, 22 September, http://www.sueddeutsche.de/panorama/amoklauf-in-loerrach-sabine-r-eine-ganz-normale-frau-1.1002922. Accessed 11 October 2010.

Expressen (1995), 'Huliganarnas egna bilder', 15 November, p. 1.

Friedman, R. (1963), 'Pictures of Assassination Fall to Amateurs on Street', *Editor and Publisher*, 30 November, pp. 16–17, 67.

'Here is New York' (2001), http://hereisnewyork.org/. Accessed 22 October 2010.

Hirsch, J. (1981), *Family Photographs: Content, Meaning and Effects*, New York: Oxford University Press.

Kadhammar, P. and Andersson, T. (1989), 'Han dör när jag tar bilden', *Expressen* 4 June, pp. 8–9.

Kobre, K. (1980), *Photojournalism. The Professionals' Approach*, Somerville, MA: Curtin & London.

Kuhn, A. (1995), *Family Secrets. Acts of Memory and Imagination*, London: Verso.

Mitchell, W. J. T. (1995), *Picture Theory: Essays on Verbal and Visual Representation*, Chicago: University of Chicago Press.

Sekula, A. (1984), *Photography against the Grain*, Halifax: The Press of Nova Scotia College of Art and Design.

Silverstone, R. (2007), *Media and Morality. On the Rise of the Mediapolis*, Cambridge: Polity Press.

Svenska dagbladet (2010), 'Stockholm i min kamera', 6 August, p. 1, http://www.svd.se/resor/nyheter/stockholm-i-min-kamera_5091795.svd. Accessed 18 August 2010.

Wardle, C. (2007), 'Monsters and Angels: Visual Press Coverage of Child Murders in the USA and UK, 1930–2000', *Journalism* 8: 3, pp. 263–84.

Zelizer, B. (1992), *Covering the Body: The Kennedy Assassination, the Media, and the Shaping of Collective Memory*, Chicago: University of Chicago Press.

Chapter 2

Amateur Photography in Wartime: Early Histories

Stuart Allan

Perceptions of photography's value for war reportage surface in accounts from the earliest days of its historical development. Illustrative of this point are the words of French chemist and physicist Joseph Louis Gay-Lussac, for example, who in proclaiming the qualities of the daguerreotype in 1839 asserted: '[A]s three or four minutes are sufficient for execution, a field of battle, with its successive phases, can be drawn with a degree of perfection that could be obtained by no other means' (cit. in Marwil 2000: 30). This chapter, in seeking to explore the role of photography as an imperative dimension of war correspondence, shall pay particular attention to contributions made by the 'amateur' to its evolution. This objective, however, is not as straightforward as it may sound. Much depends on one's interpretation of the status of the photographers in question, given that discourses of professionalism would not fully secure their purchase on photojournalism until the twentieth century was well underway. That is to say, while photography has been pressed into service to document aspects of warfare since the mid-nineteenth century, an evaluative assessment relying upon terms such as 'amateur' and 'professional' – as we are likely to understand them today – risks reifying into place certain ostensibly clear-cut categorical distinctions that do not withstand closer scrutiny. Subtle inflections of meaning where the 'competent' or 'skilled amateur' is concerned may blur into those of closely correlated notions of the 'operator', 'novice', 'hobbyist', 'enthusiast' or 'neophyte,' as well as 'non-' or 'semi-professional,' amongst others. More often than not the crux of the matter, then as today, revolved around the relative extent to which the individual photographer in question expected some form of compensation, patronage or financial remuneration when performing their craft.

In recognizing these attendant complexities, this chapter aims to draw out the conceptual tensions typically obscured by a starkly rendered amateur-professional binarism. In so doing, it will seek to identify and critique differing perspectives on the factors shaping the emergence of war photography across several conflicts, ranging from the 1840s to the close of World War I.[1] It is my contention that ongoing debates about the rise of the professional photojournalist have much to gain by tracing the evolving, still inchoate ethos of amateur photo-reportage. As I intend to show, ordinary individuals who felt compelled to bear witness to events transpiring around them, regardless of whether or not they self-identified as amateurs per se, played a vital role in helping to establish precedents of form and practice of continuing relevance today.

Pictorial Conventions

Histories of war correspondence necessarily elect to affix a starting point consistent with their conceptual priorities. It is perhaps not surprising that such accounts tend to overlook the contribution of photographers, preferring to firmly align reportage with the written word. In a British context, William Howard Russell's despatches for *The Times* on the Crimean War typically earn him the accolade for being the first 'modern' war correspondent (his self-description as 'the miserable parent of a luckless tribe' being widely endorsed over the years). Closer inspection, however, reveals alternative claims to the mantle, not least that of Henry Crabb Robinson, who found himself in Spain covering the Peninsular War shortly after its outbreak in 1808 for the same newspaper, which complicates any suggestion that Russell's role was a sudden, prodigious innovation in British journalism. Similar contingencies hold true with regard to the visual imagery of warfare, where pictorial representations of armed conflict can be traced to the earliest days of human societies (Perlmutter 1999). In a modern sense, the Dutch painter Willem van de Velde comes to mind, given the view of some historians that he was the 'first, and far away the greatest, of all the war-correspondent-artists', even though 'the sketches made on one battlefield might not have been worked up into an ambitious studio composition until years after the event' (Callender 1940: 104). It follows, then, that to contend that photography constitutes the 'first visual medium' of war reporting, as has been variously asserted over the years, is to risk overlooking the materiality – not least temporal specificity – of pictorial conventions, much to the impoverishment of any ensuing analysis.

It is worth noting for our purposes that efforts to identify the 'amateur's' contribution to the evolving dynamics of war photography will demand a careful elucidation of the basis on which this status is to be distinguished. Accordingly, while the Crimean conflict, once again, is routinely singled out as a formative occasion when photography earned its place in the history of war correspondence, it is advantageous to push back even further to discern what may appear to be, at least in retrospect, various emergent principles – if not protocols – of photojournalism's gradual consolidation in professional terms. Indeed, it soon becomes apparent that conceptions of amateurism were loosely articulated, at best, and frequently found definition to the extent that they rubbed up against those of entrepreneurism. Practical necessity, not least with regard to the costs involved, made the prospect of financial reward all but irresistible to some amateurs struggling to support their newfound hobby. A passionate commitment to photography as an art form, where the very integrity of aesthetic values was thought to be at risk of compromise by remuneration, was a luxury only the privileged could afford to sustain. Few failed to recognize the opportunity to capitalize on the skills they were acquiring with the latest technology, even when otherwise self-consciously resisting the pull towards commercialism.

Historical investigations into the origins of war photography typically begin by considering the available pictorial evidence, namely daguerreotypes or calotypes of landscapes, buildings or soldiers in uniform, formally posing for the benefit of slow shutter speeds. The camera demonstrated its potential to record important features of military life long before the images being generated were deemed to be indicative of a discrete genre in its own right. Arguably the first relevant instance occurred during the Mexican–American War (1846–48), when the US army invaded Mexico to seize control of its northern territories (Texas having been annexed by the US the year before). While little is known of the photographers involved, the images themselves reveal that American forces were accompanied by photographers – a form of 'embedding' in today's parlance – intent on documenting events, albeit typically some distance from where battle was being waged. Frequently labelled the 'first photographed war', accounts often dwell on images such as those from 1847, depicting General John E. Wool and his staff after the capture of Saltillo or another which presents the scene of a leg amputation (quite possibly a re-enactment) in a military hospital after the Battle of Cerro Gordo. Similarly worthy of note in this regard were the efforts of some American daguerreians to set up studios in Mexican towns, endeavouring to earn a commission by taking portraits of those involved in the conflict, living or otherwise. An advertisement placed in the Veracruz *American Eagle* by Charles S. Betts in April of 1847, for example, offered to produce miniatures 'to the satisfaction of the sitter or no charge made' (cit. in Palmquist and Kailbourn 2005: 107). Moreover, by special request, he was willing to 'go to the residences to take miniatures of the dead and wounded', an offer that underscored the need to earn a return on what was a substantial investment in equipment.

A series of calotype images taken by Scottish military surgeon Dr John McCosh (sometimes spelled MacCosh) during the Second Anglo-Sikh War (1848–49) and the Second Burmese War (1852–53) count as sufficient grounds, some historians maintain, to recognize him as the first war photographer known by name. A keen amateur, he actively pursued his hobby when otherwise not performing his duties for the East India Company. Most of the images attributed to him comprise landscape and architectural studies (such as the tomb of Maharaja Ranjit Singh), as well as a series of portraits. The latter include friends in the main, as well as officers, such as British commander General Sir Charles Napier, together with Indian and Burmese locals. Though Dr McCosh travelled with his camera equipment through war zones, there is no evidence that he made any effort to document the horrors of battle around him. Instead, his collection of military portraits, interspersed with occasional images of troops posing for the camera, artillery, installations and razed buildings, constitute his main involvement in war photography. Evidently aware of his limitations where photographic achievements were concerned, his enthusiasm nonetheless found expression in his book, *Advice to Officers in India*, published in 1856 following his retirement from the army. 'I would strongly recommend every assistant-surgeon to make himself a master of photography in all its branches, on paper, on plate glass, and on metallic plates', he wrote. 'I have practiced it for many years', he continued, 'and know of no extra professional pursuit that will repay him for all the expense and trouble (and both are very considerable) than this fascinating study' (cit. in Hannavy 2008: 911). McCosh was convinced that 'such a faithful collection of representations' was certain to be a 'welcome contribution to any museum'.

Notwithstanding these and related developments – such as Hippolyte Bayard and Eugene Thibault's daguerreotypes of the Paris barricades during the 1848 revolution or Stefano Lecchi's images, including salted paper prints, showing the destruction left in the wake of the siege of Rome in 1849 – it is the Crimean War (1853–56) where histories of war photography typically commence in earnest. Photographers arrived on the scene from several countries, including Britain, France, Romania, Germany and Russia, amongst others, with the aim of documenting what was happening, albeit with different motivations. The Hungarian-born Carol Popp de Szathmari, an amateur painter based in Romania, is regarded by some to be the first combat photographer because of the images he took during the first year of the Russian-Turkish War, which later extended to include the Crimea. In the British context, Gilbert Elliot, an amateur, recorded images of fortresses from aboard a ship in the Baltic Sea in 1854. Military authorities, alert to the advantages of establishing a pictorial record on favourable terms, had commissioned a small photographic unit to produce coverage of the conflict from a perspective held to be consistent with the national interest. The civilian photographer Richard Nicklin was appointed to lead it, although he and his assistants perished in November of that year when their ship sank during a hurricane striking the Balaklava harbour. Amateur-involvement also took place from within the military's own ranks, with various 'experiments' being conducted onboard vessels of the Baltic fleet. In spring of the following year, two military officers, Ensigns Brandon and Dawson, endeavoured to supplement the official record. Both had received the benefit of training from a London-based photographer before being despatched, but the relative success of their achievements is unknown (none of their work survives). Easily the most noteworthy contribution, however, is that of their fellow countryman, British-born Roger Fenton, the first war photographer to achieve fame as such. His use of the new collodion wet-plate process enabled him to create a remarkable set of some 360 images over the four months he spent in the region.

While sometimes described as a 'gentleman photographer' in light of the considerable personal wealth he enjoyed, Fenton's amateur interest gradually evolved into an abiding passion. His decision to recast his hobby in commercial terms was made in 1853, when he accepted an invitation from the British Museum to render his services as a photographer in exchange for retaining the right to sell his images to members of the public, in a kiosk in the foyer. Early the next year, Queen Victoria – an amateur photographer and enthusiast herself – commissioned him to produce a series of royal portraits, thereby enhancing his profile as a photographer of national repute. In the view of some historians, this association with the monarch (or, more to the point, an appreciation of her sensitivities where the conduct of her armed forces was concerned) decisively shaped his photographic practice in the Crimea. Royal patronage in support of his expedition to the warzone in March 1855 included letters of introduction from Prince Albert intended to help ensure the cooperation of military commanders, while related logistical challenges were eased with government assistance. Prior to his departure, a further financial arrangement had been agreed with the Manchester-based print-publishers Thomas Agnew & Sons to sell the images upon his return as mementos of the conflict (an ill-fated enterprise in the end, given waning public interest by the time the photographs were reproduced). On this basis, Fenton was able to bring with him a photographic assistant, Marcus Sparling, as well as a personal servant, together with three-dozen cases of equipment, including five cameras and over 700 glass plates. Negatives were made in his horse-drawn 'carriage,' as he called it – namely a former wine merchant's van converted into a makeshift mobile darkroom – which also enabled him to transport fragile, yet also bulky and heavy equipment.

This convergence of royal, government and financial interests, together with what were rather formidable technological constraints, helps to explain why the vast majority of Fenton's images cast the war in an ostensibly patriotic – albeit dull and uneventful – light. A further factor was his relative inexperience, both with respect to his newfound professional status (his role as photographer on assignment signalling a formal break from his amateur days) and in terms of firsthand knowledge of open hostilities in a warzone. Accordingly, while Fenton's fledgling professional approach earned considerable praise for its aesthetic and technical achievements, the scope of the ensuing coverage – 'Valley of the Shadow of Death' being a well-known exception – was kept firmly within proscribed normative limits. In marked contrast with his written observations of the tragedies endemic to warfare, as evidenced by the letters he sent home, the surviving negatives indicate that no sustained effort was mounted to document combat, let alone its devastating consequences (see also Baldwin et al. 2004). In sharp contrast with William Howard Russell's newspaper dispatches, which spoke directly to the plight of ill-equipped soldiers struggling to cope with severe extremes in weather conditions (as well as with managerial ineptitude, including inadequate medical facilities), these images appealed to different principles of reportage. Visual priorities long associated with heroic, celebratory painting – Fenton was an accomplished painter trained in the codes of realism – were reaffirmed to a considerable extent in images composed with elaborate care. Still, closer inspection could sometimes reveal subtle details in scenes, particularly those documenting day-to-day experiences of soldiers, that were transgressive of official strictures, or at least potentially so when interpreted in relation to journalistic accounts. Lurking in the shadows of the picturesque, in other words, were evidential hints of larger truths, namely the sheer scale of the human tragedy unfolding in such desperate circumstances.

By the war's final stages, amateur photographers such as Jean-Charles Langlois, a French Army officer, Italian-born Felice A. Beato and Scotsman James Robertson were bringing to bear a more robust commitment to recording both the preparations for attack and the wretched aftermath of battle (exposure times of 3–20 seconds made the active capture of movement impossible). What this imagery lacked with respect to artistic flair in Fenton's terms, it gained in its frank commitment to documentation. In 1857, Robertson and Beato, who happened to be brothers-in-law, were in India to photograph events in the First War of Independence. Beato's images of the British massacre of Indian rebels in Lucknow in 1858, providing visual evidence of the corpses left behind, was yet another grim 'first' in photographic terms in that it broke the death taboo (thereby setting 'the tone for photographic reportage of victims of the American Civil War,' Frances Fralin (1985: 34) observes). The following year, a young English amateur photographer, known only as J. L. on the basis of letters he sent to the London journal *Photographic News* from Italy, felt personally compelled to document the Second Italian War of Independence. The 'exciting prospect,' he wrote, was to 'get plates' that captured 'a field of battle' so that 'when the excitement of the conflict is past [...] they might not then perhaps talk so flippantly of war' (cit. in Hodgson 1974: 11, 22–23). Evidently J. L.'s images of those killed spared few sensitivities – Victorian or otherwise – in their graphic depiction of what had transpired, yet this amateur's early testing of proscriptive norms and values has barely registered in historical accounts written over the years.

'Volunteers for Photographic Service in the Field'

Efforts to discern the amateur's contribution to war photography encounter a myriad challenges, the resolution of which require careful consideration and, at times, informed speculation. It is often the case that important photographs are unattributed, making it difficult to locate them within a larger portfolio or collection. In some cases, prints from the plates – such as with respect to the J. L. mentioned above – no longer exist, thereby all but assuring that the circumstances of their production remain obscured in what is often called 'the fog of war.' The disappearance of an amateur photographer in a warzone would attract little attention or concern from military authorities, nor anyone else otherwise inclined towards recordkeeping. Even when certain biographical details are forthcoming, questions concerning the precise status of the photographer, including where they are situated along the amateur–professional continuum (for it is a continuum, rather than a binarism, in my view), recurrently elude confident determination. More straightforward to categorize was the civilian artist, an individual otherwise involved in the military operation, or a 'gentleman' whose self-taught hobby was appreciated amongst influential circles (several of whom deliberately sought out conflict areas when making a 'Grand Tour' of Europe).

Matters gradually improve in this regard as amateur photography raises its profile as a popular activity in its own right, albeit one still relatively restricted in class terms. This process was bolstered by the establishment of photographic clubs and associations from the early 1850s onwards in countries such as Britain, France and the United States. Membership typically encompassed a mix of professionals and amateurs, with many of the latter treating it as a serious avocation as opposed to a casual pastime or hobby (or as an indicator of 'conspicuous consumption' (Veblen 1899) in leisure activities). Photography was a dedicated pursuit for numerous scientists, academics, artists and barristers (such as Fenton), amongst others, keenly intent on advancing inventive refinements in form and practice, even where war photography was concerned. London's Photographic Society, founded in 1853, published an editorial in the 21 April 1854 edition of its journal that highlighted how members of its growing network felt compelled to become involved in the Crimean. 'We may mention [...]

Figure 2.1: Cold Harbor, Virginia (vicinity). Collecting remains of dead on the battlefield. This photograph was taken in 1865 by John Reekie. Library of Congress Prints and Photographs Division, USA.

that the patriotism and enterprise which have been so evident in all quarters in reference to the present war, is fully shared by photographers, for the brief notice in our last number was the signal for quite a shower of letters to the Secretary of the Society, from volunteers for photographic service in the field' (cit. in Green-Lewis 1996: 99). This reference to a 'shower of letters' is telling, quite possibly suggesting that the prospect of involvement rested upon a conception of war as a glorious, patriotic adventure. Presumably Fenton's personal experience of a conflict that had seen him suffering from cholera, as well as enduring broken ribs, helped to keep such enthusiasms in check for some of his fellow Society members in the years ahead.

In the 1860s there were several conflicts where photographers sought to bear witness to the human cost of conflict, such as during the latter stages of the so-called Second Opium War in China (1856–60), Franco-British bombardments on the Straits of Shimonoseki in 1864 and the War of the Triple Alliance (1864–70) amongst others. Easily the most significant for the magnitude of its photographic achievement, however, was the initiative undertaken by Mathew Brady, operator of a successful business in portrait photography, to document the Civil War (1861–65) in the United States. Following the Union army into battle, Brady and a corps of operators in his employ – which included such skilled practitioners as Alexander Gardner, Timothy O'Sullivan and John Reekie – endeavoured to record a visual legacy of a nation's tragedy. In contrast with Fenton's quasi-amateur status, Brady, who considered himself to be a pictorial historian, was soon credited with being the first professional war photographer (see also Panzer 1997; Park 1999).

Items published in *The New York Times* provide important insights into how the significance of this achievement was interpreted in journalistic terms. In 'Brady's Photographs of the War,' published on 26 September 1862, the writer observes:

> [...] Mr. BRADY is rendering us all a real service, in divers [sic] ways, by this work of his, undertaken so courageously, and carried forward so resolutely. It is no holiday business this taking the likeness of 'grim-visaged war' – and it is no mere gratification of idle curiosity which its results may afford us. We wish the artist all possible success in his task, and commend his efforts anew to the admiration and the appreciation of the American public.
>
> (*The New York Times* 26 September 1862)

War photography as a public service is contrasted here with the efforts of the casual amateur, or so it would appear depending on how one interprets the reference to 'holiday business' and the 'idle curiosity' it ostensibly gratifies. In any case, precisely what 'grim-visaged war' entailed in representational terms was spelled out more clearly in a follow-up in an editorial leader, 'Pictures of the Dead at Antietam,' published the following month where the writer observes:

> We recognize the battle-field as a reality, but it stands as a remote one. [...]
> Mr. BRADY has done something to bring home to us the terrible reality and earnestness of war. If he has not brought bodies and laid them in our dooryards and along the streets, he has done something very like it. At the door of his gallery hangs a little placard, 'The Dead of Antietam.' Crowds of people are constantly going up the stairs; follow them, and you find them bending over photographic views of that fearful battle-field, taken immediately after the action. Of all objects of horror one would think the battle-field should stand preeminent, that it should bear away the palm of repulsiveness. But, on the contrary, there is a terrible fascination about it that draws one near these pictures, and makes him loth to leave them. [...]
> These pictures have a terrible distinctness. By the aid of the magnifying glass, the very ceatures [sic] of the slain may be distinguished. We would scarce choose to be in the gallery, when one of the women bending over them should recognize a husband, a son, or a brother in the still, lifeless lines of bodies, that lie ready for the gaping trenches. For these trenches have a terror for a woman's heart, that goes far to outweigh all the others that hover over the battle-field [...].
>
> (*The New York Times* 20 October 1862)

These and related items published at the time in newspapers such as *The New York Times* afford us a glimpse of the sorts of evaluative criteria gradually coalescing into the guiding tenets of war photography as a genre of reportage. In 1867, almost two years after the surrender of the Confederate army, an article titled 'Historical Photography' appearing in the same newspaper celebrated the power of these 'war pictures' to 'tell the story of the great conflict with sad fidelity' (*The New York Times* 29 March 1867). While assertions that 'the camera is the eye of history' – words widely attributed to Brady – were countered by allegations calling into question the authenticity of certain images (corpses or weaponry being rearranged, and the like), few would dispute that war photography 'came of age' during these years, despite its glaring omissions.

In light of the estimated involvement of some 1400 photographers over the four years of the conflict (producing tens of thousands of photographs, some 3500 of which being credited to Brady), the contribution of the amateur is challenging to isolate in retrospect. Considerable effort would be required to delve into even a small number of their individual biographies. It is similarly difficult to generalize from disparate pieces of evidence, such as historical accounts offering passing observations about photographs in public exhibitions, or in the private realm of personal prints, stereo-cards or cartes-de-visite in albums and sketchbooks. Given that photographs intended to serve as the basis for wood engravings or lithographs in the press often underwent 'corrections' or 'improvements' in the course of reproduction, the specific provenance of a particular image was frequently deemed insufficiently consequential to record. Illustration was still very much the domain of the war artist, not the photographer. This remained the case where subsequent conflicts in places such as India, China, Afghanistan and the Sudan were concerned as well, despite the slow and steady progress made in photographic technique and image reproduction.

Technical innovations were largely incremental until the 1880s, when photographic practice was dramatically recast by the arrival of reliable gelatine dry-plates, and thereby hand-held cameras suitable for amateur interests. The Eastman Dry Plate Company in Rochester, New York, led the way in popularizing these developments, introducing the first folding pocket camera using roll film in 1888. Designed for 'Holiday-makers, Tourists, Cyclists, Ladies, etc.', the No. 1 Kodak box camera could be 'mastered in a few minutes' (a promise summed up in the advertising slogan 'You press the button – We do the rest'). The promise of the 'instantaneous' snapshot photograph opened up new possibilities for reportage, although the superior quality of wet-plate negatives meant that older, more established forms of camera technology took some time to displace. What each successive camera – the inexpensive 'Brownie' arriving shortly thereafter – afforded in casual portability came at the price of grainier images somewhat lacking in sharpness in comparison. Press photographs began to reflect a new aesthetic, while both professionals and 'serious' amateurs sought to differentiate themselves from the 'legions of snapshooters' caught up in the excitement of picture-making.[2] The introduction of the halftone screen made the mass reproduction of photographs technically possible, although most journals and newspapers continued to rely on engravings of artists' impressions.

By the close of the century, journal and newspaper editors were fast-becoming accustomed to casting their nets widely in the search for photographs up to the task of effectively illustrating reported dimensions of conflict. Indeed, ever-increasing numbers of amateurs were taking cameras with them on campaign – such as the Grenadier Guards during the Sudanese War of 1898 – thereby ensuring that officially sanctioned conceptions of war photography underwent rapid transformation. In the case of the Spanish–American War that same year, Susan Moeller (1989) estimates that 'three or four soldiers' brought 'their brand new Kodaks to the front' (1989: xiii). Pointing to the growing capacity of the press to reproduce photographs, she makes the related observation that distant audiences were gaining a very different order of insight into the conflict as a result. 'The invention of the half-tone', she argues, 'ushered in the first "living-room war"' (1989: 25). Closer to the home front, amateur war photography of a different order is noted in a *New York Times* article, headlined 'Happy Spaniards', published in July 1898. It describes 'a most novel and interesting picture' transpiring outside a prison, situated on Seavey's Island in the Piscataqua River in Kittery, Maine. Spanish prisoners of war 'had swarmed to the water's edge to wash their bowls, plates and spoons' following their afternoon meal, an 'animated scene' attracting the interest of those passing by on leisure boats.

> Many ladies in the boats had provided themselves with kodaks, and hundreds of pictures were taken of the prisoners that will prove valuable souvenirs of the American-Spanish war as time goes by. The Spaniards enjoyed having their pictures taken, and many of them gathered in groups and posed in picturesque attitudes and waited their turns for the camera.
>
> A colored prisoner, black as Erebus, waded out into the water up to his knees, and, striking his bowl and plate together to attract attention, placed his hands by his side, rolled the whites of his eyes heavenward, and stood expectant. Scores of kodaks snapped, and the colored sailor triumphantly rejoined his comrades on the shore.
>
> (*The New York Times* 21 July 1898)

The suggestion that these amateur snapshot 'souvenirs' held the potential to be of lasting significance to war photography is revealing. It rightly anticipates that the casual everydayness of such imagery would provide future viewers with a precious insight into this otherwise hidden dimension of the conflict.

Pictorial journalism during the Second Boer War (1899–1902) interwove the contributions of professionals and amateurs in seeking to satiate distant readers' appetite for news and images – especially as the conduct of the war became evermore controversial. It was typically the case, however, that photographs taken by professionals were static, predictable and altogether lacking in any sense of engagement – much like most of the press reporting of the time, which offered little more than celebratory treatments in the service of imperialism (the efforts of amateur journalist Emily Hobhouse to report on the desperate plight of Boer women and children starving in British prison camps being a relevant counterpoint, the appalling scenes escaping attention in the mainstream press). One exception amongst the professional photographers was Reinhold Thiele, commissioned by the *Graphic/Daily Graphic*. Thiele's work, in the words of a *Photogram* review, was 'more varied, more accurate, and more complete than anything previously attempted in the field of pictorial war correspondence [...] If war-time photography can be made a success, Reinhold Thiele is just the man to make it so' (cit. in Fralin 1985: 76; see also Lee 1985). In the main, though, titles such as the *London Illustrated News* still exercised a strong preference for artists' pictures over photographs, choosing the latter only when their visual impact was

Figure 2.2: Royal Munster Fusiliers fighting from behind the redoubt at Honey Nest Kloof, South Africa, with medics treating wounded, during Boer War. Stereoscopic photography taken by an unknown photographer on 16 February 1900. Library of Congress Prints and Photographs Division, USA.

sufficiently compelling. Significant in this context were soldiers' personal photographs, which were widely solicited by publications intent on supplementing the sorts of 'raw', 'on-the-spot' pencilled sketches otherwise provided by those in the field and trenches. The use of snapshots had advantages – they were cheaper than good drawings, for example – but risked criticism as a poor alternative when blurry, ill-composed or badly printed: 'tiresome to the eye and repugnant to the artistic sense', in the words of an advertisement in the *Sphere* periodical (cit. in Harrington 2000: 239).

A Democratization of Image-Making

By the time of the outbreak of hostilities in what would be called the First World War (1914–18), it was readily apparent that the democratization of image-making was rapidly consolidating. Amateur photography had secured a comfortable place as a popular pastime, with relatively inexpensive, reliable cameras affording the casual hobbyist as well as the dedicated enthusiast a convenient way to document everyday events of personal significance. Pictorial newspapers, led by the *Daily Mirror* in London, were creating a strong market-demand for news photographs, thanks to marked improvements in half-tone printing processes and photo-telegraphy. Moreover, there was every indication that a more formalized role for the professional photo-reporter was beckoning on the horizon.

'The War to End All Wars', having been triggered in the summer of 1914 by the assassination of Archduke Franz Ferdinand of Austria, would eventually embroil 32 countries in a conflict that would kill almost ten million military personnel and an estimated seven million civilians, by its close in November, 1918. Military censorship was strictly enforced from the start in the Allied countries, the rationale for which being aligned with interrelated objectives of controlling information perceived to be of value to the enemy while, at the same time, striving to realize the potential of frontline reports for propaganda purposes, that is, to bolster morale on the home front. Each of the different military forces from the respective countries involved experimented, to varying degrees, with 'official' photographers – typically drawn from military personnel – in order to secure a historical record of the war's conduct. Despite the number of photographs being taken, however, very few would find their way on to the pages of the press. Those which were published typically revealed little of the appalling conditions under which soldiers were being slaughtered. Self-censorship, performed under the banner of nationalism, proved to be remarkably effective, but this was only part of the story. 'In retrospect it seems unlikely that the case for halting the conflict because of visual evidence of its waste of life would have found a hearing earlier', Jane Carmichael (1989) contends, 'even had the photographers considered it their role to provide this point of view which they emphatically did not'. Quite the contrary, she adds, they 'did not consider themselves to be independent observers of the struggle but privileged participants whose skill was being put to patriotic use' (1989: 145). Further complicating efforts in this latter regard was the near-absence of dramatic imagery deemed sufficiently

Figure 2.3: Take The Soldier's Kodak With You! Published in *Evening Post*, Volume XCIV, Issue 68, 18 September 1917. National Library of New Zealand.

Take

The Soldier's Kodak
With You!

No Soldier's Kit is complete without a Vest Pocket Kodak. It weighs only 9 ounces: it will withstand the rough usage of the hardest campaign : / and it requires neither skill nor scientific knowledge to use it. When you go to the Front, carry "The Soldier's Kodak" in your breast pocket. Then you will bring back a priceless picture record of your share in the Great War.

Price 35/-

The Vest Pocket Autographic Kodak SPECIAL, with Kodak Anastigmat F6.9 Lens Price 67/6

Look for the name KODAK stamped on the Camera for your protection. KODAK PRICE LIST FREE—ASK FOR ONE!

SOLD BY ALL KODAK DEALERS, AND

KODAK (Australasia) LTD.
"The Kodak Corner"
Corner Lambton Quay and Willis Street
WELLINGTON

newsworthy by newspaper and journal editors, the realities of trench warfare affording few opportunities for photographers to capture instances of 'real action' from adequate (or safe) vantage points. Picture quality also tended to be problematic, with camera technology pushed to its limits under intense pressure in daunting conditions.

The interweaving of shared priorities among official and press photographers can be thrown into sharper relief by drawing a comparison with those embodied by the non-official photographer. Encouragement for soldiers to see themselves in these terms was widespread, not least in the case of camera manufactures. Kodak, for example, sold its Vest Pocket model as 'The Soldier's Kodak' with the tagline: 'It is as small as a diary and tells the story better'. One May 1915 advertisement stated: 'Every soldier naturally wants to keep a lasting record of the brave part he and his own Company are playing in the Great War – and he can do it well and easily with the little Vest Pocket Kodak'. Further virtues highlighted included its lightness, durability, convenience and simplicity to operate – 'You can learn to use it in half-an-hour. No skill, no practice, no scientific knowledge is needed' (*The Argus* 31 May 1915). The severity of censorship, however, meant that the price paid for soldiers (as well as civilians) caught taking photographs on the frontlines in France was instant arrest, with death by firing squad a very real possibility. Amongst those prepared to take the risk of court martial was Private F. A. Fyfe of 'Z' Company, 1/10th King's Regiment (Liverpool Scottish). A press photographer in civilian life prior to the war, evidently he smuggled a vest pocket camera to the front in his bandolier. His photographs of the Battle of Hooge, taken while lying wounded, were published in the *Northern Daily Dispatch* and the *Liverpool Daily Post* in June 1915. In relaying 'images to the home front of dead soldiers and the debris and desolation of No Man's Land', historian Mary McCartney observes, Fyfe's work 'reinforced the dual message of the heroism of the Liverpool Scots and the confusion and brutality of battle' (McCartney 2005: 108).

Given the prohibitions surrounding photography, it is hardly surprising that many soldiers kept their cameras concealed in their kitbags, not having anticipated that taking snapshots would be deemed illegal (such was also the case, many soon discovered, with regard to private diary keeping, where similar concerns about the control of information were expressed and enforced). Officers tended to be more inclined to ignore the ban, especially when on leave. They also enjoyed greater freedom of movement, were better placed to keep their cameras in working order and supplied with film and also more likely to see their negatives safely posted home to be developed (Rodger 1988). Photographs accredited to 'an officer serving at the front' occasionally found their way into print, with the local press typically being much more receptive than their national counterparts. In marked contrast with the rather mundane efforts of photographers working under military guidance, many of the amateurs taking photographs – which also included nurses, ambulance drivers and the like – brought to bear intensely personal commitments, occasionally recording in grisly detail precisely what was transpiring in all of its dreadfulness. And sometimes capturing events such as the 'Christmas truce', when enemy soldiers climbed out from their respective trenches to meet in the middle of No Man's Land, which defied belief.[3] Much more typical, however, were shots of everyday life in moments of quiet, with developed prints or postcards treated as highly valued souvenirs (even as objects of exchange for some). Comradeship meant that the dignity of the person photographed was to be respected, a sense of morality that was also extended to include the sensitivities of those who would eventually examine such images back home.[4]

Conclusion

To close, I would like to suggest that the examples under scrutiny in this chapter may be considered broadly indicative of what I am inclined to call an emergent ecology of amateur war photography. Tracing its features has proven challenging, not least because historical treatments tend to marginalize such contributions, despite the important ways in which incipient forms of professionalism prefigure, to varying degrees, various non-professional alternatives. The names of most photographers inclined to self-identify as amateurs have been long forgotten, their images and negatives – in the unlikely event that anyone thought to preserve them for posterity – typically relegated to crumbling boxes in dusty attics, or worse. Much work remains to be done to recover this material for its own sake, but also to critically examine it with an eye to delving deeper into different amateurs' desires, motivations and pretensions as they gave shape to their craft. While evidence suggests that the guiding ideals of professionalism influenced many amateurs' personal views about form and practice, for example, more needs to be learnt about the relative extent to which they embraced varied claims about visual truth or associated rhetoric concerning realism and naturalistic reproduction. To what degree, we may ask, did a journalistic impulse or ethos animate their reportorial work? Similarly, little is understood about the social connections, even networks amongst amateur photographers, their technical training (if any), or accepted norms guiding channels of distribution, sharing or exhibition and the like. What we know about the technologies involved is considerable, yet much remains to be discovered about the uneven ways in which they were taken up, modified, and recast to be judged fit for purpose.

One matter is clear, however. In fashioning an alternative, amateur-centred research agenda, any conception of 'the amateur' as a distinct figure embodying specific characteristics, effectively defined by a status held in contradistinction to the professional, is certain to be rendered problematic. In moving beyond the amateur–professional binarism, then, it is necessary to begin reading standard histories of war photography against the grain, so to speak, in order to discern otherwise implicit assumptions, values and normative proscriptions. It is in recognizing that a fluidly contingent continuum is at stake – as I have sought to suggest above – that traditional ways of thinking may be reinvigorated anew.

Notes

1. This chapter's discussion is necessarily selective in its treatment of various conflicts. Valuable surveys of war photography include Carlebach (1992), Fralin (1985), Griffin (1999), Hodgson (1974), Hüppauf (1993), Knightley (2003), Lewinski (1978), Moeller (1989), Stapp (1988) and Zelizer (2002).
2. Sarah Greenough (1991) writes that by 1890 'the commercial photographer was no longer viewed as something of a magician, the sole possessor of the secrets of drawing with light, but instead was often seen by the public as little better than an amateur hack who pushed the button and let Kodak do the rest' (1991: 260). For a further discussion of Kodak's influence on amateur photography, see also Collins (1990).
3. For an account of German amateur photography at the Western Front, see Remus (2008). Further examinations of this period include Carmichael (1989), Holmes (2008) and Taylor (1991).
4. This relationship found its reverse when citizens at home were encouraged to send soldiers photographs of their loved ones. 'Snapshots from Home' is the title of an August 1915 article from *Amateur Photographer* magazine reproduced in Mary Warner Marien's (2002) account, which describes the YMCA's coordinated volunteer drive to lend soldiers support with comforting imagery.

References

Baldwin, G. et al. (2004), *All the Mighty World: The Photographs of Roger Fenton, 1852–1860*, New Haven: Yale University Press.

Callender, G. (1940), 'Willem van de Velde the Elder and His Art', *The Burlington Magazine for Connoisseurs*, 76: 445, pp. 104–10.

Carlebach, M. L. (1992), *The Origins of Photojournalism in America*, Washington: Smithsonian Institution Press.

Carmichael, J. (1989), *First World War Photographers*, London and New York: Routledge.

Collins, D. (1990), *The Story of Kodak*, New York: Harry N. Abrams, Inc.

Fralin, F. (1985), *The Indelible Image: Photographs of War – 1846 to the Present*, New York: Harry N. Abrams.

Green-Lewis, J. (1996), *Framing the Victorians: Photography and the Culture of Realism*, Ithaca, NY: Cornell University Press.

Greenough, S. (1991), '"Of Charming Glens, Graceful Glades, and Frowning Cliffs": The Economic Incentives, Social Inducements, and Aesthetic Issues of American Pictorial Photography, 1880–1902', in M. A. Sandweiss (ed.), *Photography in Nineteenth-Century America*, Fort Worth: Amon Carter Museum.

Griffin, M. (1999), 'The Great War Photographs: Constructing Myths of History and Photojournalism', in B. Brennan and H. Hardt (eds), *Picture the Past: Media, History, and Photography*, Urbana: University of Illinois Press.

Hannavy, J. (2008), 'McCosh, John (1816–1894)', in J. Hannavy (ed.), *Encyclopedia of Nineteenth-Century Photography*, London and New York: Routledge.

Harrington, P. (2000), 'Pictorial Journalism and the Boer War: The London Illustrated Weeklies', in J. Gooch (ed.), *The Boer War: Direction, Experience and Image*, London: Frank Cass.

Hodgson, P. (1974), *Early War Photographs*, London: Book Club Associates.

Holmes, R. (2008), *Shots from the Front*, London: Harper Collins.

Hüppauf, B. (1993), 'The Emergence of Modern War Imagery in Early Photography', *History and Memory*, 5: 1, pp. 130–51.

Knightley, P. (2003), *The Eye of War: Words and Photographs from the Front Line*, Washington, D.C.: Smithsonian Books.

Lee, E. (1985), *To the Bitter End: A Photographic History of the Boer War 1899–1902*, Harmondsworth: Penguin Books.

Lewinski, J. (1978), *The Camera at War: A History of War Photography from 1848 to the Present Day*, London: W & J Mackay.

Marien, M. W. (2002), *Photography: A Cultural History*, London: Lawrence King Publishing.

Marwil, J. (2000), 'Photography at War', *History Today*, June, 30–37.

McCartney, M. (2005), *Citizen Soldiers: The Liverpool Territorials in the First World War*, Cambridge: Cambridge University Press.

Moeller, S. (1989), *Shooting War: Photography and the American Experience of Combat*, New York: Basic Books.

Palmquist, P. E. and Kailbourn, T. R. (2005), *Pioneer Photographers from the Mississippi to the Continental Divide: A Biographical Dictionary, 1839–1865*, Stanford: Stanford University Press.

Panzer, M. (1997), *Mathew Brady and the Image of History*, Washington, D.C.: Smithsonian Books.

Park, D. (1999), 'Picturing the War: Visual Genres in Civil War News', *The Communication Review*, 3: 4, pp. 287–21.

Perlmutter, D. D. (1999), *Visions of War*, New York: St Martin's Griffin.

Remus, S. (2008), *German Amateur Photographers in the First World War: A View from the Trenches on the Western Front*, Atglen: PA: Schiffer Military History.

Rodger, A. C. (1988), 'Amateur Photography by Soldiers of the Canadian Expeditionary Force,' *Archivaria*, 26, pp. 163–68.

Stapp, W. (1988), 'Subjects of Strange … and of Fearful Interest: Photojournalism from its Beginning in 1839,' in M. Fulton (ed.), *Eyes of Time: Photojournalism in America,* Boston: A New York Graphic Society Book/Little, Brown & Company.

Taylor, J. (1991), *War Photography: Realism in the British Press*, London: Routledge.

Veblen, T. (1899), *The Theory of the Leisure Class*, New York: Macmillan.

Zelizer, B. (2002), 'Finding Aids to the Past: Bearing Personal Witness to Traumatic Public Events,' *Media, Culture & Society*, 24: 5, pp. 697–714.

Chapter 3

The Eyewitness in the Age of Digital Transformation

Mette Mortensen

With mobile cameras always at hand, we are all potential eyewitnesses today. The emergence of digital technologies and participatory journalistic practices secure the vitality of eyewitnessing as a keyword in the present-day media landscape. In a culture marked by compulsive picture taking and sharing, bearing witness is invariably an option, whether we find ourselves situated as bystanders to history in the making, an unfolding crisis or merely in the humdrum of everyday life. As a tangible result of this development, the amount of non-professional photos and videos is growing apace across a broad spectrum of media: from personal websites and blogs to social media platforms to the established news media.

Currently, it is critical for us to determine how we might define and theorize the non-professional producer of images arising over the past decade. Recent technological advances have of course facilitated the unprecedented scale and scope of amateur visuals in the public realm. However, technology-led modes of explanation hardly exhaust the political, social and cultural impact of amateur images in our present age of digital transformation. This chapter's examination of the contemporary citizen photojournalist takes its point of departure in a critical assessment of the theoretical work pertaining to the eyewitness. With first-hand experience of events as the entrance card to taking on the role of citizen photojournalist, the new picture producer is often regarded as a successor to the long-standing figure of the eyewitness. For instance, citizen photojournalism is commonly associated with the tradition of bearing witness in media discourse when phrases such as 'eyewitness photography' and 'eyewitness accounts' are applied to news pictures taken by non-professionals. Yet, with a few exceptions (Zelizer 2007: 421–24), the assumption that the citizen photojournalist is a web 2.0 incarnation of the eyewitness has no theoretical underpinnings. This is all the more surprising considering the rich literature in the field that examines issues concerning the special position for experience and narration held by the witness, as well as this figure's moral, cultural and political significance, which are also vital for defining the present-day citizen photojournalist. This research tradition serves as a starting point for conceptualizing arguably the most groundbreaking change regarding the eyewitness today. Eyewitnesses no longer just settle for making appearances in the media as sources of information and experience; they are themselves capable of creating and distributing media content. Consequently, the aim of this chapter is to formulate a definition of the first-person recorder of current news events and consider the moral and political implications of the new centrality of the eyewitness as media producer.

This chapter consists of three sections. In the first section, the theoretical framework of the eyewitness is introduced. The second section defines the present-day picture producer and begins by criticizing the most widespread designations, 'citizen journalist' and 'citizen photojournalist' for their imprecision. The 'eyewitness picture producer' is then introduced as probably a more accurate term. The six defining traits of the 'eyewitness producer' – presence, communication, competence, relationality, participation and subjectivity – are then delineated. The third section discusses the radical transformation whereby the eyewitness is becoming self-mediated and self-authorized to a still greater degree. On the one hand, this development challenges the ideals and the normative perception of this character, while on the other hand, it increases the eyewitness' direct impact on media and politics.

Theorizing the Witness

The prominent place the eyewitness, and more broadly the witness, occupies in western culture has not passed unnoticed in academia during the past two decades. In the 1990s, the witness became a major topic in literary, psychoanalytic and philosophic thinking. Scholarly interest was primarily directed at the genre of witness literature, which spawned of World War II with authors such as Paul Celan, Primo Levi, Victor Klemperer and Imre Kertész (Felman and Laub 1992; Agamben 1999; Ekman and Tygstrup 2008). The literary scholar Shoshana Felman and psychoanalyst Dori Laub published the pioneering work *Testimony: Crises of Witnessing in Literature, Psychoanalysis and History* under the auspices of this school in 1992. The book explores the way testimonies from Holocaust survivors continue to reverberate in art, culture and politics, despite – or, perhaps, because of – the 'crisis of witnessing' broached in the title, for example, the impossibility of bearing witness to traumatic events which have left the victims speechless.

In the 2000s, media scholars also took an interest in the witness. As opposed to perceiving the Holocaust survivor as *the* prototypical witness, John Ellis, John Durham Peters and others greatly expanded the field of witnesses and events being witnessed. In his influential book *Seeing Things: Television in the Age of Uncertainty* (2000), Ellis declares the 20th century to be 'the century of witness' (2000: 9). Ellis argues for witnessing as a new, generalized mode of experiencing media characterized by the safety and the powerlessness of the viewer (see also Boltanski 1999; Sontag 2003; Chouliaraki 2006; Frosh 2006; Ellis 2009a; 2009b). In this connection, he proposes his often-cited stance, which encapsulates the complicity involved with witnessing mediated events: 'We cannot say that we do not know' (Ellis 2000: 1).

Partially as a response to Ellis, John Durham Peters published his seminal essay 'Witnessing' in 2001, which presents the historical foundation of witnessing and a typology of four witnesses deduced from their spatial and temporal relation to an event:

To be there, present at the event in space and time is the paradigm case. To be present in time but removed in space is the condition of liveness, simultaneity across space. To be present in space but removed in time is the condition of historical representation: here is the possibility of a simultaneity across time, a witness that laps the ages. To be absent in both space and time but still have access to an event via its traces is the condition of recording.

(Peters 2001: 720)

The distinctions made by Peters concerning first-hand eyewitnesses (present in time and space), live transmitted witnesses (present in time, removed in space), historical witnesses (present in space, removed in time) and witnessing a recorded event (removed in time and space) call for a differentiated application of the term seldom seen. One notable exception is apparent in the article 'On "Having Been There": "Witnessing" as a Journalistic Key Word' (2007) by Barbie Zelizer, which accounts for four phases in the deployment of eyewitnesses by journalism. This includes a contemporary period, in which eyewitnessing maintains its significance in 'a curious combination of technology and nonconventional journalistic practices' (Zelizer 2007: 421).

Most recently, the volume *Media Witnessing: Testimony in the Age of Mass Communication* (2009b) edited by Paul Frosh and Amit Pinchevski was published. The concept of 'Media Witnessing' involves both specific witnesses (media personas or producers) and a media audience. In the words of the editors, it '[…] casts the audience as the ultimate addressee *and* primary producer, making the collective both the subject and object of everyday witnessing, testifying to its own historical reality as it unfolds' (Frosh and Pinchevski 2009b: 12). Albeit acknowledging the richness of thinking involved in the broad concept of media witnessing, the current chapter distinguishes between the witness as a sender and a recipient in order to walk down a path largely untrodden: the theoretical implications of the eyewitness producing media content.

A New Figure, a New Vocabulary

Citizen photojournalist, citizen journalist, eyewitness photographer, non-conventional photojournalist – an abundance of terms is at hand to describe the new producer of images, not to mention the practices and proliferating genres and subgenres of non-professional visuals. At this point, the expressions are applied more or less at random, and point to a lack of clarity and conceptualization. No unanimous horizon of expectations exists between picture producers and media platforms, let alone between media users and the visuals. In brief, the basic definitory work still needs to be carried out. A first step in this direction is to identify three problems present in the present terminology: (1) 'citizen photojournalist' and 'citizen journalist' are used indiscriminately, (2) many of the picture producers in question do not qualify as ordinary 'citizens' and (3) the picture producers are operating increasingly in a professional manner and thus the commonly applied adjectives of 'private', 'amateur' and 'non-professional' are becoming less adequate.

First, 'citizen photojournalist', which derives from 'citizen journalist', is starting to gain ground as the agreed-upon designation (Liu et al. 2009). Citizen journalist became a widespread denomination in the aftermath of the South Asian tsunami of December 2004, when first-person accounts by tourists on the scene were recognized as an extraordinary contribution to the coverage by mainstream journalism. According to Stuart Allan, 'citizen journalism' seizes the essence of the phenomenon, which he sees as an extension of the ethos for bearing witness: 'Despite its ambiguities, the term "citizen journalism" appeared to capture something of the countervailing ethos of the ordinary person's capacity to bear witness, thereby providing commentators with a useful label to characterize an ostensibly new genre of reporting' (Allan 2009: 18). However, from the perspective of this chapter, the notion of citizen journalism is extremely broad given that media and academic discourse alike miss a clear distinction between citizen journalist and citizen photojournalist. Citizen journalist is applied somewhat gratuitously to producers of both written and visual material, for instance to the creators of amateur photos from the South Asian tsunami, Hurricane Katrina (2005) or the bombings in London's public transport system (2005) (see, among others, Allan 2009; Ellis 2009a). This usage is oblivious to the conditions for operating as a citizen photojournalist and the special status held by visual material. Citizen photojournalists regularly alter the food chain of news, given that they are on the spot before professional photographers arrive; for example, this was true of 9/11, the London bombings and the 2008 Mumbai attacks. For this reason, citizen photojournalists occasionally produce pictures which achieve a position similar to professionally produced ones, that is, amateur footage as breaking news (Pantti and Bakker 2009: 485). Moreover, citizen photojournalists

Figure 3.1: Tourists' videos made the South Asian tsunami a crucial turning point in the use of amateur photography by mainstream news organizations. This is a screen grab from an amateur footage of the first of six waves that hit the beach at Krabi, Thailand.

reach a much larger audience than ordinary citizen journalists, as visuals cross national and regional borders and address spectators in a seemingly immediate and direct manner.

Second, simply employing the terminology 'citizen photojournalism' does not solve the problem, given that 'citizen' and 'photojournalism' also suffer from imprecision. 'Citizen' stems from a notion of a subject in a nation state carrying rights and obligations, which is not universally applicable. Likewise, 'photojournalism' does not give a proper impression of the variety of material in question, including videos, edited photo slide shows etc. Even if we bracket these reservations, large groups of picture producers hardly meet the criteria for ordinary citizens. In particular, amateur visuals from areas of unrest or armed conflicts are not usually taken by people compelled to bear witness.

Often picture makers blur the boundaries between documenting a conflict and taking part in it. In some of the most high-profile media cases generated by amateur images, photographers were on-site by virtue of their occupation. To name but a few, a cargo worker employed by a US military contractor took the pictures of caskets draped with American flags lined up in a military aircraft, which featured on the front page of *The Seattle Times* in 2004. The photos spurred controversy for violating the media prohibition enforced between 1991 and 2009 against publishing pictures of fallen soldiers being returned to the United States. Another famous instance of an individual seizing the opportunity to tape otherwise unobtainable images by virtue of his profession is the security guard from the Iraqi Department of Justice behind the bootleg video of the hanging of Saddam Hussein in 2006 (Mortensen 2007; Bakir 2009). The video's revelation of the disorderly manner in which the hanging took place delivered a powerful counter narrative to the official video of the event issued just hours before by the Iraqi government.

Apart from the one-off cases, soldiers and veterans make up a large group of picture producers from areas of war and conflict. Military personnel have uploaded such substantial

Figure 3.2: Gunmen opened fire on two of Mumbai's best known luxury hotels, the Taj Mahal and the Oberoi, in November 2008. This is a view of the Taj hotel in flames, captured by Arun Shanbhag who live-blogged the crisis. Permission to reproduce granted by Arun Shanbag.

amounts of stills and videos to both commercial and military sites for picture sharing that one can begin to see various genres: triumphant or scorning videos, memorials to fallen soldiers, documentary-like recordings of combat or everyday life in the camp etc. (Christensen 2008; Andén-Papadopoulos 2009a, 2009b; Mortensen 2009; see also Kennedy in this volume).

With the same dual perspective of observer and participant, activists comprise another significant supplier of non-professional images. Notably, digital activism from countries with restricted press freedom has infiltrated mainstream media in recent years. Images by activists grant the public insight into areas of tension, to which the media has no other access. A clear case in point is the June 2009 uprising in Iran following the assumed electoral fraud, which secured another term in office for the president in power, Mahmoud Ahmadinejad (see also Chapter 5). In the global media's coverage of the protests, on-site activists turned into essential sources of information due to the government's ban on independent and foreign media reports on non-official events. Likewise, the international media relied on the reporting of the so-called VJs (Video Journalists) during the revolts in Burma (Myanmar) in the fall of 2007, when their images of monks clad in red marching through Rangoon in silent protest against the military regime were aired again and again.

Third, the often-applied adjectives 'amateur', 'non-professional' and 'private' have now lost their significance. To a still greater extent, activists engage on a semi-professional level in producing and distributing images targeted at the global media in order to raise awareness of their causes. For instance, digital activism from Burma emanates from a tightly structured network of citizen photojournalists on the ground, supplying recordings for the Oslo-based organization *Democratic Voices of Burma*. The Oscar-nominated documentary film *Burma VJ* (2008) by the Danish director Anders Østergaard presents the way in which Burmese VJs work goal oriented towards capturing the attention of the global news networks.

While it may not cut the Gordian knot of defining citizen photojournalism once and for all, I propose the term 'eyewitness picture producer'. Apart from shunning the problematic designation 'citizen', it introduces the term 'eyewitness', which enables a better understanding of contemporary media protagonists and practices.

The Eyewitness Picture Producer

'Eyewitness' has become an inescapable keyword in the contemporary media landscape. Formats such as 'eyewitness News', 'eyewitness reports', 'eyewitness photography', 'eyewitness accounts' and 'citizen eyewitness' share a sense of immediate vicinity to unfolding events – and not much else. Arguably, the current preoccupation with the eyewitness reflects the tendency in many news and entertainment formats to focus on singular, individual experiences, which may or may not hold the potential for putting larger political, societal or cultural issues into perspective.

Historically, witnessing originates from law and theology.[1] On the one hand, most known legal systems have depended on the witness as an indispensable source of information. On the other hand, the witness – especially in the form of the martyr – is featured in various religious traditions. Etymologically, this is indicated by the term 'martyr' deriving from the Greek word 'μάρτυρ', meaning 'witness', that is, one who attests to the truth by suffering (Thomas 2009: 95).

Particularly since World War II, the media has constituted another essential framework for witnessing. While 'the act of witness is never itself unmediated', as Ellis observes (2000: 11), issues relating to the representation of traumatic events and the media in question gained more urgency after the war, when visual and eventually also audiovisual media turned into the favoured platforms for delivering testimony. One could make cases both for and against the media as a separate realm for witnessing. In his insightful article 'Witnessing as a Cultural Form of Communication', Günter Thomas convincingly argues that law and religion appear on dual sides of today's audiovisual media system. Fact-oriented, forensic witnessing re-emerges in journalism, whereas the transformations of religious witnessing appear in talk shows (Thomas 2009: 105). No doubt numerous other examples of the two historical traces of witnessing being revitalized by the media could be listed. Nevertheless, since media witnessing has entered our everyday lives, and we have ourselves become impending witnesses, we should view the audiovisual media as an institution for witnessing in its own right. The media vouch for the identity and legitimacy of the person testifying. Furthermore, the media counterbalance the eyewitness' notoriously subjective disposition by offering a role governed by rules and rituals (Thomas 2009: 101), which frames and structures witnessing as a public, performative act with a 'communicative intent' (Ellis 2009a: 77). When media networks open their doors to witnesses, experiences are transformed into discourse and events are turned into stories (Peters 2001, 2009).

Today, eyewitnessing is performed by, in and through the media (Frosh and Pinchevski 2009a: 296). As Peters suggests, it is 'a strange but intelligible sentence to say: the witness (speech-act) of the witness (person) was witnessed (by an audience)' (Peters 2001: 709). Eyewitnesses to particular incidents are presented as privileged *sources of information* in news items. *Media producers* also assume the part of eyewitness, when documenting or reporting from the scene of a crime, crisis or war. This applies to professional as well as non-professional producers, owing to, on the one hand, the centrality of live coverage and, on the other hand, the growing amount of user-generated content (UGC). Finally, a *media audience* is situated as 'eyewitnesses' or 'witnesses' to events unfolding on the screen. The multiple meanings testify to the way in which the eyewitness lies at the heart of today's media experiences and addresses complex notions of reality, technology and communication. However, they also lay bare the prevailing lack of precision when trying to clarify whether 'witness' refers to an eyewitness or to a media audience.

In order to pursue the argument that the new picture producer is an heir to this tradition, it is beneficial to first outline the basic traits of the eyewitness as proposed by Tamar Ashuri and Amit Pinchevski[2]: *Presence, communication* (rhetoric), *habitus* and *competence* (Ashuri and Pinchevski 2009: 137–38). *Presence*, or first-hand experience, is the 'entry card' to coming forward as an eyewitness. *Communication* is likewise essential; someone must recall what took place and have a desire to report. *Habitus*, or the moral integrity of the eyewitness, is highly valued, seeing as this character is traditionally on the right side of history. Lastly, *competence* is necessary in order to make a public statement.

If we focus on defining the eyewitness picture producer specifically, this figure acting as a producer is by and large a novelty, which calls for a revision of the designation put forward by Ashuri and Pinchevski (2009).[3] While presence, communication and competence are still imperative for the eyewitness picture producer, habitus is of less importance. Besides, supplementary defining traits need to be added, bringing us to a total of six: presence, communication, competence, relationality, participation and subjectivity.

First, with *presence*, in comparison with the classical understanding of an eyewitness as someone who is or has been physically present in time and space at an occurrence, the attendance of the eyewitness picture producer tends to be more reflexive and active. While events are still unfolding, he or she decides to digitally secure the visual or audiovisual traits.

Second, *communication* has become considerably more complex. Communication used to involve the speech-act of witnessing within a predefined, institutional context. Today, communication is expanded by the eyewitness' own production and distribution of testimonies to a broad range of institutions, from news networks to new media like Twitter, YouTube, LiveLeak and Facebook. Moreover, once they have been published, reports by eyewitnesses flow between institutional settings according to the logics of media convergence, for example, the news media's frequent broadcast of YouTube clips.

Third, in terms of *competence*, attendance alone does not foster eyewitness picture producers. Even though new easy-to-use technology has entailed the dramatic growth of eyewitness imagery, the individuals in question still need to master recording devices and enjoy access to the media or digital channels for self-publication. Rather than an existential category granted by faith, eyewitnessing is to be understood as a skilled and performative act. Along the same lines, Ashuri and Pincheviski go against the essentialist perception of witnessing as 'a position one already holds, not something one must obtain', which is to be found in much of the existing literature (Ashuri and Pinchevski 2009: 135).

Fourth, witnessing is *relational* to the event being witnessed, and the position of eyewitness picture producer may be filled in numerous ways. In other words, an eyewitness does not exist 'separately from its contextual specificities' (Ashuri and Pinchevski 2009: 135). Different places, circumstances and technologies enable different kinds of witnesses and witnessing.

Fifth, eyewitness picture producers are *participatory*. This is regardless of whether they see themselves as neutral observers or activists, although degrees of participation vary. Every act of witnessing is tied to a 'transformation' (Thomas 2009: 96). Witnessing becomes part of the event, changing both the course of the event and the witness' perception of the event. The mere presence of a camera is often sufficient to exert an influence, most dramatically in countries where it is interpreted as a sign of dissent in public spaces, but also when people become conscious of themselves as future images. Events take place in front of the lens, which would otherwise not have happened in that way, or, perhaps, would not have happened at all.

Sixth, *subjectivity* is a strong feature of traditional and contemporary eyewitnesses alike. One cannot usually draw final conclusions or obtain definitive evidence based on the testimony of just one person (Felman 1992: 5). Eyewitnessing is characterized by tunnel vision, or, in the words of Ashuri and Pinchevski, '"being there" entails proximity, which means involvement, and hence the annihilation of perspective' (Ashuri and Pinchevski 2009: 140). The trademark of subjectivity has intensified today, given the diversity of institutions accommodating eyewitness despatches. In particular, online sites for UGC do not filter or edit clips, let alone identify their producers.

Presence, communication, competence, relationality, participation and subjectivity – these six characteristics may explain the modus operandi of the eyewitness picture producer. Be that as it may, they leave the no-less important question regarding the incentive for taking on this role unanswered. Moving on to the third and final section of this chapter, the issue to be examined concerns the moral and political implications of the shift from an exclusive to an inclusive group of eyewitnesses.

Contested Realities

If we recall the defining traits of the eyewitness introduced by Ashuri and Pinchevski (2009), this chapter has so far left perhaps the most challenging one in brackets: habitus. In light of the moral authority and obligation attributed to the eyewitness, how might the new picture producer be placed in the evolution of this figure?

Traditionally, the moral constitution of the person presenting herself or himself as an eyewitness has been of great importance, because witnessing was conceived as a civil, courageous achievement for the common good. Witnessing is thus conventionally the lot of the victim rather than the perpetrator, as it ultimately concerns who has the moral right to tell the version of events that is recorded in history books.[4] Furthermore, an obligation rests upon, for example, survivors of manmade catastrophes, to give evidence according to the Roman rule *'de visu suo et auditu'* ('what he saw and heard for himself') (Peters 2009: 47). The burden of the witness is 'a radically unique, noninterchangable and solitary burden', since the testimony cannot be repeated or reported by another (Felman 1992: 3). Paul Celan gives voice to this experience as well in his famous poem *Ashglory* (*Aschenglorie*) from 1965: 'No one / bears witness for / the witness' (*Niemand / zeugt für den/ Zeugen*).

The ascribed moral superiority of the witness ought not to be confused with romanticism. Personal integrity is vital when bearing in mind that witnessing always takes place in situations of contested realities, where it is yet to be established what is true, real and just. If consensus rules and all facts are verified, the witness is superfluous. According to Thomas:

> Any act of witnessing presupposes the instability, ambiguity, and actual indeterminacy of reality *and* a structural (legal or political) attempt to steer toward stability and

determinacy. Any act of witnessing, confession, or testimony – even in 'historical' cases – relates to disputed, unstable, conflicting, or transitory realities.

(Thomas 2009: 96)

Even though many methods have been developed for testing and securing the truthfulness of the witness, from calling in more witnesses, to swearing on the Bible, to polygraphs, the disputed reality is often settled by putting faith in one particular witness.

When every onlooker, every participant is free to join the ranks of the eyewitnesses, it is questionable whether the moral claim still holds, since the basic 'who' and 'why' of picture makers often hang in the balance. As far as the 'who' goes, the producers often remain anonymous and withhold any information that may disclose their identity, for reasons of safety, for example, in the case of Iranian and Burmese activists, but also as something of a genre convention. The lack of a steady figure or institution responsible for the images prevents the media user from testing the reliability of the source, which obviously renders its value as a news story or a contribution to one much more complex.

Concerning the 'why', eyewitnessing functions as a means of self-expression in several ways. Giving testimony situates one's identity in relation to an event, with a toolbox of verbal and visual rhetoric readily at hand to narrate, but secondarily also to express personal feelings and promote political viewpoints. Assuming the part of eyewitness picture producer may be spurred by the urge to document significant occurrences or reveal conditions that are open to criticism. Transforming the passive role of merely being present to the active one of recording may also work as a way of coming to terms with the possible traumas afflicted by attending violent and dramatic occurrences. However, much contemporary eyewitnessing appears to be an extension of the mundane habit of visually documenting our lives, that is, when passers-by photograph a fire or a traffic accident with their mobile phones. As Zelizer writes, '[C]onventional journalists no longer determine what counts as an eyewitness report. With private citizens now increasingly filling in as eyewitnesses, the proximity and immediacy they provide qualify as grounds for eyewitnessing' (Zelizer 2007: 421). Being there, and being able, at times appears to be a sufficient motive for an eyewitness. At the same time, the eyewitness' ability to exert a direct influence on politics and the media is greater than ever before.

Conclusion

The eyewitness producing media content has become a central figure in journalism. In recent years, we appear to have taken a giant leap towards the situation anticipated by the German historian Leopold von Ranke in the first half of the 19th century: 'I see a time coming when new history will be built on the reports of eyewitnesses' (cit. in Zelizer 2007: 411). Digital technologies and participatory journalistic practices have paved the way for a new and powerful media protagonist, and it has been the objective of this chapter to conceptualize and contextualize this character as a web 2.0 version of the eyewitness.

Subjective and involved, eyewitness picture producers challenge the conventional scales for measuring reports, for example, whether a witness has a moral right to be seen and heard, or whether the citizen contributing to a news story is impartial and acting out of civil courage. Despatches migrate between different institutional settings, and no guarantees are offered insofar as the authenticity and legitimacy of the eyewitness are concerned. Obviously, this does not render the space of witnessing any less contested. In recent years, the involved parties often let a conflict play out in the media by offering diverging visuals of an episode, or diverging interpretations of the same visuals of an episode. When Israeli naval forces attacked a convoy of aid ships in Gaza in May 2010, the army and activists each submitted their own footage to the global media in order to substantiate their versions of the events. The two videos of the killing of the Iranian woman Neda Agha Soltan during an anti-government demonstration in Tehran in June 2009 recorded by bystanders is another example. While European and US news media agreed that the clips documented the appalling killing of an innocent woman, the Iranian state media offered other explanations. The newspaper *Javan* wrote that a woman by the name of Neda Agha Soltan had presented herself at the Iranian embassy in Greece, maintaining she was the person depicted in the pictures that falsely documented her death (BBC Monitoring Middle East 2009). Another story published in the pro-government paper *Vatan-e-Emrooz* claimed that the recently expelled BBC correspondent Jon Leyne had hired a contract killer to shoot Agha Soltan in order to film the shooting (Fletcher 2009). Other media agreed with the version put forward by the Iranian security forces that the videos in themselves proved the killing had been staged, because the filmmakers must have been forewarned (Dehghan 2009). These are just two examples of the contested realities to which eyewitness picture producers currently respond and/or contribute.

Ten years ago, Peters (2001: 722) observed that most eyewitnesses are not aware of themselves as such until after the closing of an event. This no longer holds true. Eyewitnessing has become a choice, an option and a mass phenomenon. By all appearances, we have only seen the beginning, rather than the end, of this development.

Notes

1. According to Peters, the moral and cultural force of the eyewitness originates from three sources: law, theology and atrocity (2001: 708–09). However, I agree with Thomas that 'atrocity' ought not to be regarded as an independent field of witnessing in line with the two others, as it dates back to a specific historical event (Holocaust), and is not a fundamental institution in historical and modern societies. Moreover, Thomas (2009: 93, note 2) argues that bearing witness to atrocities has developed out of both these domains (Thomas 2009: 93, note 2).
2. I have altered Ashuri and Pinchevski's second category from 'rhetoric' to the broader category of 'communication'.
3. Of course, one should not be ignorant of significant historical predecessors of eyewitnesses behind the camera. To name one famous example, the photographs by German conscripts documenting

their war crimes on the East Front during World War II were highly debated in the mid-1990s when they were included in a travelling exhibition (Heer and Naumann 1995; Heer et al. 2008).

4. To this day, it is controversial when perpetrators assume the role of eyewitness. For instance, the historical fiction novel *The Kindly Ones* (*Les Bienveillantes*, 2006) by Jonathan Littell called for a heated debate on account of the narrator, a former SS officer, who conveys his involvement in massacres without regret.

References

Agamben, G. (1999), *Remnants of Auschwitz: The Witness and the Archive*, New York: Zone Books.

Allan, S. and Thorsen, E. (eds) (2009), *Citizen Journalism: Global Perspectives*, New York: Peter Lang.

Allan, S. (2009), 'Histories of Citizen Journalism', in S. Allan and E. Thorsen (eds), *Citizen Journalism: Global Perspectives*, New York: Peter Lang.

Andén-Papadopoulos, K. (2009a), 'Body Horror on the Internet', *Culture, Media & Society*, 31: 6, pp. 921–38.

Andén-Papadopoulos, K. (2009b), 'US Soldiers Imagining the Iraq War on YouTube', *Popular Communication*, 7: 1, pp. 17–27.

Ashuri, T. and Pinchevski, A. (2009), 'Witnessing as a Field', in P. Frosh and A. Pinchevski (eds), *Media Witnessing: Testimony in the Age of Mass Communication*, Houndmills: Palgrave Macmillan, pp. 133–57.

Bakir, V. (2009), 'Tele-Technologies, Control, and Sousveillance: Saddam Hussein – De-Deification and the Beast', *Popular Communication*, 7: 1, pp. 7–16.

BBC Monitoring Middle East (2009), 'Iran Paper Says Neda's Death during Post-Poll Protest "Suspicious"', July 1.

Boltanski, L. (1999), *Distant Suffering: Morality, Media and Politics*, Cambridge: Cambridge University Press.

Chouliaraki, L. (2006), *The Spectatorship of Suffering*, London: Sage.

Christensen, C. (2008), 'Uploading Dissonance: YouTube and the US occupation of Iraq', *Media, War & Conflict*, 1: 2, pp. 155–75.

Dehghan S. K. (2009), 'Thousands Defy Ban to Take to Tehran Streets on Day of Remembrance for Fallen Protesters', *Guardian International*, July 31.

Ekman, U. and Tygstrup, F. (eds) (2008), *Witness: Memory, Representation, and the Media in Question*, Copenhagen: Museum Tusculanum Press.

Ellis, J. (2000), *Seeing Things: Television in an Age of Uncertainty*, London: I. B. Tauris Publishers.

Ellis, J. (2009a), 'Mundane Witness', in P. Frosh and A. Pinchevski (eds), *Media Witnessing: Testimony in the Age of Mass Communication*, Houndmills: Palgrave Macmillan, pp. 73–88.

Ellis, J. (2009b), 'What Are We Expected to Feel? Witness, Textuality and the Audiovisual', *Screen*, 50: 1, pp. 67–76.

Felman, S. (1992), 'Education and Crisis, or the Vicissitudes of Teaching', in S. Felman, and D. Laub (eds), *Testimony: Crises of Witnessing in Literature, Psychoanalysis, and History*, New York: Routledge, pp. 1–56.

Felman, S. and Laub, D. (1992), *Testimony: Crises of Witnessing in Literature, Psychoanalysis, and History*, New York: Routledge.

Fletcher, M. (2009), 'Neda Died in My Hands', *The Times*, June 26.

Frosh, P. and Pinchevski, A. (2009a), 'Crisis-Readiness and Media Witnessing', *The Communication Review*, 12: 3, pp. 295–304.

Frosh, P. and Pinchevski, A. (eds) (2009b), *Media Witnessing: Testimony in the Age of Mass Communication*, Houndmills: Palgrave Macmillan.

Frosh, P. (2006), 'Telling Presences: Witnessing, Mass Media, and the Imagined Lives of Strangers', *Critical Studies in Media Communication*, 23: 4, pp. 265–84.

Heer, H., Manoschek, W., Pollak, A. and Wodak, R. (eds) (2008), *The Discursive Construction of History: Remembering The Wehrmacht's War of Annihilation*, Houndmills: Palgrave Macmillan.

Heer, H. and Naumann, K. (eds) (1995), *Vernichtungskrieg: Verbrechen der Wehrmacht 1941–1944*, Hamburg: Hamburger Edition HIS Verlagsges.

Liu, S., Palen, L., Sutton, J. Hughes, A. and Vieweg, S. (2009), 'Citizen Photojournalism during Crisis Events', in S. Allan and E. Thorsen (eds), *Citizen Journalism: Global Perspectives*, New York: Peter Lang.

Mortensen, M. (2007), 'Krigen på billeder. Visuel krigsførelse i digitaliseringens og globaliseringens tidsalder', *Kritik*, 186, pp. 7–17.

Mortensen, M. (2009), 'The Camera at War: When Soldiers Become War Photographers', in R. Schubart, F. Virchow, D. White-Stanley and T. Thomas (eds), *War Isn't Hell, It's Entertainment: War in Modern Culture and Visual Media*, Jefferson: McFarland.

Pantti, M. and Bakker, P. (2009), 'Misfortunes, Memories and Sunsets: Non-professional Images in Dutch News Media', *International Journal of Cultural Studies*, 12: 5, pp. 471–89.

Peters, J. D. (2001), 'Witnessing', *Media, Culture & Society*, 23: 6, pp. 707–23.

Peters, J. D. (2009), 'An Afterword: Torchlight Red on Sweaty Faces', in P. Frosh and A. Pinchevski (eds), *Media Witnessing: Testimony in the Age of Mass Communication*, Houndmills: Palgrave Macmillan, pp. 42–48.

Sontag, S. (2003), *Regarding the Pain of Others*, London: Penguin Books Ltd.

Thomas, G. (2009), 'Witness as a Cultural Form of Communication: Historical Roots, Structural Dynamics and Current Appearances', in P. Frosh and A. Pinchevski (eds), *Media Witnessing: Testimony in the Age of Mass Communication*, Houndmills: Palgrave Macmillan, pp. 88–111.

Zelizer, B. (2007), 'On "Having Been There": "Witnessing" as a Journalistic Key Word', *Critical Studies in Media Communication*, 24: 5, pp. 408–28.

Part II

Practices

Chapter 4

Amateur Images and Journalistic Authority

Helle Sjøvaag

This chapter asks to what extent journalistic authority is threatened by the substitution of user-generated content (UGC) for professionally collected images in the coverage of breaking news stories. Because journalism is not a profession in the strict sense – as there are no barriers to entry, no required exams or mandatory licences needed in order to practise journalism – the vocation is sustained by a strong professional ideology that protects journalists from outside threats to their authority as newsmakers (Raaum 2001: 67). Online and mobile technology has over the past 10–15 years brought about frequent threats to this authority – from bloggers, citizen journalists, Google news services and amateur video-makers on YouTube, to name a few. As journalism will always need the cooperation of citizens as sources and witnesses, unsolicited contributions to the news product from such amateurs should be welcomed. Journalists cannot be everywhere at once, and sometimes news organizations rely on amateur recordings to convey big breaking news stories to the public. Such cases might indicate that journalism is letting go of some of its control over the news agenda. However, as the two case studies presented in this chapter demonstrate, mainstream news organizations are able to retain gatekeeping control over the type of visual amateur material that effectively makes a big breaking news story. Mainstream television news exercises this professional authority by using narrative strategies to incorporate amateur images into the journalistic product, thereby retaining narrative authority over visual sources not captured by a professional journalist.

The cases chosen to analyse how the two main Norwegian television news organizations, NRK and TV 2, narratively incorporate amateur images into their breaking news coverage are the 7/7 London bombings in 2005 and the assassination of Benazir Bhutto on 27 December 2007. The cases are similar in that they are framed as terror events, and they both happen abroad, making the news organizations reliant on secondary sources such as television channels in the United Kingdom and Pakistan for amateur footage. The cases are thus similar in being characterized by amateur videos of the event – recordings that have news value in themselves. The images furthermore fall into two recognizable narrative frameworks. The Bhutto case represents the political assassination where the moment of death is captured on tape, while the 7/7 case represents the post-9/11 terror attack characterized by the bombing of urban infrastructure.

Journalism as Institution

Journalism's legitimacy is primarily founded on the premise that information is vital to the health of democracy and its citizens. The authority with which journalism maintains this social contract rests on the professional ideals, practices and ethics that legitimize the editorial power of the news institution. These professional standards are communicated to the public and thus also maintained in the public sphere through journalistic ideology – a narrative or *mythos* whose premise rests on the fundamental tenets of journalism. These include ethical standards such as truth, facts, accuracy, impartiality and independence. In practical terms these ideals are managed through professional practices in the gathering and dissemination of news. Virtues inherent in this process include covering contemporary and timely events, immediacy, exclusivity, investigation and breaking news coverage (c.f. Kovach and Rosenstiel 2001: 37; Schudson 2003: 40; Zelizer 2004: 72). When journalism is regarded as an institution, the practices and conventions, rules and norms of that institution function as the carriers of the profession's ideology (Cook 2005: 66–67; Eide 2001: 18, 31).

Journalistic authority is founded on this ideology. This authority is maintained partly by the perceived exclusivity of what journalists do. As mainstream news faces growing challenges from amateurs and citizen journalists, however, this impression of exclusivity of the knowledge and practice of journalism is weakened, something that also confronts the news value paradigm (Fry 2008). Internet and mobile technologies therefore raise questions regarding some of the fundamental premises of journalism, namely, says Mark Deuze, that 'the professional journalist is the one who determines what publics see, hear and read about the world' (Deuze 2005: 451). The result is a greater emphasis on journalistic methodology as a guarantee of accurate and ethically collected information and on the institution as a production framework for news of relevance, importance and resonance. The institutional framework does not only mean that the news presented to us is produced according to certain practices, standards and ethics. It also entails a cultural form that operates according to a set of narrative frameworks in news production (Schudson 2003: 190). The cognitive schemes handed down to journalists by the institution enable 'adequate action in the social situations in which journalists work', including the knowledge of how to complete journalistic processes and an understanding of how news is made and displayed (Hjarvard 1999: 28–29). As news is preoccupied with events, says Schudson, 'journalists handle the anarchy of events by depending on available cultural resources, the treasurehouse of tropes, narrative forms, resonant mythic forms and frames of their culture' (Schudson 2007: 254). Moreover, narrative frames that explain events in a way we can understand are innate to journalism and exist naturally in the mind of the news worker (ibid.: 256).

Protecting the Profession

Today we frequently hear arguments asserting that UGC may contribute to alter 'the established modes of journalism' (Hermida and Thurman 2008: 344). In addition, professional journalistic attitudes to amateur content see it at best as complementary to journalism, and at worst as potentially damaging to the news brand (ibid.: 349–50). Studies of newsroom approaches to UGC however conclude that journalists manage to retain the traditional gatekeeping function of the news organizations even in the face of growing volumes of amateur contributions (Gordon 2007: 308; Harrison 2009: 2; Hermida and Thurman 2008: 353). Nevertheless, witnesses to major events have always been important to the newsgathering process and have served as sources for news reporting that legitimize the information presented and thus the journalistic institutions reporting them. Mastering this new environment entails assuming editorial and narrative control over the many contributions from non-professionals. When successful, containing the news narrative ensures journalistic authority and asserts the continued function of the profession in the public sphere (Knight 2008).

Inclusion of amateur images and recordings in mainstream news coverage not only signals the scarce availability of professionally shot footage of the event but also implies the value of such material to the news agenda. As Herbert Gans explains, journalistic products imply a process of exclusion and inclusion that signifies the degree of value placed on these news items. News decisions thus involve judgements about importance, as value inclusion goes hand in hand with value exclusion (Gans 1980: 203). Moreover, journalism is intentional. It involves judgements about relevance, has narrative structure that consists of a plot or story, presentational form and a discourse of its own (Ekström 2000: 567, 472–73). Editing enables this narrative structure, creates dramatic sequences and establishes the communicative strategies of the journalistic institution. Consequently, the narratives journalism creates help us understand the reality in which we live (ibid.: 474). So when amateur images are included in mainstream news coverage, it conveys the value and relevance of this material to the journalistic narrative.

In facing up to new digital technologies and how these enable citizens to participate in the news agenda, news institutions often focus their ideological branding efforts on journalistic methodology as a measure to protect their professional claim. The value of the professional journalistic treatment of news stories is founded on the advantages created by the editorial system of the news institution. Mainstream news organizations not only produce news based on the enduring standards of journalistic ideology, they also denote a collective of professional knowledge and habits that function to ensure the ethical quality of the news product. Whereas citizen journalism and UGC certainly have their values, professional journalism's strength rests with its methodology. This methodology, performed within the framework of an institution, ideally ensures that facts are checked, that sources are verified and that stories are presented with some degree of impartiality and balance. Accuracy is thus ensured by the professionalism that guarantees that content, angle and framing are delivered on the basis of sound journalistic criteria. Whereas amateur contributions to news content can be regarded as traditional sources, amateur production nevertheless implies a partial selection of objects, images or information that lie beyond the control of the news institution. In order to restore the veracity of such material, and remove doubt over its authenticity or 'objectivity', journalists can impose the necessary frames or narratives on such amateurism and thus legitimize the objects as journalistically relevant to the story.

Narrative Strategies

Television news has certain enduring generic genre traits, of which having good visuals is one of the fundamental news criteria. Moving images, remarks John Corner (1995), 'give to viewers a sense of independent surveillance and evidence' (p. 13). Images bring dramatic effect to the news narratives, which shape news accounts with a sense and significance that render cultural resonance to the report. Narratives are affective; they add coherence and offer a 'scheme for organising comprehension' (ibid.: 57). As most unscheduled events lack pictures to illustrate the action at the heart of the story, visualization here usually assumes a symbolic form. The visual recipe for such events is to use footage surrounding the event – reporter on the scene, stock footage, images of the aftermath, interviews with witnesses etc., 'over which a *spoken* exposition can be delivered' (ibid.: 60). Such secondary footage is symbolic rather than iconic, and serves as placeholder for events rather than representing them (ibid.). 'Where they *do* contain images and sequences of a strongly evidential character or of a strongly affective kind, this broadly demonstrative function becomes more particularised and intense, radically altering the image/word balance and the grounding of news *truth telling*', writes Corner (1995: 61).

Such imagery serves the function of witness – a function with an inherent proximity to the facts that are so central to the legitimacy of journalism. The witness function of images that catch events live as they happen represents, as John Durham Peters says, 'the paradigm case of a *medium*: the means by which experience is supplied to others who lack the original' (Peters 2001: 709). The potential impact of such images thus speaks to their affective and evidentiary force as pieces of information or, particularly, as focal points of debate, political discussion and public reaction (Corner 1995: 61). The use of narrative frames to engage interpretation and moral evaluation of an event reduces the possible understandings and explanations for these events. As such, says David D. Perlmutter (1998), '[W]hich visual images do and do not appear in the press, what is and is not said about them, the context which they are said to represent and the context in which they appear, constitute media frames' (p. 7). Whereas the amateur images used in mainstream media coverage of the 7/7 London bombings and the Bhutto assassination perhaps do not achieve the iconic status attributed to the professionally shot 'icons of outrage' identified by Perlmutter, they do attain the 'nodal' status for new information, event impression and deliberation described by

Corner (1995: 61). Moreover, these amateur images are incorporated into the open-ended and continuously updated news narrative through two particular narrative strategies.

Narrative strategies in news can be described as the result of aesthetic-analytic work practices with which journalists make news reports. The terms used to describe the narrative strategies for the purpose of this analysis – the embedding and the embellishing of amateur images into mainstream news broadcasts – serve a purpose through their simplicity. To embed indicates to include or insert into a whole. At the same time embedding suggests restriction and entrenchment. The term thus implies that the use of amateur images is limited, and that such footage is visually and orally negated. Here, the embedded narrative technique textually ignores the amateur origin of pictures and refrains from the endless repetition of such imagery in news broadcasts. Embedding expressly denies the obvious difference between amateur and professional footage, both visually through montage editing, and orally by refraining from comments as to the source of the material. Hence, embedding ignores the very presence of the amateur, thereby ensuring journalistic authority over the professional process. This strategy also protects the professionalism of source relations and fact verification and maintains control over the narrative frame for the event. In narrative embedding journalists secure gatekeeping power by treating the news value of amateur images in a non-sensational manner.

To embellish, on the other hand, means to enhance, expand or elaborate on the object in question. The embellished narrative technique thus gives prominence to pictures and videos of amateur origin, primarily through repetition, close analysis and speculation as to their origins. Visually embellished, amateur images are placed at the top of the inverted pyramid, signalling their relevance to the story. They are used to demonstrate the effect of events, or serve as evidence to claims made by parties to the story. Contextualization takes place both visually and orally as such footage is repeated, commented on and analysed by experts. The prominent treatment of such material hence creates a narrative frame from within which the images can be understood. The embellished strategy emphasizes the uniqueness of the footage by focusing on its many un-journalistic qualities, thus maintaining the distinction between professional and amateur. Both narrative techniques described here serve to render authority to the broadcaster. One emphasizes the professional importance of the journalistic institution by ignoring the fact that television news sometimes relies on amateurs to communicate breaking news properly. The other uses amateur images as proof that there is no professional account of the event, thereby positioning itself as the necessary and trustworthy legitimating function of amateur sources (Bridge and Sjøvaag 2010).

Study

Two case studies analysing the narrative techniques used to incorporate amateur images into professional news coverage found that there are variations as to how amateur images are used by mainstream television. The analysis looks at how two Norwegian broadcasters used amateur footage in their coverage of the London Underground bombings and the assassination of Benazir Bhutto. NRK (The Norwegian Broadcasting Corporation) is the licence-fee-funded public service broadcaster and number one in the market for television news, while TV 2 is the commercial public service broadcaster and number two in the market, behind NRK. The comparative study found both similarities and differences in how the channels incorporated the amateur contributions into the prevailing news narrative.

Both case studies here represent the terror event as narrative frame, where the Bhutto case falls under the category of political assassination and the 7/7 bombings embody the post 9/11 terror attack. The political assassination as terror event entails the ideologically motivated targeting of political figures with the intent to kill. The post-9/11 terror attack represents the seemingly random and violent destruction of infrastructure such as buildings and transportation systems, with potentially fatal consequences for innocent bystanders. The two cases differ in time frame. This analysis looks at the first day of coverage of the London bombings and the first five days of coverage of the Bhutto assassination. This is because the two events also differ in time frame regarding the use of amateur images in the coverage. In both cases there are only two amateur contributions used. However on 7/7 these images were reported within hours of the event, while in the Bhutto case amateur footage did not emerge until a few days later. For the Bhutto assassination both NRK and TV 2 used the embedding technique to frame the event narratively. Because the treatment of the amateur videos from the Bhutto murder is fairly similar across the two channels, their narrative strategies are treated together. In the case of the 7/7 bombings, NRK employs an embedding technique coupled with an accuracy approach that stands in contrast to TV 2's embellishing and immediacy approach. Because of the difference in narrative strategy employed in the 7/7 case, the two are treated separately.

In the Bhutto case study, analysis of Norwegian coverage includes NRK's news broadcast *Dagsrevyen* (30-minute prime time evening news bulletin) and *Kveldsnytt* (15-minute late evening news update) from 27 to 31 December 2007, and TV 2's news broadcast *Nyhetene 18:30* (30-minute early evening news bulletin) and *Nyhetene 21:00* (30-minute main evening news bulletin) from 27 to 31 December 2007. The case comprises 10 broadcasts from each channel – 20 broadcasts in total. In the 7/7 case study, analysis of Norwegian coverage includes nine NRK bulletins broadcast from 12 noon to 23 p.m. on the day of the attack (189 minutes in total) and nine TV 2 bulletins broadcast from 12:17 to 23:55 on the same day (171 minutes in total). In both case studies the content of the broadcasts surveyed was logged frame-by-frame according to visual content (what the images displayed), technical signature (whether the images were amateur, professional, in-studio, press conferences etc.) and voice-over contextualization (journalistic story and narrative framing). Findings were analysed within the sociology of news framework and related to professional ideology.

The Assassination of Benazir Bhutto

In the Bhutto case, two amateur videos emerged that had captured the shooting itself – one of the suspected murder weapon and one of the suspected killer and the moment of death. The shooting happened at an election rally, and as such, the videos display all the hallmarks of amateur footage – blurry, shaky and unfocused images of a chaotic scene. The Bhutto case departs from other cases of amateur images dominating news coverage of terror events mainly for two reasons. First, there is a time-lag between the captured event itself and the mainstream news dissemination of the video evidence. Second, the videos did not travel via the Internet. Instead, they were submitted directly to the television channels. This fact demonstrates a particular point in relation to this case, namely that traditional news media here function as the defining disseminator and thus gatekeeper of important events.

Both channels use embedding techniques on the amateur footage of Bhutto's murder. NRK and TV 2 both focus most of their coverage on the 'gun video' and stills from the 'suspected killer video'. Both frame the amateur-captured images within the context of the disputed cause of death, and within the political framework of the event. The first day predominantly features reaction coverage to the event, with a visual focus on events before and after the assassination. Images show the election rally where Bhutto was killed and street riots and the general aftermath of the bomb blast. On 28 December, both channels use images from the Pakistani Interior Ministry's press conference, where their spokesperson Javed Iqbal Cheema claims Bhutto was killed by the impact of the bomb blast. Here, the 'gun video' is introduced; however the focus is not on the gun being fired, but on the lever where Bhutto allegedly hit her head. As such, the 'gun video' is not itself the focus of the news, it is merely referred to as the Pakistani authorities' claim to evidence.

Later that evening, a dispute arises as to the cause of death, and both channels turn their attention to shots being fired from the crowd in the 'gun video'. NRK focuses purely on the content of the clip, displaying the encircled gun repeatedly and in slow motion. TV 2 also directs the viewer's attention to the highlighted handgun, but keeps cutting back and forth

Figure 4.1: This still image from an amateur video of the Bhutto assassination highlights the suspected killer aiming a gun. The video was first aired on the Pakistani television channel Dawn News.

between the 'gun video' and Cheema's statement. This underscores the disputed cause of death as narrative frame for the report. On the 29th, both channels use still photos from the 'suspected killer video' as witness to the claim that Bhutto died from gunshot wounds. NRK employs a textual strategy that cuts back and forth between the 'gun video' and the 'suspected killer' stills to support the narration that 'new images show that there may have been two assassins', and that doubt is cast on the official version. TV 2 also focuses on the potential effect of the new images on the stability of Pakistan.

Comments by journalists or commentators regarding the amateur status of the clips themselves are largely absent. The tapes are presented as 'new evidence' in reports about the disputed cause of death of Benazir Bhutto. As such, there is little contextualization of the amateur quality or witness status of the tapes in coverage on either channel. Furthermore, the amateur footage is used 'indirectly', meaning that audiences are made aware that NRK and TV 2's sources are not the original recorders themselves, but rather that they have been obtained through other news organizations. This entails a conspicuous contrast to the proximity established through original close-up shots of comments made by official sources and spokespeople in Norway and live stand-up feeds from correspondents reporting from Pakistan.

The main aesthetic differences between primary witness imagery and secondary commentators are that in the first case they are shaky, unstable and blurry pictures of an unpredictable event – sometimes even filtered through a secondary source; and that in the second case they are stable and clear close-ups of known figures doing and saying predictable things. The aesthetic quality of the amateur footage thus creates a nearness to the event through the role of the footage as witness. The two Norwegian channels edit the amateur images into their reports in a manner that secures the institutions' credibility. Both channels mix the amateur footage with visual content that grounds the event in a fairly predictable narrative frame. The use of amateur footage here alludes to the political assassination narrative. The images are edited into montages that resemble countless accounts of the Kennedy assassination, where the famous Zapruder tape captured the moment of death. The Bhutto footage is thus first shown in its entirety, then in slow motion, followed by zoom-ins on suspect and victim, followed again by stills displaying shots fired – all the time with the object of interest either highlighted or encircled in red pen. This 'Zapruder style' editing thus further supports the rhetorical amateur status of the images, although in this case there is no identifiable Zapruder. The tapes are nonetheless portrayed as hard visible evidence with a claim to factuality (Bridge and Sjøvaag 2010).

Having said that, both NRK and TV 2 clearly attempt to treat the amateur videos in a non-sensational manner and succeed in doing so through taking a detached approach to the shock value of the footage. Norway has a relatively large Pakistani community, and both channels have determined the relevance of the story to lay in its potential political consequences. Although the predominant narrative frame here is the political assassination, the subsequent focus is on the political fallout and the possible ensuing power play within the Pakistani People's Party, not on placing blame for the murder. The sensitivity with which the two channels treat the footage and the story itself suggests audience considerations play a part in the narrative strategy. The editorial decisions to assume a non-sensational approach are therefore likely to be what also inspired the channels to adopt the embedding strategy towards amateur footage capturing the moment of death.

The 7/7 London Bombings

The amateur images used in the coverage of the 7/7 London bombings allowed for a particular proximity to the events, both in time and space. The first amateur image, of passengers escaping through the underground tunnels, was shown on Norwegian television just four hours after the event. The other amateur footage, a mobile phone video taken from inside one of the trains after the blast, reached Norwegian screens two hours later. Overall, NRK and TV 2 display dissimilar approaches to the 7/7 London bombings. NRK uses the amateur recordings in a more limited way than TV 2 and employs the embedding strategy by editing the footage uncommented into a continuous montage flow that runs in the background of each bulletin. The montage serves to accompany studio interviews, commentary and telephone reports from London. The channel uses the video from inside the train in three of its special bulletins (at 16:00, 16:24 and 17:00). In the first bulletin, the video is placed at the end of the broadcast; while subsequent bulletins repeat the video, this time earlier in the broadcast. Although the 'train video' is clearly identifiable as amateur and can be easily distinguished from footage taken above ground – primarily of rescue workers and police securing the scene – it is difficult to identify exactly which, if any, of the other images used in NRK's montage packages are amateur in origin. Other professionally captured footage frequently used includes visuals outside the train stations, Sky News helicopter footage of Aldgate tube station and witness statements outside on the streets. In addition there are the clearly professionally shot images of 'official' events such as the Metropolitan Police's press conference, statements by Prime Minister Tony Blair and other world leaders gathered for the G8 meeting in Scotland that same day, as well as reactions from politicians and officials in Norway. NRK's narrative frame focuses less on the victims and more on the official statements by police and politicians. Thus, official sources are given more prominence than witness statements or amateur recordings of the event.

After the initial 'breaking news' bulletin at 12:00, which primarily consists of immediate information, NRK also quickly shifts its primary news angle away from the blasts themselves, and onto how this affects Norwegians holidaying in or travelling to or from London on that day; commuting problems in and around the UK capital; general security in London and in US cities; and whether or not this 'could happen in Norway'. Overall, NRK's visual rhetoric falls into the post-9/11 terror attack narrative. Scenes of chaos, rescue efforts, police roadblocks and the occasional amateur evidence of panic and distress all serve to bring the event closer to viewers watching in Norway. A focus on the safety of Norwegians further supports this narrative. Rhetorically the images present a familiar scene – one we have seen before in television coverage of terror events in New York, Madrid and Israel. What fuels the coverage throughout the day is the fear created by event proximity. The urge to attribute responsibility and accountability for the chaos is a common journalistic reaction to such events. The post-9/11 terror attack narrative thus supports the embedding strategy, where scarce focus on amateur recordings is substituted by a focus on institutional response, infrastructure and safety issues.

In contrast, TV 2 uses an embellishing strategy regarding amateur images from the 7/7 bombings. Whereas NRK uses the 'train video' only three times, TV 2 airs it nine times during the day, in seven of its bulletins. First at 14:55, an hour before NRK, and then repeated in nearly all of its subsequent bulletins. Here, it opens the main report on the bomb blasts whereas NRK puts it towards the end of its montages. When it comes to the amateur footage used, TV 2 has at least three times more than NRK. TV 2 also contextualizes the images whereas on NRK they remain uncommented. TV 2's reporter mentions seven times that 'this mobile phone video shows the situation underground this morning'. An amateur still was used in TV 2's coverage even earlier. The 13:55 bulletin shows the mobile phone photo taken by tube passenger Adam Stacey in the tunnel at King's Cross. TV 2's reporter comments that 'this fresh mms image clearly shows the panic that spread underground this morning'. TV 2 uses this image nine times throughout the coverage, whereas NRK excludes it from its broadcasts. TV 2's coverage thus tends to highlight amateur footage, particularly by placing it early in the news reports and prominently in the general coverage. The amateur origin of the footage is noted specifically and is commented upon by reporters and commentators. This type of imagery is also repeated more often than in NRK's embedded narrative.

In addition to differences in the visual narrative approach to the amateur footage, the analysis reveals how these strategies also reflect the different ethical decisions of the two channels. NRK takes a cautious approach regarding information about the number of blasts, and about the number of dead and wounded. Its information during the first few

Figure 4.2: Commuter Alexander Chadwick took this now famous image of passengers walking to safety along the tracks at King's Cross station with his cameraphone and sent it to the BBC.

hours of coverage comes largely from official channels and is thus more or less accurate. TV 2 takes the opposite approach – valuing speed and immediacy over accuracy. Thus, hindsight reveals that during its first few hours of coverage, the information disseminated by TV 2 was somewhat speculative. TV 2 initially reported six blasts on underground trains, three bus explosions and up to 1000 wounded, when in reality the figures were three blasts underground, one bus explosion and 700 wounded. NRK's reports, on the other hand, never exceeded the final figures.

TV 2's immediacy approach also reveals a greater willingness to incorporate amateur images into the news coverage than NRK's accuracy approach. The difference between the two approaches is clearly reflected not only in the degree to which amateur footage is used, but also in the overall visual representation of the event. TV 2's coverage is saturated with images, while NRK's coverage is more thematically concentrated. TV 2's visual coverage has an emphasis on the wounded, while NRK's visual profile is dominated by images of police and ambulance services. TV 2's coverage has a faster pace than NRK, meaning TV 2 has edited more images into reports and montage sequences than NRK. TV 2 also has a tendency to display more images of the wounded and witness accounts taken from tube passengers, moments after they emerged from the tube stations. In terms of journalistic ethics, this approach could be seen as somewhat problematic, as some of the initial estimates of damages and casualties were overstated. There is also the issue of victims' and witnesses' state of mind. On the other hand, information was broadcast quickly, and audiences were given an immediate impression in terms of temporality and proximity as to the unfolding events in London on the day in question. The connection of this emphasis on the amateur footage to the immediacy approach can be seen in the speed with which these images were disseminated after initially reaching the newsroom. This approach, where getting the information out fast is a primary news value, might be seen to be reflected in the channel's procedures for fact verification of the initial information broadcast to audiences.

TV 2 also mobilizes the post-9/11 terror attack narrative for the event, but with a more pronounced focus. Reports here frequently refer to the Madrid train bombings and 9/11 as narrative contexts to the 7/7 bombings, both visually and orally. This gives the viewer a recognizable and familiar reference point, as well as a political and cultural context. The overall visual focus is on the victims and the wounded, the immediate aftermath and the rescue operations and on the amateur videos and pictures taken underground. TV 2's narrative tells the story of individual plight, thereby drawing viewers closer to the story. The amateur footage from inside the train serves a similar purpose. TV 2 thus treats the existence of these images as news in itself. They have a shocking effect. And although we actually see very little of the drama that is unfolding underground in these stills and videos, they help us imagine the situation. The wobbly, blurred quality conveys confusion, chaos and panic. These visual cues hold claims to authenticity in terms of the witness status of the images on the screen. They carry with them emotional as well as narrative and institutional arguments. The visual signature of the amateur video is easily recognizable as a non-journalistic product. By embellishing the amateur footage from the

7/7 aftermath, TV 2 thus bestows upon the images their witness status, authenticates the source of the images and establishes the narrative frame within which the images are to be understood.

Both the embedding and the embellishing strategies convey strong institutional arguments that serve to protect the authority of the journalistic profession. TV 2's significant use of the amateur images first communicates the fact that no journalists were on the scene to record the events, and second, that TV 2 still fulfils its duty to report by bringing us the next best thing – namely the amateur recordings of the event. NRK's limited use of the amateur images – where the footage is embedded, its origins uncommented and its witness status negated – contains the same claim to professional authority as the embellishing strategy. Here, however, editorial control, accuracy and sobriety as to the sensational aspects of the story are the primary arguments. Whereas NRK's embedding and accuracy approach did ensure audiences received true, timely and relevant information, TV 2's embellishing and immediacy approach – although more dramatic and immediate than NRK's coverage – provided audiences with exaggerated and inaccurate accounts of the effect of the blasts during the initial hours of coverage. The two approaches nevertheless served the needs of both institutions in communicating their professional identities to their audiences.

From an institutional point of view, the variation in how NRK and TV 2 treat amateur footage of the 7/7 bombings can be linked to differences in the two channels' identities and market positions. NRK is the licence-fee-funded public service broadcaster and has an ethos of public responsibility that entails a detached and neutral style of news reporting. Its strong public service culture can be said to include a desired image of sobriety and level-headedness that perhaps inspires its embedded visual narrative. This could also be what encourages such caution and restraint with regard to the news value of the amateur footage. Attention to verified facts, the predominant use of official sources and the seemingly critical attitude towards the status of amateur images as sources suggest that NRK perhaps assumes an overly cautious approach to UGC from the 7/7 London bombings. Accuracy and responsibility as public service values do not in themselves preclude giving UGC prominent coverage, all the while the projected gatekeeper ideology carries a claim of trust that entails audiences can rely on the veracity of the information disseminated. Here, journalistic procedures and methods have traditionally been kept out of news reports and thus hidden from audiences. With increased participation and collaboration between news organizations and audiences, however, the methodologies of journalism necessarily become more transparent. This particularly entails greater openness about the use of sources in the journalistic work process. TV 2 seems to account for this trend in its treatment of amateur images from the 7/7 London bombings to a greater extent than NRK. TV 2 is a commercial public service broadcaster and has a watchdog approach to news that first of all makes for a more engaged style of reporting. TV 2's watchdog identity furthermore assumes a partnership with the audience that perhaps renders the channel more open to UGC collaboration. This projected identity, coupled with the number two position in the market, could be what inspires TV 2 to assume a more inclusive attitude towards collaborative developments within its journalism. Channel identity in a de facto duopoly such as the Norwegian television market is important to retain audience shares, and TV 2 could therefore gain from branding itself as being at the forefront of journalistic and technological developments.

At the same time, both broadcasters need to keep the online news services at arm's length. Timeliness, liveness, immediacy and visual imagery are news values that need to be fulfilled in order to attract audiences in a breaking news situation (Couldry 2004: 356, 360; Eide 1992: 27; Hoskins 2006: 453). This is because images represent physical reality. They bring viewers into direct contact with the outside world and create a communicative connection between the news organization and its audiences (Hjarvard 1999: 35–36). In fact, in a television environment, images are important for an event to become newsworthy in the first place (ibid.: 22). More than anything else, the videos analysed here serve in a witness capacity, as they were captured by people close to the event. As there is no professionally shot footage available, such amateur footage has the ability to become iconic. In this context, amateur images are valuable to broadcasters insofar as they are newsworthy and serve to retain audiences and higher status among competitors.

The Significance of Amateur Images

The increasing importance of live coverage of event-driven news often means such stories are characterized by the saturation of images that are indelible and endlessly replayed (Livingstone and Bennett 2003: 366, 375). Contradictory and disruptive images affect the public imagination and contribute to our historical consciousness; particularly as such imagery is often highly migratory (Andén-Papadopoulos 2008: 6). Thus, over the years, amateur images have come to significantly determine our visual and cultural memory of disruptive events (Hansell 2006). Yet, without the mass dissemination of amateur images by mainstream news organizations, such imagery can find little cultural significance. In fact it becomes difficult to imagine, or even to remember, historic events of the modern age outside or separate from the media that 'produce' them (Hoskins 2006: 458).

The use of UGC in the mainstream media on 7 July 2005 has been referred to as a 'tipping point' in the growing symbiosis between journalism and the audience. The reasons used to explain such a profound shift are, first of all, the speed with which the images and videos were sent to newsrooms, and the subsequent immediacy of the event for audiences online and watching television. The sheer volume of images and videos submitted is seen as significant, given that this arguably led to a comprehensive impression of the events. Researchers and commentators thus stress that news journalism has – as a result of the contribution of the amateur in the coverage of the 7/7 London bombings – experienced a profound democratization of news coverage (Allan 2007). New technology, however, is only democratically potent if it reaches critical mass. In order for this new technology to communicate the effects of major accidents, disasters and social upheaval to a wider audience, witnesses to such events need a large-scale one-to-many disseminator. For most people, this medium is still television.

Even though UGC may pose a threat to the gatekeeping privileges of the mainstream news media, these case studies demonstrate how the journalistic narrative as an institutionalized practice manages to balance this threat through editing and framing. As the visual signature of the amateur image in itself signals that a professional was not at the scene, amateur footage in fact validates itself while at the same time validating the mainstream media institution broadcasting it. Even more importantly, the existence of amateur recordings of large-scale events such as the 7/7 London bombings and the Bhutto assassination is news in itself. It brings valid and important information about the situation that according to standard news values needs to be highlighted in any mainstream news coverage. As such, the true democratic potential of amateur images lies in its inherent information value for the public.

Conclusion

This chapter has asked to what extent journalistic authority is threatened by the inclusion of amateur images of events where professional reporters were not themselves present to record the scenes. This question is founded on the premise that journalism has a weak professional status, which makes its gatekeeping authority vulnerable to outside challenges. Rather than regarding UGC of the sort analysed here as a threat, we should acknowledge that both the embedding and embellishing strategies display journalism's ability to retain editorial authority over amateur images of these terror events. Breaking news stories such as these represent events that are disruptive to the regular news agenda. In these cases amateur videos and pictures are valuable to the news coverage. Audience contributions of this kind will remain equally valuable in the future, and the spread of mobile and Internet technologies across the globe is only likely to increase the amount of such material flooding into newsrooms in times of breaking news.

References

Allan, S. (2007), 'Citizen Journalism and the Rise of "Mass Self-Communication": Reporting the London Bombings', Global Media Journal, Australian Edition, 1: 1, pp. 1–20.

Andén-Papadopoulos, K. (2008), 'The Abu Ghraib Torture Photographs: News Frames, Visual Culture, and the Power of Images', Journalism, 9: 5, pp. 5–30.

Bridge, J. and Sjøvaag, H. (2010), 'Amateur Images in the Professional News Stream' in J. Gripsrud (ed.), Relocating Television: Television in the Digital Context, London: Routledge.

Cook, T. E. (2005), Governing with the News: The News Media as a Political Institution, 2nd Edition, London: University of Chicago Press.

Corner, J. (1995), Television Form and Public Address, London: Edward Arnold.

Couldry, N. (2004), 'Liveness, "Reality", and the Mediated Habitus from Television to the Mobile Phone', *The Communication Review*, 7: 4, pp. 353–61.

Deuze, M. (2005), 'What is Journalism? Professional Identity and Ideology of Journalists Reconsidered', *Journalism*, 6: 4, pp. 442–64.

Eide, M. (1992), *Nyhetens interesse: Nyhetsjournalistikk mellom tekst og kontekst* (*News Journalism between Text and Context*), Oslo: Universitetsforlaget.

Eide, M. (2001), 'Journalistisk makt. Et oppslag' ('Journalism and Power'), in M. Eide (ed.), *Til Dagsorden! Journalistikk, makt og demokrati* (*Journalism, Power and Democracy*), Oslo: Gyldendal Akademisk, pp. 13-59.

Ekström, M. (2000), 'Information, Storytelling and Attractions: TV Journalism in Three Modes of Communication', *Media, Culture & Society*, 22: 4, pp. 465–92.

Fry, K. G. (2008), 'News as Subject: What is It? Where is It? Whose is It?', *Journalism Studies*, 9: 4, pp. 545–60.

Gans, H. J. (1980), *Deciding What's News*, New York: Pantheon.

Gordon, J. (2007), 'The Mobile Phone and the Public Sphere: Mobile Phone Usage in Three Critical Situations', *Convergence*, 13: 3, pp. 307–19.

Hansell, S. (2006), 'Have Camera Phone? Yahoo and Reuters Want You to Work for Their News Service', http://www.nytimes.com/2006/12/04/technology/04yahoo.html?ex=1322888400&en=949fa991657f9851&ei=5088&partner=rssnyt&emc=rss. Accessed 25 June 2008.

Harrison, J. (2009), 'User-Generated Content and Gatekeeping at the BBC Hub', *Journalism Studies*, 11: 2, pp. 243–56.

Hermida, A. and Thurman, N. (2008), 'A Clash of Cultures', *Journalism Practice*, 2: 3, pp. 343–56.

Hjarvard, S. (1999), *Tv-nyheder i konkurrence* (*TV News in Competition*), Fredriksberg: Samfundslitteratur.

Hoskins, A. (2006), 'Temporality, Proximity and Security: Terror in a Media-Drenched Age', *International Relations*, 20: 4, pp. 453–66.

Knight, A. (2008), 'Who is a Journalist? Journalism in the Age of Blogging', *Journalism Studies*, 9: 1, pp. 117–31.

Kovach, B. and Rosenstiel, T. (2001), *The Elements of Journalism*, London: Atlantic Books.

Livingstone, S. and Bennett, W. L. (2003), 'Gatekeeping, Indexing, and Live-Event News: Is Technology Altering the Constriction of News?', *Political Communication*, 20: 4, pp. 363–80.

Perlmutter, D. D. (1998), *Photojournalism and Foreign Policy: Icons of Outrage in International Crisis*, London: Praeger.

Peters, J. D. (2001), 'Witnessing', *Media, Culture & Society*, 23: 6, pp. 707–23.

Raaum, O. (2001), 'Se opp for etterligninger: Journalistikk som merkevare' ('Beware of Immitations: Journalism as Brand'), in M. Eide (ed.), *Til Dagsorden! Journalistikk, makt og demokrati* (*Journalism, Power and Democracy*), Oslo: Gyldendal Akademisk, pp- 59-85

Schudson, M. (2003), *The Sociology of News*, New York: W. W. Norton & Company.

Schudson, M. (2007), 'The Anarchy of Events and the Anxiety of Story Telling', *Political Communication*, 24: 3, pp. 253–57.

Zelizer, B. (2004), *Taking Journalism Seriously: News and the Academy*, Thousand Oaks: Sage.

Chapter 5

Transparency and Trustworthiness: Strategies for Incorporating
Amateur Photography into News Discourse

Mervi Pantti and Kari Andén-Papadopoulos

The Iranian street protests in the wake of the disputed presidential elections in June 2009 have been singled out as yet another crucial turning point in the relationship between established news media and 'citizen journalists'. As some foreign journalists were forced to leave Tehran, and others were confined to their hotel rooms and offices, professional news organizations increasingly relied on Iranians themselves to provide information and, most importantly, images from the street protests. As *New York Times* blogger Brian Stelter (2009) observed, '[T]he combination amounts to the biggest embrace yet of a collaborative new style of news gathering – one that combines the contributions of ordinary citizens with the reports and analysis of journalists'. We argue in this chapter that the use of non-professional images of the Iran-election crisis also became a test case for the traditional journalistic standards of accuracy and responsibility.

In the reporting on the Iranian protests citizen-shot photos and videos became a crucial means of 'true witnessing' for mainstream news organizations, that is, of being present at the event in time and space (Peters 2001: 38). Yet at the same time these images raised important questions regarding our camera-mediated knowledge of crisis events, and more specifically, regarding professional journalistic norms of accuracy and responsibility. The authenticity of citizen eyewitness imagery pouring out of Iran proved to be difficult or impossible to verify. Some news organizations tried to solve the problem of publishing unconfirmed images by taking measures to ensure transparency, that is signalling with caveats and labelling that the authenticity of published footage could not be verified (Newman 2009: 8, 28; Stelter 2009; Stöcker, Neumann and Dörting 2009).

Our aim is to provide a comparative view of how different mainstream news organizations integrated the eyewitness footage captured by 'ordinary' Iranians into their news narrative and whether they were adhering to the same professional practices and ethical standards. For this purpose, we have analysed the news coverage of the transnational channel CNN and three national public service news channels, YLE in Finland, SVT in Sweden and BBC in the United Kingdom. We ask the following questions: How is citizen imagery integrated into the news discourse and what truth-status is given to it? How do these news organizations handle the challenges that amateur eyewitness imagery raises for professional ethics, specifically for the standards of accuracy and the use of graphic images? And to what extent do they adhere to the increasingly important ethical norm of transparency in responding to these challenges?

The Challenge of Non-Professional Imagery

What sets citizen-shot news photographs and videos apart from other types of audience content in the mainstream news media (such as comments and non-news photography) is the discursive authority that rests on eyewitnessing. Therefore, they sometimes gain a status equivalent to professional material and feature in broadcast news and on the front pages of newspapers around the world. The importance of citizen images of breaking news events, thus, lies in the fact that they help to establish journalism's own claim to authority. As Barbie Zelizer notes, the figure of the citizen journalist 'has allowed the news media to claim that they "have been there" as witnesses of events that they have not witnessed' (2007: 425).

News organizations undeniably appreciate citizen-shot news imagery because it facilitates immediate newsgathering. Besides immediacy, the images are believed to lend a heightened sense of 'reality effect' to news reporting, deriving from the subjective point of view, 'raw' emotions and poor technical quality of the amateur footage (Pantti and Bakker 2009; see also Williams et al. in this volume). However, because of the problems of securing the origin and reliability of such content, and because of their typically subjective character, they are also understood to present a risk to the trustworthiness and brand of a news organization (Allan 2006: 156; Pantti and Bakker 2009; Williams et al. 2010). The task of establishing who produced a particular photograph or video clip (and why, when and where) is undoubtedly an intricate one, since amateur contributors often remain anonymous, sometimes because of safety concerns but also as a genre convention of sorts (Bridge and Sjøvaag 2009). Journalists, however, underscore the need to check (visual) audience content with the same rigour as material from other news sources. They emphasize that, in the end, it is the journalistic standards of accuracy and the fact-checking that set them apart from citizen journalists (Pantti and Bakker 2009; Williams et al. 2010). However, despite professional journalists' discourse, the trend in journalism is claimed to be towards 'a more relative and post-modern view on accuracy' (Witschge and Nygren 2009: 46).

The increasing availability of amateur images also raises the question of responsible representation, of what is deemed acceptable to show to the public. What appears on websites or is solicited and obtained directly from the public does not necessarily adhere to the standards of 'good taste and decency' that govern mainstream news media. According to John Taylor (1998), journalists' codes of practice have traditionally restricted them from displaying dead bodies, dying people or gory details of a violent event. News organizations face a constant need to make decisions whether or not to show violent images, which ones to use and why, where to show them (in broadcast news bulletins or online news sites) and how to present them (e.g. should they be digitally edited to reduce their horror-factor; how should they be captioned and contextualized) (see Perlmutter and Hatley 2004). While these decision-making dilemmas prompted by images of death and violence are far from new, the fact that graphic, newsworthy images are today 'everywhere' to be seen makes established media organizations' decisions more important – and difficult. As Risto Kunelius (2009) argues, in the networked era the acts of publishing are not simply about the public's right to know and, hence, about revealing new information, but about performing a distinct speech act that will be judged on normative grounds. For example, by publishing (or not) a horrific image which is already available to be seen in the public domain, news organizations make a statement about their ethics and professional codes. What is at stake, then, is the authority and trust in a news organization.

The crucial question is whether the profusion of amateur images constitutes a change in the standards and ethics exercised in newsrooms across the world. What happens to the key principle of responsible reporting – 'Avoid using violent material simply because it is available' (Taylor 1998: 75) – is in question at a time when personal cameras produce not only exclusive and immediate images of breaking news events but also images that may subvert the official representations and shape public perceptions of historic events. It has been suggested that for news organizations wanting to appear respectable, the figure of the amateur provides 'an ethical bumper' for publishing graphic images: 'The amateur, willing to point his or her camera at anything, shoulders the ethical responsibility of producing such footage. Meanwhile, the network can frame such footage with multiple disclaimers about its "disturbing content," while simultaneously reaping the benefits of presenting a more graphic picture of a given event' (Bridge and Sjøvaag 2009).

Transparency as Strategic Ritual

The idea of objectivity has been a guiding principle of journalistic professionalism in the western hemisphere throughout the twentieth century, made operational through various 'strategic rituals of objectivity'. These typically include the corroboration of facts with multiple sources, the balance of viewpoints and keeping the journalist's view out of the news story (Schudson 2001; Tuchman 1978). It has been suggested, however, that in the networked-media environment the authority of journalism should rest more on the openness of journalists and journalistic institutions. As Jane Singer states, '[S]erving today's public means conveying not just the "news" itself but also as much as we can about the people, process, and products that shaped it' (2008: 75). Indeed, the notion of transparency has recently received attention as a necessary – if not sufficient – condition for building credibility and trust with audiences and for reinforcing *journalism's* standing in society (Allen 2008; Craft and Heim 2009; Karlsson 2010; Phillips 2010; Plaisance 2007).

Above all then, transparency is a mechanism between journalists and the audience. It serves as a means through which journalists attempt to earn trust from the audience and the audience can assess journalists' performance. Transparency is at the heart of ethical communication, since, as Patrick Lee Plaisance writes, '[t]ransparent interaction is what allows us as rational, autonomous beings to assess each other's behaviour' (2007: 187). On the other hand, transparency can also been seen as an opportunity for journalism to improve in a way that reinforces a more discerning public (Kovach and Rosenstiel 2001: 83).

The idea of transparency as a norm has *so far* been studied in an online news environment but it warrants further examination with regard to the use of audience material in the 'old' news media. Transparency entails explaining and being open about the methods of selecting and producing the news, and it can also include making tough ethical decisions public. It necessarily includes letting the public know where information comes from. As with the notion of journalistic objectivity, transparency is an abstract concept that needs to be translated into standardized rituals that can be used in everyday journalistic work and be recognized and understood by users (Karlsson 2010).

Study

The purpose of this study is to describe, analyse and compare how different television news organizations incorporated footage captured by ordinary Iranians into their news narrative. The following analysis will focus on the coverage of CNN, BBC One, The Swedish Broadcasting Corporation (SVT1) and The Finnish Broadcasting Company (YLE TV1). The comparative logic of the analysis is based on contrasting a transnational, US-based commercial 24-hour news channel with three national public-service broadcasting channels, and comparing the national public-service news with each other. The study is based on close analysis of news reports from the 14th to the 24th of June. Analysis of YLE coverage included nine YLE TV1's news broadcasts at 20:30 (the main news broadcast) and one late television news broadcast at 23:15 on June 17 (because there was no story on Iran in the main news bulletin) – 10 reports in all. The SVT coverage included ten SVT1 Rapport programmes at 19:30 (main bulletin) and the BBC coverage included 20 news reports from 18:00 and 22:00 bulletins. The CNN coverage includes two broadcasts per day, which generated 20 news reports in total.

The content of the news stories was analysed according to visual content and verbal contextualization: We have looked at what kind of status is given to amateur images and how they are identified and contextualized – or not – in news narratives and to what extent news organizations addressed the specific challenges that eyewitness imagery from Iranian citizens raised for journalism's trustworthiness. The use of anonymous amateur video of the death of the Iranian woman Neda Agha Soltan on the evening of 20 June 2009 has been singled out to analyse how these news organizations handled extremely violent, yet compelling, citizen imagery.

Measures of Transparency in the Iran Protest Reporting

In covering the Iran post-election protests, CNN made extensive use of amateur imagery it acquired from two main sources: through CNN's own online news community iReport and social networking sites such as YouTube, Twitter and Facebook. In CNN's coverage, the role of social media and personal cameras in organizing the protest movement became a sensational topic of news in its own right. Accordingly, citizen eyewitness images were referred to as objects to be explained and analysed rather than as supportive evidence (cf. Bridge and Sjøvaag 2009).

CNN's strategy for incorporating amateur images into its news stories was to draw attention to the difference between citizen-shot imagery and professional footage by using *transparency* as a strategic ritual. An illuminating example of CNN's performance of transparency is a newscast from 17 June, titled 'Internet's Role in the Iranian Protest' in which the news anchor Tony Harris and the reporter at CNN's Iran desk, Isha Sesay, establish amateur videos as 'unverified material'. Sesay says on-camera: 'We want to share with our viewers two compelling pieces of video that are coming in to us. We need to stress, and we continue to do so, that CNN cannot independently *verify* this stuff. But we feel it is important that people see this, see and hear what is coming in to us.' The report then cuts to the first video, which allegedly shows a burned down dormitory in the aftermath of a raid at Tehran University. All amateur material was prominently labelled in CNN's coverage, and Sesay is careful to spell out that the video, which also carries the 'iReport' logo, is shot by one of CNN's iReporters. The reporter's narration in this story exemplifies the problem of veracity that CNN's ecstatic approach to amateur videos presents: 'As you look at these pictures it looks like a warzone! Everything in bits. You could assume that maybe there was a fire because things certainly seem charred there on the ground [...] really giving you a sense of what took place there [...] something dramatic took place here.' She then adds, in an evident attempt to verify the video: 'And according to numerous media reports there was a raid on that dormitory.'

While broadcasting the second amateur video, which shows a crowded metro station with people chanting, the journalists perform a casual, yet clearly calculated conversation about the difficulties of verifying such material:

Sesay: Look at that scene Tony, and listen! Do you hear the chanting? That's from inside a metro station.

Harris: Yes. Do we know what they're saying?

Sesay: No, we haven't been able to make out exactly what they're saying. We just see that platform full of people chanting in unison [...] and protesting [...] what's playing out in Iran at this point. These are the sights and sounds that the Iranian authorities don't want the rest of the world to see, Tony.

Harris: So, the reality is that they could be chanting Mousavi or they could be chanting Ahmadinejad, we just don't know, we can't make it out.

Sesay goes on to explain that there had been pro-Ahmadinejad rallies and that a large number of people indeed voted for him. The news anchor continues to stress the unverifiable nature of amateur images in a pedagogical manner, and the discussion ends with a declaration of CNN's commitment to the strategy of transparency:

Harris: So when we say unverified material […] let's try to be clear here: someone claims, makes a claim about the video that we are showing you. And we are not able to independently confirm the claims that are being made, the representations of the video, correct?

Sesay: Well, absolutely, because we are confined, we are limited in our ability to do so. The very fact of the matter is […] that international media is confined to their offices, to their bureaus, so they can't get out on the streets. So, we are unable to go out and shoot this stuff and be present as these scenes play out. […] And also, because of those restrictions in getting in touch with people there on the ground in Iran, even as we get this stuff via the web we can't ask those probing questions as we would like to because basically we are very very limited.

Harris: So we just want the viewers to be aware of that and keep that in mind as we get those images and put them on air through the Iran desk.

Sesay: Absolutely. Here at the Iran desk it's all about transparency, giving context of what we see.

Harris: Transparency, let's do that!

By emphasizing and dramatizing its own performance of transparency, CNN was able to simultaneously publish unverified amateur footage and protect its professional authority. The repeated use of verbal and textual disclaimers about the videos being 'unverifiable', and the continuous discussion of the constraints imposed on foreign journalists in Iran allowed CNN to sidestep issues of accuracy and bias. In being open about the uncertainty pertaining to the meaning and truth-value of the amateur footage, CNN effectively strived to defuse any potential critique.

While citizen images certainly play an important role in all three public service broadcasters' reporting, they are not presented with a similar hype as in CNN's content. Rather than gaining prominent status as an independent object of analysis and fascination, they are mainly used as supporting evidence – and obviously also to add to the visual style and dramatic impact of the overall story. However, there are considerable differences between the public-service broadcasting organizations in how they incorporate amateur images into their news narrative and, consequently, what truth-status is given to them.

The first difference concerns the *identification* and *contextualization* of amateur visuals. None of the public service broadcasters adopted a similar rigorous labelling of amateur images as CNN but in the BBC and SVT coverage the non-professional status of visuals is pointed out in the verbal narrative. Here is an example of BBC's news story from 21 June. The reporter's narration is overlaid a video showing a long-shot overview of a street protest: 'Pictures of what happened on Saturday are still being posted on websites. The BBC did not film this material but you get a good idea what was happening.' The reporter then continues to explain what is actually happening in the picture – protestors and the police fighting to gain control over a street – and concludes by spelling out the greater meaning of the scene shown: 'What made this [protest] very significant for the future of

Iran is that they were there at all, defying authorities.' In a similar way, SVT attempted to provide context to the images it used. In a report from 20 June we see an amateur video taken from within the basement of a building (the camera view is framed by the dark rims of an opening in the façade) which shows a group of protesters carrying sticks and throwing stones at the government forces up the street. The reporter's voice-over states: 'The images that are coming are filmed in secret, since all foreign and oppositional press are now forbidden in Iran. Today thousands of people gathered again in the capital Tehran to demonstrate against the election results'.

In both respects, YLE stood out as it largely refrained from identifying the non-professional images. Instead of systematically identifying amateur material as such, YLE seemed to trust that viewers are capable of telling amateur material apart from professional footage on the basis of their narrative context and different aesthetics. The use of amateur material in the story from 15 June demonstrates YLE's overall strategy to seamlessly embed amateur visuals into the narrative. The story starts with professional footage of Moussavi's supporters on the streets and Ahmadinejad's supporters protesting in front of the British and French embassies in Tehran. With the reporter's narration 'foreign channels are being interfered, websites have been closed down' the professional footage changes seamlessly into a 10 second clip of a low quality amateur video displaying similar images of fires and violence on the streets that were seen in the professional footage. Against a backdrop of the following narrative 'our reporter who returned from Tehran yesterday describes the situation as chaotic' the package switches back to using professional footage: a studio interview shot with the YLE reporter Jukka Niva, who explains that the Iranian police had been confiscating cameras and tapes from foreign journalists. The restrictions on foreign media, then, serve as verbal transitions from professional material to amateur video, and amateur videos function mainly as an illustration of the journalist's verbal narration.

Unlike CNN, which repeatedly commented on and discussed the problems of ensuring the accuracy and verification of amateur footage, the public service broadcasters typically did not point out these difficulties in their coverage. The amateur footage that SVT and YLE used in their reporting came from transnational news agencies, often with warnings that the time, place or reliability of the amateur content was not guaranteed. The two Nordic public service news organizations, however, excluded any backstory about the acquisition of amateur footage and refrained from referring to the problem of authenticity. SVT and YLE, then, authenticated amateur images by relying on the established legitimacy of the news provider itself (we show it, therefore it is true). There is only one exception to this traditional strategy: In SVT's report from 22 June the reporter says in voice-over: 'It is ordinary demonstrators with mobile cameras that today document what is taking place on the streets of Tehran. This video of a clash this weekend has been released by the news agency AP who interviewed the filmmaker to confirm the veracity.' Considering that all SVT's broadcasts between 14 and 24 June contain amateur videos, it seems that the issue of authenticity made it into the news only when it was affirmed. The BBC, on the other hand, received an unprecedented amount of amateur recordings through its own Persian

TV (BBC 2009) and showed more willingness to share not only the source of the imagery but also doubts over its authenticity. The latter was communicated in the verbal narrative by using words that express uncertainty, as the following examples show: 'This video sent to the BBC *appears* to show shooting from the military base last week.' (22 June, our emphasis) and 'Iranians have been posting more pictures of the security forces in action [...] This *appears* to show the violence last Saturday' (23 June, our emphasis).

To be sure, the media's restricted working conditions became a central narrative frame in all news organizations' coverage, with news anchors and reporters routinely calling attention to the incapacitating conditions under which news organizations had to operate. This narrative frame worked to legitimize the use of amateur footage. However, this openness regarding the production of news was limited to highlighting the difficulties foreign news media faced in obtaining adequate information about the unfolding events inside Iran in a very general manner. When news organizations took the viewers 'behind the scenes' of news production it was done either in order to promote the news organization's advanced news-gathering and 'participatory' practices (CNN) or to add extra weight and drama to the story by highlighting the censoring of the media (BBC, SVT, YLE). For example, on 20 June BBC's John Simpson tells the story of protesting and police violence of that day with reference to the BBC's own problems of getting good pictures: 'It was too dangerous to use a professional television camera and like so many people in the crowd we had to use a mobile phone.' What was not included was the discussion of editorial policy or individual decisions concerning the use of amateur material.

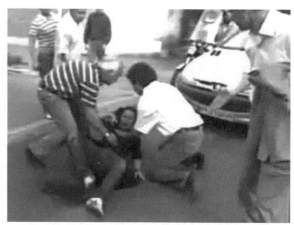

Figure 5.1: Neda Soltan's final moments were captured on a cell phone video and disseminated rapidly across the Internet, transforming her into an icon of the protests against the Iranian regime.

To Show or Not to Show

As with the practices of identifying, authenticating and contextualizing amateur images, a variety of editorial procedures and ethical standards exist to accommodate the use of graphic amateur visual material. CNN's use of graphic amateur material is another indication of the ritual of transparency functioning simultaneously as a source of legitimacy and a justification for exploiting the sensational value of such material. The channel persistently used preceding warnings and voice-over narrative to explicate the violence shown and, in the most disturbing cases, chose to pixelate parts of the content. CNN broadcasted the video of Neda's death in its entirety the same day she was shot. Initially, the video was framed through CNN's own continuous monitoring of the social networking sites. Reporter Josh Lewis introduced the video:

> One of the top topics on Twitter, in the whole Twitter universe tonight is the name of a girl who Twitter says is the one featured in a video. I'm going to show you a clip now [...] this is disturbing, I want you know that [...] and we have blurred out her face out of respect. This is possibly the most seen piece of video out of Iran in the world today.

The next day, on 21 June, CNN aired a non-edited version of the video with repeated warnings about graphic content. The news report, titled 'Her name was Neda', displayed a version of the video in which Neda's face is fully visible as she appears to lose consciousness and blood begins to pour from her mouth and nose. The airing of the footage illustrates the claim made by some critics in the US context that news organizations adopted a new strategy of publishing first and asking questions later in their reporting on the street protests (Stelter 2009). The reporter Octavia Nasr clearly strives to provide context to and explain the dramatic video as it unfolds but there is confusion in her interpretation (the men on the video Nasr identifies here as her father and a stranger were later identified as a doctor and her singing instructor):

> Her name is Neda. The facts surrounding her life and her death are difficult to verify. She appears to have been a young student who joined thousands of her countrymen to voice her disapproval of Iran's election results. Eyewitnesses say a Basij militiaman, hiding on a building roof top shot Neda in her chest, silencing her forever. A man who appears to be her father, desperately calling on her to open her eyes. A stranger begging her to stay awake. 'Don't be afraid, don't be afraid, Neda' the man says. But Neda doesn't respond. She dies, right there, on the streets. Another protester capturing her last moments on a cellphone camera. And just like that, Neda who came to the square thinking she is one voice among thousands, turned into the voice of an entire opposition movement.

The shooting of Neda continued to be a CNN top story for the following days, and the channel covered it from different viewpoints and used political experts, quotes from inside

Iran and phone interviews to assess the impact of the video. An essential part of CNN's reporting was devoted to the meta-story of how the video rapidly spread across the global mediascape and gained iconic status – all the while exploiting the visual power of the video by constantly airing it (along with dramatic frame grabs from the video).

Of the three public-service broadcasters, only SVT transmitted the video of Neda's death in its entirety. The Swedish news channel reported on the case of Neda only when the video had already gone viral on the Internet and had drawn the attention of the international news media. In its 22 June report, SVT broadcasted the uncensored video of Neda's last moments. However, it is interesting to note that SVT showed it without any attempt to explain or provide context to the disturbing footage, other than a brief, unaffected annotation (voice-over): 'This young woman Neda has for many Iranians become the symbol of the brutality of the regime. She was shot to death by the dreaded Basij militia this Saturday.' While CNN guided the viewer through the video simultaneously playing up its sensational content, SVT took a detached stance to the shock value of the footage, framing the imagery in a more matter-of-fact manner.

In both the BBC's and YLE's reporting the shock value of the video is diminished even further: the BBC showed only still images taken from the Neda video, and YLE showed the first few seconds of the video playing on a small YouTube window. In the BBC bulletin aired on 21 June the anchor builds up the drama stating that 'more dramatic footage of the violence of recent days has emerged' and the on-location report from Jeremy Bowen displays two still images taken from the video, the first one a long-shot from the beginning of the video in which Neda is about to collapse to the pavement with a large bloodstain at her feet and the second one a blurry close-up of her face from the end of the video before blood streams out of her nose and mouth. While the images are being showed, Bowen's voice-over puts them in perspective: 'These were the last moments of one young woman's life. Her name was Neda Aghan Soltan and her death on Saturday flashed around the world on the Internet has made her into an icon for some of the demonstrators.' The images of Neda dying are then contrasted with two beautiful portraits of Neda that highlight the tragedy and build the human-interest angle, which is further developed via phone interview with the victim's fiancé describing what had happened to her. In its visual decisions regarding this much publicized video, BBC seemed to follow accurately the broadcaster's ethical guidelines which state that the reality of tragedy can be achieved without showing blood through good scripting and the use of still images which are not believed to shock to the same degree as video (Taylor 1998: 75).

YLE clearly took a more 'rational' approach refraining from using the video of the dying woman to create a human-interest angle to the story. However, when it comes to showing this video and other graphic amateur imagery, YLE adopted the questionable double strategy of not 'publishing' the original video by visually referencing a YouTube posting of the video. Like SVT, YLE reported on the case of Neda only when the video had already gained significant international attention. The first time it appeared was on 23 June when Neda's story was specifically linked to US President Barack Obama's reaction to the violence in Iran and in particular to her killing. After Obama's speech, the voice-over states that the 'female student's death was captured in cell phone videos and spread over the Internet' while a YouTube page on a computer screen with search results of the Neda video is displayed and subsequently the first few seconds of the video running in a small YouTube window. In the following bulletins, images of Neda appear in the reporting on demonstrations in Helsinki on 23 and 24 June where Iranian residents in Finland carry still images taken from the Neda video. While YLE obviously had no control over the visuals the protestors were carrying, it was a deliberate choice to zoom in on a poster with a close-up image of Neda's bloody face. This strategy of 'showing what other media are showing' allowed YLE to highlight its journalistic restraint and ethical sensibility while still showing the shocking images. As Kunelius and Eide (2007: 13) have argued, this kind of 'photographic citation' can be seen as a 'strategic ritual' that is used to fend off criticism and circumvent responsibility (cf. Tuchman 1978).

Conclusion

We have explored how major national and international news organizations address the specific challenges that citizen imagery raises for professional journalism. Our study shows that while these images play an essential role in today's breaking news story, there is a variety of editorial strategies and ethical standards to accommodate non-professional eyewitness images. It also shows that these differences cannot be explained simply by assumed differences between public service broadcasters and commercial broadcasters.

As we have shown, the two Nordic public service broadcasters, SVT and YLE, both used amateur imagery to reinforce a verbal discourse, and refrained from explicitly addressing the possible inaccuracy and partiality that characterize this type of citizen-shot footage. Moreover, the both omitted any backstory *regarding* the acquisition of the amateur footage. The basic explanation for this is that in the absence of direct sources (all amateur material coming from international news agencies), the responsibility of the sources was seen to lie with the supplier – the news agencies. This traditional way of making news – what Jay Rosen (2005) calls 'trust me journalism' – requires the public to trust the news institution because of what it is and does not include any pursuit for transparency. SVT, however, did enlist a more significant measure of transparency than YLE by singling out the amateur-shot footage as such in the verbal narrative. As a global news organization BBC had direct access to amateur footage through BBC Persian TV, and unlike its Nordic counterparts, it made more of an effort to build a relationship with the images by contextualizing them – educating audiences about what they are seeing and what it means – and also communicating uncertainties around authenticity. In this way, BBC can be seen to give their viewers the means to make their own judgement about the truth-value of the amateur imagery.

CNN put on an elaborate ritual of transparency, evidently placing heavy emphasis on communicating its editorial deliberations to the audience. The US-based global news channel manifestly set the amateur videos apart from professional material and took every opportunity to discuss openly the problems of verification and interpretation attached to this type of imagery. Furthermore, in establishing as one of its main narrative news frames the 'revolutionary' role of social media in mobilizing and publicizing the Iran anti-government protests, CNN continuously made the amateur videos the focus of the news, presenting them as giving us privileged access to reality *per se*. While the emerging ethical norm of transparency calls for journalists to disclose their methods of newsgathering, so that the accuracy of their work can be assessed, we should, however, not be naive about the power of transparency rituals *to improve* the ethical standards of journalism. CNN's ritual of transparency can also be seen as a way to abdicate the gatekeeping role. Some have cautioned that that transparency can also function as a method of circumventing responsibility: 'There is a point at which the pursuit of transparency veers into the absurd, and instead of clarifying the question of what journalists do and why, can only obfuscate' (Cunningham 2006: 9, cit. in Plaisance 2007: 193). By rhetorically distancing itself from the potential deception of the amateur imagery CNN could capitalize on the dramatic 'reality effect' of the subjective and at times shocking amateur videos.

CNN's dramatized performance of transparency also reveals how amateur images, regardless of their content (e.g. whether they reveal new information) can be rendered sensational through news narratives. The channel continuously explicated the scenes shown, a device that no doubt has an educational dimension to it. However, it was carried out in such a manner that it functioned more to dramatize than to contain the potential shock value of the imagery. CNN's framing of the video of the death of Neda is a case in point. The channel was careful to contextualize and narrate the violent content of the footage as it unfolds – but it did so in a strikingly melodramatic manner that played up the tragedy of the event. On the other hand, one could argue that SVT's choice to broadcast the graphic video of Neda's death without much of an attempt at providing interpretative guidance to it, forces the disturbing scenes on the viewers in a blunt and potentially agonizing manner. The strategy to let even the most graphic amateur images 'talk for themselves' is clearly a way for a news organization to distance itself from and downplay the shock value of the footage. It does, however, also read as an abdication from the fundamental task of explaining and providing context to visuals in the news, especially disturbing ones, to enable viewers to put into perspective potentially overpowering scenes of violence. Moreover, the second-hand representation of shocking images – as demonstrated by the coverage of Finnish public service broadcaster YLE – can be seen as a form of circumventing full responsibility for their broadcast. Clearly, it is also an indication of a difficult ethical dilemma a news organization has faced.

News competition primarily concerns immediacy, and in today's digital environment amateur contributions are certainly prized assets. CNN's strategic ritual of transparency can be interpreted as an answer to the increasing use of amateur sources, with potentially compromising effects to the traditional concepts of accuracy and responsibility. However, from an ethical viewpoint, this type of strategy of transparency does transfer the responsibility of assessing the truth-value of amateur images from the news organization to the audience. On the other hand, the lack of transperancy regarding the origin of news images is similarly problematic as it hides not only the potential problems of accuracy involved in amateur eyewitness footage but also its interested perspective. Traditionally, there has been a strong belief in the veracity of the news image; news images have been understood to offer a literal and neutral reflection of reality (e.g. Becker 2008: 122). The perspective provided by the amateur footage from the unfolding crisis in Iran is clearly that of involved, interested actors in – rather than detached observers of – the events. This is also to say that the amateur footage invites a shared stance or point-of-view with the anti-government protesters, who more often than not are the ones capturing the Iranian unrest on their mobile phones and personal cameras. Being banned from on-the-ground reporting, professional news organizations subcontracted the key role of eyewitnessing to the Iranian protesters themselves. In the field of media witnessing the mediator is in a dominant position as it determines who or what we see and hear in the media or, in other words, who is a 'trustworthy' witness (Ashuri and Pinchevski 2009). Amateur images potentially offer invaluable knowledge of the event and they can have the potential to focus public debate (e.g. Perlmutter 1998), but their 'amateurishness' or 'rawness' does not gurantee an undistorted view of reality. The significance and truth-value of amateur images become understandable only when they are critically interpreted in their historical and social context, and this should be the responsibility of journalists.

References

Allan, S. (2006), *Online News: Journalism and the Internet*, Maidenhead and New York: Open University Press.

Allan, S. and Thorsen, E. (2009), *Citizen Journalism: Global Perspectives*, New York: Peter Lang.

Allen, D. (2008), 'The Trouble with Transparency:The Challenge of Doing Journalism Ethics in a Surveillance Society', *Journalism Studies*, 9: 3, pp. 323–40.

Ashuri, T. and Pinchevski, A. (2009), 'Witnessing as a Field', in P. Frosh and A. Pinchevski (eds), *Media Witnessing: Testimony in the Age of Mass Communication*, London: Palgrave Macmillan, pp. 133-57

BBC (2009), 'Young Iranians Use Video to Tell Story', BBC 16 June 2009, http://news.bbc.co.uk/2/hi/middle_east/8102676.stm. Accessed 4 August 2010.

Becker, K (2008), 'The Power of Pictures in Journalistic Discourse: As News, as Commentary, as Art', in E. Eide, R. Kunelius and A. Phillips (eds), *Transnational Media Events: The Mohammed Cartoons and the Imagined Clash of Civilizations*, Göteborg: Nordicom, pp. 117-32

Bridge, J. and Sjøvaag, H. (2009), 'Amateur Images in the Professional News Stream', in ICA, *Keywords in Communication, 59th Annual Conference of the International Communication Association*, Chicago, United States, 20–25 May.

Craft, S. and Heim, K. (2009), 'Transparency in Journalism: Meanings, Merits, and Risks', in L. Wilkins and C. Christians (eds), *The Handbook of Mass Media Ethics*, New York: Routledge, pp. 217-28

Karlsson, M. (2010), 'Rituals of Transparency: Evaluating Online News Outlets' Uses of Transparency Rituals in the United States, United Kingdom and Sweden', *Journalism Studies*, 11: 4, pp. 535–45.

Kovach, B. and Rosenstiel, T. (2001), *The Elements of Journalism: What Newspeople Should Know and The Public Should Expect*, New York: Crown Publishers.

Kunelius, R. (2009), 'Lessons of Being Drawn In: On Global Free Speech, Communication Theory and the Mohammed Cartoons', in A. Kierulf and H. Rønning (eds), *Freedom of Speech Abridged? Cultural, Legal and Philosophical Challenges*, Göteborg: Nordicom, pp. 139-51

Kunelius, R. and Eide, E. (2007), 'The Mohammed Cartoons, Journalism, Free Speech and Globalization', in R. Kunelius, E. Eide, O. Hahn, and R. Schroeder (eds), *Reading the Mohammed Cartoons Controversy: An International Analysis of Press Discourses on Free Speech and Political Spin*, Bochum: Projektverlag, pp. 9–24.

Newman, N. (2009), *The Rise of Social Media and Its Impact on Mainstream Journalism*, Reuters Institute for the Study of Journalism, University of Oxford.

Pantti, M. and Bakker, P. (2009), 'Misfortunes, Sunsets and Memories: Non-Professional Images in Dutch News Media', *International Journal of Cultural Studies*, 12: 5, pp. 471–89.

Perlmutter, D. (1998), *Photojournalism and Foreign Policy: Icons of Outrage in International Crisis*, London: Praeger.

Perlmutter, D. and Hatley Major, L. (2004), 'Images of Horror from Fallujah: "The Transparency of Angst and Indecision about the Fallujah Images Have Been Good for Journalism"', *Nieman Reports*, 22 June 2004.

Peters, J. (2001), 'Witnessing', *Media, Culture & Society*, 23: 6, pp. 707–23.

Phillips, A. (2010), 'Transparency and the New Ethics of Journalism', *Journalism Practice*, 3: 4, pp. 373–82.

Plaisance, P. (2007), 'Transparency: An Assessment of the Kantian Roots of a Key Element in Media Ethics Practice', *Journal of Mass Media Ethics*, 22: 2, pp. 187–207.

Rosen, J. (2005), 'After Trust Me Journalism Comes Openness: Rather Report Released', *Pressthink* 10 January 2005, http://journalism.nyu.edu/pubzone/weblogs/pressthink/2005/01/10/cbs_rept05.html. Accessed 15 September 2010.

Schudson. M. (2001), 'The Objectivity Norm in American Journalism', *Journalism*, 2: 2, pp. 149–70.

Singer, J. (2008), 'The Journalist in the Network: A Shifting Rationale for the Gatekeeping Role and the Objectivity Norm', *Trípodos*, 23, pp. 61–76.

Stelter, B. (2009), 'Journalism Rules Are Bent in News Coverage from Iran', *New York Times*, 29 June 2009, http://www.nytimes.com/2009/06/29/business/media/29coverage.html?pagewanted=1&_r=1&fta=y. Accessed 13 July 2010.

Stöcker, C., Neumann, C. and Dörting, T. (2009), 'Iran's Twitter Revolution: Ahmadinejad's Fear of the Internet', *Spiegel Online International*, 18 June 2009, http://www.spiegel.de/international/world/0,1518,631170,00.html. Accessed 20 June 2010.

Taylor, J. (1998), *Body Horror: Photojournalism, Catastrophe and War*, Manchester: Manchester University Press.

Tuchman, G. (1978), *Making News*, New York: Free Press.

Williams, A., Wardle, C. and Wahl-Jorgensen, K. (2010), 'Have They Got News for Us? Audience Revolution or Business as Usual at the BBC?', *Journalism Practice*, iFirst: http://www.informaworld.com/smpp/content~content=a921303452~db=all~jumptype=rss. Accessed 30 June 2010.

Witschge, T. and Nygren, G. (2009), 'Journalism: A Profession Under Pressure?', *Journal of Media Business Studies*, 6: 1, pp. 37–59.

Zelizer, B. (2007), 'On "Having Been There": "Eyewitnessing" As a Journalistic Key Word', *Critical Studies in Media Communication*, 24: 5, pp. 408–28.

Chapter 6

Pans and Zooms: The Quality of Amateur Video Covering a Breaking News Story

Ray Niekamp

In the early morning hours of Saturday, 13 September 2008, Hurricane Ike slammed into the US coastline near Galveston, Texas. Ike churned north through Houston, and remained a strong storm as it moved up the Ohio River valley towards Canada and finally out into the Atlantic Ocean. Hitting a major metropolitan area as it did, the storm caused a lot of damage. It also brought out scores of amateur videographers and their camcorders. For the amateurs, Ike provided a 'cannot miss' opportunity to chronicle a major event. Many of them posted their video to YouTube, CNN's iReport or the websites of local television stations.

Much has been written about 'citizen journalism,' and the new perspective offered by non-journalists on issues of public importance. A breaking story is something different, however. The pictures become the most important contribution from citizens because they are able to be places and get scenes professional news organizations cannot. This chapter examines amateur videos of the Hurricane Ike story and the different standards applied to video shot by non-professionals compared to professional shooting and editing standards. Specifically, it will examine the aesthetic quality of amateur video in terms of its photography and editing. It will also look at the reporting submitted along with the video. The study asks two questions. First, how do amateur video standards for reporting compare to the standards of the professional world? In addition, the editorial judgements of mainstream media regarding the acceptability of amateur video will get some attention. The second question is as follows: How do news outlets decide whether to use video submitted by amateurs, especially if that video does not conform to the quality standards applied to professionally shot and edited video?

Mainstream news organizations have set up online sites that solicit video contributed from citizens. One of the most notable of these sites is iReport, a feature of Cable News Network (CNN). iReport accepts video and still photos without editing, screening or fact-checking them before they are put up on the site. However, CNN will vet iReport stories and will use some of them on their cable TV newscasts. At the time of Hurricane Ike, those stories were marked with an 'On CNN' stamp on the iReport web site (at present, the stamp reads 'CNN iReport'). Videos of Hurricane Ike started appearing on iReport even before the storm hit in the Caribbean Sea, as residents of islands in the path of the storm readied for its impact. Over the almost three-week period that the storm affected the Caribbean, the United States and Canada, more than 200 videos were posted on iReport.

The aesthetic and journalistic quality of amateur video submitted to iReport varied widely. Some were shot and edited to almost professional standards, with steady camera shots, matching action edits and clear sound. Occasionally, the contributor even supplied narration and interviews with the video. Most videos, though, had a 'home movie' feel, with constant back-and-forth pans and zooms and shaky shots. Still, many of these videos were used on mainstream television news programmes.

Making Judgements about Video Quality

Gatekeeping theory is an appropriate basis for researching citizen journalism because even though laypersons contribute videos and information, someone at the television station or network must decide what will be used on the air, and how it will be used. The sociologist Kurt Lewin (1947) introduced the term 'gatekeeping' but David Manning White (1950) first applied it to journalism. White's 'Mr. Gates' was a newspaper wire editor, who combed through 12,000 inches of copy per week, but chose only a tenth of it for publication. His reasons for not using material often related to a lack of space in the newspaper, but he also judged stories based on 'clarity, conciseness and angle' (White 1950: 390). White concluded that the gatekeeper's job was highly subjective and relied on value judgements that came from his own experiences. Gieber (1964) showed that a wire editor's job might not be as subjective as White presented it, since all wire editors made similar decisions based on a narrow range of choices. In doing so, they adhere to a set of professional values that guide them in their story selection.

Gieber and several other scholars (e.g. Epstein 1973; Tuchman 1978; Gans 1980; Berkowitz 1990; Shoemaker and Reese 1996) also indicated that gatekeeping is not the function of a single decision maker, but rather is a group process. Berkowitz (1990) found that the gatekeepers might change from day to day – for example, a key member of the team might be absent on a particular day – and decisions on story selection might change because of changing circumstances, such as a 'slow' news day compared to a busy one, or the need to respond to breaking news and drop stories that had been selected earlier in the day. One method of determining which stories are selected for use and which are discarded is for an organization to fall back on its routines, a pre-established and generalized set of practices about how the work is to be done, including its 'news values' (Berkowitz 1990; Shoemaker and Reese 1996). The television station Berkowitz used in his study, for example, tended to cover stories about government and politics, accidents and disasters and crime more than other types of stories. Newscast producers also favoured stories with visual impact. According to one producer: '[T]he more visual a story, the less important it needs to be to get on the air; the less visual, the more important it has to be' (cit. in Berkowitz 1990: 65). Organizational routines would also require a degree of transparency in the newsgathering process, such as the name of the reporter and attribution of sources (Kovach and Rosenstiel 2001), and these routines would also determine whether material from other media is used, such as material submitted by amateurs.

One factor that must be considered in gatekeeping and new media is whether the theory even applies any longer. The Internet has made massive amounts of information available online, with no one to tend it (Williams and Delli Carpini 2000). The traditional approach of 'we write, you read' journalism is undermined by the arrival of user-generated content (UGC) (Deuze 2003). Instead of filtering information before it gets to the public, the emphasis in citizen journalism is on publishing (Bowman and Willis 2003). Citizen contributors can post directly to online sites without having their video reviewed for quality by someone with editorial authority. Journalists, however, still value the role of the gatekeeper. Their notion of gatekeeping has expanded from news judgement calls, to inclusion of quality control and increasing the value of the product so it becomes easier to find in the flood of information currently available (Singer 1997). Journalists in general find little value in material contributed by amateurs. A recent study by Jane Singer found that one statement with which journalists were most in agreement was 'The quality of user-generated content is generally lower than the quality of what our journalists provide' (2010: 133).

Quality can be considered from two viewpoints: *content quality* and *aesthetic quality*. Most gatekeeping studies regard quality as dealing with content (e.g. Carroll 1985; Gladney 1990; Zelizer 1993; Shoemaker and Reese 1996; Gladney, Shapiro and Castaldo 2007; Belt and Just 2008) and the mix between stories about politics, government and issues of public importance. These studies generally regard traditional news values – what Belt and Just (2008: 196) describe as 'hard news', or issues of public policy – as indicative of quality, while 'soft news' – crime, lifestyle and entertainment stories – reflects a lack of quality. Gladney (1990) found that the top standards for quality were strong local news coverage, accuracy, good writing, visual appeal, community focus, news interpretation, lack of sensationalism and comprehensive coverage. In recent years, the amount of monetary investment television stations put into news coverage has come to be regarded as an indicator of quality (Scott, Gobetz and Chanslor 2008), with the Pew Center for Excellence in Journalism (PEJ) devoting much of its annual reports on the state of journalism to the dwindling revenues and news budgets faced by both network and local television, and their ability to cover news with fewer resources.

Aesthetic Quality

Gatekeeping studies generally do not consider the production quality of the story elements. Studies have been conducted on professional journalism enterprises, whether print or broadcast, which are expected to adhere to professional standards. For example, local television newscasts are judged to be of lower quality when technical mistakes are made during newscasts (Roberts and Dickson 1984). Those standards may be changing. Capps (2009) suggests that a new standard for quality is simply 'good enough'. The 'good enough' revolution values immediacy and output over the standards that had been in place over time.

Bare bones functionality and a cheap price are the drivers of this revolution, and quality is relegated to a minor consideration:

> We get our breaking news from blogs, we make spotty long-distance calls on Skype, we watch video on small computer screens rather than TVs, and more and more of us are carrying around dinky, low-power netbook computers that are just good enough to meet our surfing and emailing needs.
>
> (Capps 2009)

This 'good enough' world represents a paradigm shift in the production of images, according to Karen Ritzenhoff: 'Instead of celebrating perfection, as a society we are celebrating amateurishness and imperfection' (2008: 139). Other observers also have reservations about lower quality. The *New York Daily News* TV critic Richard Huff (2010) complains that new technologies such as Skype and cell phone video are not the cutting-edge breakthroughs they have been presented as, but rather, are lowering the quality of TV news. 'What's the sense of having high definition television if the stations are presenting low definition newscasts?' he asks.

However, this lack of aesthetic quality is often viewed as adding 'authenticity' to the video (Pantti and Bakker 2009; Pauwels and Hellriegel 2009), a home-made feel that provides a sense of immediacy and heightened emotional impact missing from professional video. 'In terms of aesthetics, all amateur images are praised as being more "authentic" than professional photography and, thus, they are believed to offer special value to the audience' (Pantti and Bakker 2009: 486).

That authentic quality can come into conflict with professional video standards. Professionals are in agreement on basic rules of shooting video in the field. First and foremost, a tripod must be used for steady camera shots. Indiscriminate shooting must be avoided, as well as panning and zooming. Each shot must be held long enough for editing; ten seconds per shot is the general advice (Shook 2005; Compesi 2003; Medoff and Tanquary 1998). CNN's iReport suggests most of these rules on its site. A section of the site is reserved for the 'iReport Toolkit,' which tells users that to tell a story 'like a pro,' the videographer should, for example, avoid pans and zooms and hold shots steady (iReport 2008a). Despite such guidance, amateur video is easily distinguished from that shot by professionals:

> Out of focus is a common problem in amateur video, as is poor lighting. For video shot by a hand-held camcorder, shaky camera motion can be observed. The video content may shake, which is caused by the instability of hands.
>
> (Wu et al. 2009)

Mainstream news outlets regard aesthetic video quality as an important consideration, and are often reluctant to lower their standards except when the news value of the video outweighs the quality issue: 'Professional photojournalists will often do a better job recording a news event than citizens because they are trained and better equipped' (Lyon and Ferrara 2005: 17). Many have used poor quality video from citizen journalists in the past, but usually when there is no professionally produced video available. During the terrorist bombings in London in 2005, dim, grainy, shaky video submitted by eyewitnesses was judged more compelling because they showed what was happening as it was happening (Allan 2007).

For this study, a content analysis was done of videos related to Hurricane Ike appearing on iReport.com between 31 August 2008 (the first day a report appeared on the site) and 18 September 2008, when hurricane reports drastically fell off. Videos were searched by accessing the iReport site and selecting the word 'Ike' from a list of tags describing the videos posted on the site. The purpose of the content analysis was to determine what kinds of video stories were submitted to iReport, and what kinds of stories were most likely to be used on CNN's regular newscasts. In all, 120 different video clips were examined.

Videos were coded for length; story type, either silent or natural sound video without narration, or an edited package, a self-contained story with narration and/or interviews; whether the video was edited before being uploaded to the site; whether information about the story was supplied with the video; whether the information was gathered by the contributor; whether the information was attributed to a source; and whether the video was aired as part of a newscast. In the case of iReport, an 'On CNN' stamp indicated it was. To learn why and how amateur video is used on CNN's newscasts, an interview was conducted with Lila King, the director of participation for iReport. King heads a team of journalists who draw on their experiences to make determinations about video submissions. In addition, news executives from small, medium, and large market US television stations answered the same questions asked in the King interview, to learn whether the standards for use of amateur video on commercial broadcast stations are similar to those used by CNN.

Amateur Video Submitted During Hurricane Ike

The majority of videos on iReport were not edited. A very liberal view of editing was adopted for this study – if a video had even one edit, it was counted as an edited video. It did not have to be a polished, finished piece. An estimated 18% of the iReport pieces were edited. All of the unedited videos were a single, continuous shot. In some cases, the camera was mounted on a tripod and left running. In most cases, the camera was hand held, and the videographer panned across the field of view, seemingly without purpose. The result was an unsteady camera shot that did not draw the viewer's eyes to a particular focus of attention. Many citizen contributors had some good material to work with, such as wind blowing signs or storm debris, downed power lines and emergency vehicles, but the videographers did not concentrate on those elements and instead panned away to something else.

Another characteristic of amateur video is the lack of information that accompanies the pictures. Each iReport video is embedded on a page that includes a box with information about the contributor (usually a user name), the date the video was shot, the date uploaded and perhaps a short description of the video. If the contributor supplied information about the event beyond those basic entries, it was counted as 'information'. Sometimes, that information was lifted from other news sources. For example, the contributor might include an unspecific attribution in the information box, such as 'the radio says'. In a few instances, the contributor narrated over the video, and referred to reports seen on television. In most cases, however, the information box lacked even a brief description of the scene. If contributors included information found on their own, it was coded as 'original' information. Original information by this criterion could include a first-person account or information from a source contacted by the contributor, including interviews with witnesses to the storm. Of the 120 videos, 21 included original information. Fewer than half the stories – 43% – included any information beyond what the viewer could see in the video.

Whether the amateur videographer includes original reporting along with the video may not matter, in any case. Information is one area where journalists still cling to the gatekeeper function. Clearly, they are distrustful of non-journalists' ability to deliver factual reporting. In the words of a former executive producer from a large US television market: 'I would not use amateur reporting unless it was something related to something easier – like whether the tornado really did sound like a freight train' (2010). A medium market executive producer expressed a similar point of view: 'Honestly, it's doubtful that we would use their on-camera reporting in the sense of a standup or a live-look' (Kearney 2010). But she added that if information provided by an amateur can be verified, it would be considered for use on the air if it added something their own reporting did not already have. A small-market news director said some situations would lend themselves to the use of information supplied by non-journalists:

> Is it a first hand or eyewitness account of something that happened? We often interview people at the scene of a story who were there when we weren't. What's the difference if they interview themselves or describe what happened, and send it to us? Video most often speaks for itself. However, information or dialogue supplied by random citizen/ reporter/videographer would need some level of confirmation.
>
> (Baxter 2010)

CNN does try to confirm information supplied by iReporters, by interviewing them to find the story behind their video. That information is compared to what CNN already knows about the story: 'We consult internal experts, local news organizations and others as needed to confirm details just as we would for a story from any other source' (King 2010).

Most citizen-generated videos did not attempt to mimic journalistic style. The ones that did stood out because of their relative rarity. One iReport contributor, Charles Vienn, who used the moniker 'uplift', filed ten pieces done in the style of a television news live shot, with an ad lib, on-camera introduction, an interview with someone close at hand and an on-camera close. When he did edit his reports, the edits were minimal, and often involved just the addition of text information from a character generator. He also signed off with his real

Figure 6.1: An iReporter who calls himself 'uplift' (right) interviews a friend as a storm approaches. Permission to reproduce granted by CNN.

name. Five of his ten stories carried the 'On CNN' stamp, but it is not clear whether those reports were used in their entirety. In the report, he interviews a man whom he identifies as his friend, 'Steve'. The report was filed from Houston before Ike hit, and 'uplift' asks 'Steve' about safety. 'Steve' urges people to get to a 'well-secured area', and to have 'your water, your food, and a little entertainment' handy: 'Make it a mini-vacation', he suggests. Vienn wraps up the report by addressing the camera: 'Check this out, man – I'm your host, Charles Vienn, an' we reportin' an' gettin' the story from the street, y'all! This is Charles Vienn, puttin' it out there, God bless you all, and y'all stay safe' (iReport 2008b).

An early piece from Grand Turk Island north of Cuba featured a man behind the wheel of his car, driving through neighborhoods preparing for the storm and narrating on camera what he saw. He also used his real name. The citizen journalism story that looked most like a professionally done news package was a piece from San Antonio, Texas, on Ike evacuees. It was a fully edited news package, with a reporter standup, B-roll of an evacuation centre and even an on-camera interview with the mayor of San Antonio. IReport encourages contributors to provide stand-ups and narration with their stories, and if several are submitted for the same event, they are often edited together into a video package: 'The combination of a personal take, footage and the story behind it makes these sorts of iReports among the most powerful kinds of content we can receive' (King 2010).

The amateur quality of the videos was emphasized by the lack of adherence to professional journalists' standards of transparency. IReport allows contributors to use their user names, rather than their real names, when uploading video. In 24 of the 120 iReport videos, the citizen journalist supplied his or her real name, either in an on-camera standup, or as part of information posted online. Otherwise, the viewer was given only a user name such as 'lilcoco77070' or 'IkeTracker'. Most of the videos that provided additional information let the viewer know who supplied the information. Five of the videos named independent sources. When vetting iReport video for possible use on CNN, the iReport staff requires the contributor to supply his or her real name, although iReport might not share the name (King 2010).

Overall, the aesthetic quality of video reports submitted to iReport did not fare well when judged by contemporary television news production standards. The author and a graduate student assistant – who both previously worked in television news – assigned a rating to each story: excellent, good, mediocre or unacceptable. These ratings are subjective, but are based on their experiences with current practices in commercial television news in the United States. Stories graded 'excellent' featured well-composed and steady pictures and provided original information. 'Good' videos lacked original information, but the video's aesthetic quality was acceptable. Both excellent and good videos would likely be used in newscasts at a small market station. 'Mediocre' video included minimal information, was shot with a hand-held camera, and may or may not have been edited. 'Unacceptable' video was very shaky, included no information beyond the contributor's user name and consisted of one continuous unedited shot with pointless panning and zooming.

About half the pieces on iReport were considered to be unacceptable, when judged according to professional television news standards. Among the 120 iReport pieces, nine, or 7.5%, were rated 'good' or 'excellent'. A 'mediocre' rating went to 52 videos, and 'unacceptable' to 59 videos. The average rating fell between unacceptable and mediocre. Unacceptable video by these standards would include the case of a woman who walked across her street with the camera rolling, shooting downed trees and power lines and some damage to neighbouring houses. But she moved the camera constantly, so the viewer could not take in the extent of the damage. A similar video from a different city showed a parked car with a tree trunk through its windshield, as though it had been hurled there like a javelin. But instead of holding the shot so the viewer could appreciate the seriousness of the damage, the camera jerked away immediately to broken tree branches littering a nearby lawn. Other videographers shot from their front doors during the height of the storm, to show high winds and lashing rain, but because the cameras were hand held, the video was shaky and did not concentrate on a point of interest.

One might be inclined to assume that the iReports pass some kind of quality test to make air. CNN did broadcast both stories rated 'excellent' in this study. However, almost 60% of the pieces reviewed for this study carried the 'On CNN' stamp. Almost half of the stories rated as 'unacceptable' – 29 – were used on the air. Two stories rated as 'good' were not used on CNN. Editing improved the chances of a video being used on CNN, but was no guarantee. As many as 15 edited pieces carried the 'On CNN' stamp, amounting to 21% of the videos used. Six edited videos, or 8.5% of the total, did not make it to a CNN newscast. King (2010) said CNN typically vets between 5 and 10% of the videos submitted to iReport for possible inclusion on air:

> Simply put, we treat iReport footage like any other CNN footage, in the sense that we look at it, find the best part or the part applicable to the current situation, and we use that. We generally can't use the whole thing on air, but we can use parts.
>
> (King 2010)

Use of Amateur Video in Newscasts

If the amateur video on a visually arresting subject like a hurricane is so poor, compared with quality standards for professional news video, why is it used on the air? Observers of the television news industry long ago recognized that the business is hungry for gripping images to broadcast. The use of amateur video has been around for years, the most notable being the Abraham Zapruder film of the assassination of President John F. Kennedy in 1963. David Johnston, director of technology for ABC affiliate WFAA-TV in Dallas-Forth Worth, said, 'It's like having extra camera crews. Viewer-shot video is definitely important, because the more sources you can get news content from, the better' (Careless 2008).

CNN has had a mechanism in place for soliciting and using amateur video since at least 1990, but it was often relegated to spot news coverage, such as sports, weather, and natural disasters (Ouellette 1995). Then, as now, amateur coverage was considered 'accidental', shot by people who happened to be in the right place at the right time. It was clear what TV stations wanted: '[…] anything that has smoke and fire coming out of buildings, or people hanging from the sides. They want the major trauma, that's what brings in the ratings' (Ouellette 1995). CNN continues to value such spot news coverage, and gets more video of weather events than traditional hard news: 'Some topics are just more iReporty [sic] than others' (King 2010).

The aesthetic quality issue is getting more attention now because of the proliferation of small video recording devices, such as the Flip camera, that are easily affordable and easily operated (Capps 2009). Brian Kennedy, director of digital newsgathering at CBS News, said, '[U]sing their cell phones and camcorders, people are providing us with a wider range of breaking news video than we could ever generate ourselves. And they are there when it happens, which we can't always be' (Careless 2008). Although the newer generation of these miniature devices can capture sharp, clear video, television news executives are willing, even happy, to use grainy, shaky video:

> There was a time when amateur video was frowned upon, because of its poor quality. Those days are long gone. Now that home video cameras are so prevalent, and news operations are slimmer, newsrooms rely on amateur video more and more, not just for tornadoes, but also for whatever spot news may occur. We used to warn people *not* [his emphasis] to take pictures of tornadoes and get to safety instead. TV meteorologists don't even bother warning people to do that any more.
>
> (Hartley 2010)

Even so, it must fulfil some needs. Primarily, amateur video is used when the television station or network does not have something equivalent. Lee Giles, the former news director at WISH-TV in Indianapolis, stated: 'When we don't have our own video, we look hard for an amateur who may have shot something' (Prato 1991). A good example is found in an iReport video shot by a person with the user name 'katelott'. Her family had a beach house on the Bolivar Peninsula east of Galveston. When they went to check on the condition of her house after the hurricane moved through, they saw a Texas Game Warden rescuing a three-meter long alligator that had been washed up on the beach by the storm. She shot some still pictures, and an 11-second video that she uploaded to iReport. The video is unedited and shaky, but CNN used it. Katelott furnished the following information to iReport concerning the incident:

> A Texas Game Warden had the situation under control. He immediately called for help to rescue the lost alligator who was tossed into the Gulf during Hurricane Ike. Within minutes, four more game wardens arrived. They rescued the gator and later released him back to his natural habitat. The alligator would have died without food or water. Good job Texas Game Wardens.
>
> (iReport 2008c)

iReport tries to provide some kind of context to the rough videos it uses early in a spot news event. As Lila King, the director of participation for CNN's iReport, explains: '[E]arly on in a breaking news story, often there isn't much imagery available. We may have to rely on that first shaky image that comes in, and we have to give it context. Helping our audience to see and understand what's happening is the most important thing we can do (King 2010).

The authentic characteristic of amateur video is one of the features that make it desirable to use on the air. While some professionals dismiss the notion of authenticity – 'I don't believe it's any more authentic than video shot by a professional' (Baxter 2010) – the 'eyewitness' flavour of poorly shot video offers an attraction for news outlets that adds to the impression of being on the scene of a breaking story. IReport encourages contributors to voice their own narration while shooting video of an event: 'Anything that gives a personal

Figure 6.2: In this iReport Texas game wardens capture an alligator that was washed ashore in Galveston by the hurricane Ike. Permission to reproduce granted by CNN.

perspective on a snowstorm or other news event is valuable. It makes the footage much more meaningful and gives it a unique quality that you just don't get from a traditional news package many times' (King 2010).

Conclusion

This study demonstrates that amateur videographers are responding to breaking news in their hometowns and are contributing their content to online video sites. But it also shows that the aesthetic quality of citizen video is far below the standards viewers are used to from the mainstream media. Professional news organizations do not expect amateurs to have the skills necessary to produce work that meets professional expectations. Hetrick (2006) notes that people not socialized in television news values do not emulate television news style. That is not necessarily bad, just a different way of doing things. She points out that television is hardly the only field where professionals and amateurs have different standards for what is acceptable.

The miniaturization, ease of use and wide availability of video cameras can be expected to contribute to an increase in the amount of amateur video both online and on the air. Mainstream media organizations such as the BBC in the United Kingdom and PBS in the United States are trying to come to terms with the apparent shift in standards for acceptable video, and not only from amateurs, but from their own employees. A BBC producer and reporter recently shot news packages leading up to the UK general election, using small flip-style cameras. On a BBC blog, a producer asked the question: 'How perfect do we need to be?' (Sharma 2010). On the PBS MediaShift website, Legrand (2009) characterized the choice between 'rough' or 'slick' video as the 'big' video debate: 'Do we always need slick, television-style video, which require more specialized skills, or will our community accept "rougher" video, made by amateurs using less sophisticated cameras?' He concluded that non-professionals are enthusiastic about the simple consumer-grade cameras, but professionals were not, and the audience was more interested in the content than in the aesthetic quality of the video. The potential for individuals to carry small cameras with them even more commonly than is done now will lead to more amateur video being contributed to mainstream media outlets, and to more of it being used in newscasts. Since professional journalists see more value in spot news shot by amateurs, compared to amateur coverage of public policy issues, it is likely they will continue to feature fires, disasters both man-made and natural and mayhem that amateurs encounter before the professionals do.

Although amateurs are quick to upload their video to online sites like iReport, they are not so quick to provide information to go along with the video. Schaffer (2007) has noted that amateurs avoid the heavy lifting of reporting. They generally do not produce stories with leads, middles and ends, and do not call people for interviews. Schaffer concludes: 'Amateurs do not do the hard work of journalism. They do not like to do interviews'. If amateur videographers do not want to be journalists, what are they contributing to online video sites? With minimal reporting or even information, the focus is on the video. The picture becomes the important feature of user-generated video. Bentley (2008) suggests that citizen journalists do not report stories so much as they 'share' them. The video reviewed for this study featured pictures that did not originate with mainstream media. By uploading the video to iReport, amateur videographers shared their eyewitness experiences.

Video might be the best way for amateurs to participate in media at the same level as the professionals. Submitting video to news organizations, such as CNN, amounts to a win-win – the professionals get video they would not otherwise be able to get on their own, and at the same time amateurs can participate in the newsgathering process (Reich 2008). Furthermore, video submitted by amateurs bolsters the veracity of information presented by the professionals, by adding visual backing to that information (Pantti and Bakker 2009). Under this scenario, gatekeeping by professional news organizations becomes less of a burden. Some observers contend that moderation of amateur video is necessary to maintain journalistic standards (Paulussen and Ugille 2008). But it could be argued as well that concentrating on the video lessens the risk of using amateur material and provides viewers with a different angle than the professional news organization can provide on its own. Amateur video, regardless of its deficiencies in artistic quality, will likely show up on mainstream news outlets more often, as the image becomes the overriding criterion of the gatekeeper.

This study is limited by its selection of videos. While every effort was made to access every video on Hurricane Ike uploaded to iReport, some pieces were inevitably excluded. The findings cannot be applied to citizen journalism sites in general, since each can be expected to have different policies for story acceptance and to draw from different pools of contributors. The small sample of television news executives commenting on the use of amateur video cannot be generalized to the television news industry as a whole. Future studies could examine the accuracy of amateur video reports and the motivations for uploading video to online sites. Future research could examine more systematically and in more detail the decision-making process involved in selecting amateur video for use in television news broadcasts. Focus could also be shifted to the audience, to determine whether the aesthetic quality of video makes a difference in their perceptions of a news organization's accuracy and credibility, and whether amateur video is a factor in deciding to watch a given station's news.

Citizen journalism represents a new option for the consumer to get information about breaking news events. Traditional standards professionals have applied to video are changing. Images that would not have been allowed on the air in the past are passing muster now because of their immediacy and authenticity. But the material supplied by amateurs in a breaking news event like Hurricane Ike is mostly video. The amateur videographer will not do the job of gathering and verifying information. That has traditionally been the work of the journalist, and therefore amateur videos like the ones contributed during Hurricane Ike are really examples of citizen *media* – not journalism.

References

Allan, S. (2007), 'Citizen Journalism and the Rise of "Mass Self Communication": Reporting the London Bombings', *Global Media Journal*, Australian edition, 1: 1, pp. 1–20.

Baxter, L. (2010), Interview, 6 August.

Belt, T. and Just, M. (2008), 'The Local News Story: Is Quality a Choice?', *Political Communication*, 25: 2, pp. 194–215.

Bentley, C. (2008), 'Citizen Journalism: Back to the Future?' *Discussion paper prepared for the Carnegie-Knight Conference on the Future of Journalism*, June, http://www.hks.harvard.edu/presspol/carnegie_knight/Conference%20June%202008/Bentley.%20Citizen%20Journalism.pdf. Accessed 14 November 2008.

Berkowitz, D. (1990), 'Refining the Gatekeeping Metaphor for Local Television News', *Journal of Broadcasting & Electronic Media*, 34: 1, pp. 55–68.

Bowman, S. and Willis, C. (2003), *We Media: How Audiences are Shaping the Future of News and Information*, Reston, VA: The Media Center at the American Press Institute, http://www.hypergene.net/wemedia. Accessed 14 November 2008.

Capps, R. (2009), 'The Good Enough Revolution: When Cheap and Simple Is Just Fine', *Wired Magazine* 17.09, http://www.wired.com/gadgets/miscellaneous/magazine/17-09/ff_goodenough. Accessed 2 November 2009.

Careless, J. (2008), 'Stations and Nets Crave Unexpected Video', *TV Technology*, 1 October, http://www.tvtechnology.com/article/67830. Accessed 2 October 2008.Carroll, R. (1985), 'Content Values in TV Newsrooms in Small and Large Markets', *Journalism Quarterly*, 62: 4, pp. 877-938.

Compesi, R. (2003), *Video Field Production and Editing*, sixth edition, Boston: Allyn & Bacon.

Deuze, M. (2003), 'The Web and Its Journalisms: Considering the Consequences of Different Types of News Media Online', *New Media & Society*, 5: 2, pp. 203–30.

Epstein, E. (1973), *News From Nowhere*, New York: Vintage Books.

Gans, H. (1980), *Deciding What's News*, New York: Pantheon Books.

Gieber, W. (1964), 'News is What Newspapermen Make It', in L. Dexter and D. M. White (eds), *People, Society, and Mass Communications*, New York: Free Press.

Gladney, G. (1990), 'Newspaper Excellence: How Editors of Small and Large Papers Judge Quality', *Newspaper Research Journal*, 11: 2, pp. 58-72.

Gladney, G., Shapiro, I. and Castaldo, J. (2007), 'Online Editors Rate News Quality Criteria', *Newspaper Research Journal, 28: 1, pp. 55-69.*

Hartley, L. (2010), Interview, 5 August.

Hetrick, J. (2006), 'Amateur Video Must Not Be Overlooked', *The Moving Image*, 6: 1, pp. 66–81.

Huff, R. (2010), 'Local Newscasts Have an Image Problem: Fuzzy Graphics Plague Outlets', *New York Daily News*, 30 April, http://www.nydailynews.com/entertainment/tv/2010/04/30/2010-04-30_local_newscasts_have_an_image_problem_fuzzy_graphics_plague_outlets.htm. Accessed 22 August 2010.

iReport (2008a), *Shoot Better Video. iReport Toolkit*. http://www.ireport.com/toolkit-video.jspa. Accessed 5 November 2008.

iReport (2008b), *Hurricane Ike Report 5*, http://ireport.cnn.com/docs/DOC-84593. Accessed 17 February 2011.

iReport (2008c), *Hurricane Ike and Alligators!* http://ireport.cnn.com/docs/DOC-95486. Accessed 17 February 2011.

Kearney, B. (2010), Interview, 6 August.

King, L. (2010), Interview, 13 September.

Kovach, B. and Rosenstiel, T. (2001), *The Elements of Journalism: What Newspeople Should Know and the Public Should Expect*, New York: Three Rivers Press.

Legrand, R. (2009), 'The Big Video Debate: Rough or Slick?' *PBS MediaShift*, 23 January, http://www.pbs.org/mediashift/2009/01/the-big-video-debate-rough-or-slick-023.html. Accessed 1 September 2010.

Lewin, K. (1947), 'Frontiers in Group Dynamics', *Human Relations*, 1: 2, p. 145.

Lyon, S. and Ferrara, L. (2005), 'With Citizens' Visual News Coverage Standards Don't Change', *Nieman Reports*, 59: 4, pp. 16–17.

Medoff, N. and Tanquary, T. (1998), *Portable Video: ENG and EFP*, third edition, Boston: Focal Press.

Ouellette, L. (1995), 'Camcorder Dos and Don'ts: Popular Discourses on Amateur Video and Participatory Television', *Velvet Light Trap*, 36, p. 44.

Pantti, M. and Bakker, P. (2009), 'Misfortunes, Memories and Sunsets: Non-Professional Images in Dutch News Media', *International Journal of Cultural Studies*, 12: 5, pp. 471–89.

Paulussen, S. and Ugille, P. (2008), 'User Generated Content in the Newsroom: Professional and Organizational Constraints on Participatory Journalism', *Westminster Papers in Communication and Culture*, 5: 2, pp. 24–41.

Pauwels, L. and Hellriegel, P. (2009), 'Strategic and Tactical Uses of Internet Design and Infrastructure: The Case of YouTube', *Journal of Visual Literacy* 28: 1, pp. 51–69.

Prato, L. (1991), 'Red Alert: Amateur Videos', *American Journalism Review*, November, http://www.ajr.org/article.asp?id=171. Accessed 12 August 2010.

Reich, Z. (2008), 'How Citizens Create News Stories: The "News Access" Problem Reversed', *Journalism Studies*, 9: 5, pp. 1–20.

Ritzenhoff, K. (2008), 'Visual Competence and Reading the Recorded Past: The Paradigm Shift from Analogue to Digital Video in Michael Haneke's Film Cache', *Visual Studies*, 23: 2, pp.136–46.

Roberts, C. and Dickson, S. (1984), 'Assessing Quality in Local TV News', *Journalism Quarterly*, 61: 2, pp. 392–98.

Schaffer, J. (2007), *Citizen Media: Fad or the Future of News?*, College Park, MD: J-Lab: The Institute for Interactive Journalism, http://www.kcnn.org/research/citizen_media_report. Accessed 8 October 2008.Scott, D., Gobetz, R. and Chanslor, M. (2008), 'Chain Versus Independent Television Station Ownership: Toward an Investment Model of Commitment to Local News Quality', *Communication Studies*, 59:1, pp. 84-98.

Sharma, R. (2010), 'Pocket-Size Video Journalism', *BBC College of Journalism*, http://www.bbc.co.uk/journalism/blog/2010/06/pocket-sized-video-journalism.shtml. Accessed 1 September 2010.

Shoemaker, P. and Reese, S. (1996), *Mediating the Message*, second edition, White Plains, NY: Longman.

Shook, F. (2005), *Television Field Production and Reporting*, Boston: Allyn & Bacon.

Singer, J. (2010), 'Quality Control', *Journalism Practice*, 4: 2, pp. 127–42.

Singer, J. (1997), 'Still Guarding the Gate? The Newspaper Journalist's Role in an On-line World', *Convergence*, 3: 1, pp. 72–89.

Tuchman, G. (1978), *Making News: A Study in the Construction of Reality*, New York: Free Press.

White, D. (1950), 'The Gatekeeper: A Case Study in the Selection of News', *Journalism Quarterly*, 27: 4, pp. 383–96.

Williams, B. and Delli Carpini, M. (2000), 'Unchained Reaction: The Collapse of Media Gatekeeping and the Clinton-Lewinsky Scandal', *Journalism*, 1: 1, pp. 61–85.

Wu, P., Taipanich, T., Purushotham, S. and Kuo, J. (2009), 'Separation of Professional and Amateur Video in Large Video Collections', in P. Muneesawang et al. (eds), *PCM 2009, LNCS 5879*, Berlin Heidelberg: Springer-Verlag, pp. 33–44.

Zelizer, B. (1993), 'Journalists as Interpretive Communities', *Critical Studies in Mass Communication*, 10: 2, pp. 219–37.

Chapter 7

'You Will Die Next': Killer Images and the Circulation of Moral Hierarchy

Johanna Sumiala

The historian of photography Allan Sekula (1986) claims that every society has its 'shadow archives' containing images of the heroes, leaders and moral exemplars of society as well as images of its poor, diseased, insane, criminal and somehow radically 'inferior' members (Lury 1998: 44). According to Sekula, every portrait has to take its place either implicitly or explicitly in this social and moral hierarchy of visual representation. In the late modern society of high media saturation the media consisting of different branches of old and new, mainstream and social media have taken the place of the cultural archive to a great extent (see also Seaton 2005).

Crime news offers a particular case for the analysis of the moral and social hierarchy of visual representation by giving a face to the 'deviant other'. In his article 'Crime, Media and Community' the criminologist Chris Greer explains the interconnectedness between crime, media and the moral struggle over collective identity in today's world in the following manner:

> One important way in which people are afforded a sense of collective identity and social cohesion is via the mediatised construction of deviant and idealized identities. These constructions achieve much of their potency through the selective creation of binaries – the 'idealized victim' and the 'absolute other', a 'utopian' past and a 'dystopian' future. Both old and new media technologies present opportunities to engage collectively in the affirmation of virtuous identities through insisting on the non-identity of those 'not like us'.
>
> (Greer 2004: 110)

Eamonn Carrabine (2009) similarly points out in his book *Crime, Culture and the Media* that collectively shared cultural narratives that claim to describe, respond to or even displace crises in the moral order are typically structured by social conflict between different actors and identities; heroes, villains, good and evil, self and other, fate and choice, home and abroad. Crime news, too, are always played out in this field of moral struggle (pp. 7–8). One way of approaching the construction of moral hierarchy in crime news is to look at how news media representations of crime offer a point of negative identification, the image from which we want to distinguish and distance ourselves. But, it has to be acknowledged that not every crime can have that function in the media. Thus, we should pay special attention to crime that appears so utterly and unconditionally heinous in the media that it takes on an almost sacrilegious status, thus forcing the society to take a moral stand (Greer 2004: 113; Hancock and Matthews 2001). School shootings are an interesting case in point.

In this chapter, I attempt to demonstrate how the media construct a visible image of the 'absolute other' in the case of the two Finnish school shootings in Jokela (2007) and Kauhajoki (2008). The analysis focuses on the self-portraits of the killers. How were they incorporated into crime news? What types of media were used in this incorporation and how did the incorporation take place? Finally, I will discuss what kind of ethical implications were evoked through the incorporation of the killers' images in the crime news. The chapter draws on a larger empirical study of the coverage of the Jokela and Kauhajoki school shootings in the Finnish media. The data include news material as well as material gathered from social media. The print news data consist of 68 Finnish newspapers (nationwide, tabloids, regional and local papers), and they were collected from the first week after the shootings. The electronic news material consists of television news broadcasts from the Finnish Broadcasting Company (YLE) channels 1 and 2, from MTV3 and Channel Four Finland (the two nationwide commercial channels in Finland) and from the Finnish News Agency (STT) from the first two days after the shootings. News material has also been collected from the websites of the Finnish Broadcasting Company (YLE), MTV3 Finland and Channel Four Finland and the online editions of *Iltalehti* and *Ilta-Sanomat* (the two Finnish tabloids) and *Helsingin Sanomat* (the largest daily in Finland) from the first days of the Jokela and Kauhajoki school shootings, 7–8 November 2007 and 23–24 September 2008. In addition, the material includes compilations on the yle.fi, mtv3.fi, nelonen.fi, hs.fi, iltalehti.fi and iltasanomat.fi websites. The data from the social media have been gathered from eight websites in the period between November 2007 and February 2009: YouTube, Facebook, IRC-Gallery, MuroBBS (Finnish discussion forum frequented by computer enthusiasts), murha.info (trans. murder.info), spreerkillers.org, respectance.com and mahalo.com. In this article special focus is given to the visual media performance of the first two days after the shootings.

Incorporation by Circulation

My starting point for the analysis is that the incorporation of the Jokela and Kauhajoki killer images into the mainstream news media took place first and foremost through and due to a certain logic of image circulation. Mark Allen Peterson (2005) describes the complex media logic of circulation in the present era by stating:

[T]he circulation of media images has slipped from the leash of the political economic structure and threatens to multiply, mutate, and transform itself at an inhuman speed. Not only do texts slip rapidly from context to context, but the contexts of consumption are themselves shifting in uncontrolled ways and at unparalleled rates. People and texts circulate simultaneously, old traditions are dismantled and new ones invented, and identities are constructed, deconstructed, and reconstructed in increasingly facile ways.

(pp. 251–52)

So, if circulation is to serve as a useful analytic construct for the analysis of the media coverage of crime news, it needs to be conceived of as more than simply the movement of killer images from one medium to another. It is necessary to analyse image circulation as a communicative process with its 'own forms of abstraction, evaluation, and constraint' (Lee and LiPuma 2002: 192). It is the dynamic structures of image circulation that we have to look for: Who are circulating killer images? What kind of images are being circulated? And what purpose does the circulation of the killer images serve in the crime news (see also Spitulnik 1997; Sumiala 2008)?

In the history of crime news there is an established tradition of circulating killer images as a visual chronicle of people potentially dangerous to a society (Wardle 2007). In the pre-digital era the killer images incorporated into the news coverage of high-profile crimes have typically contained pictures and photographs from family photo albums as well as official records. The process of news circulation, including image production, visual representation, selection and modification, has characteristically been controlled and managed by the news institutions themselves, involving editors, journalists and producers (Wardle 2007: 265). The mainstream media in the era of mass communication have been a key gatekeeper in controlling and managing the circulation of criminal imagery. However, with recent developments of mobile and digital communication technology the circulation of killer images has started to slip from the leash of the mainstream news media towards social media and non-professional newsmakers.

This type of mobile amateur 'mass self-communication' (Castells 2009) is a new phenomenon in the history of crime news, and it reflects unexpected trends growing out of the soil of the social media and the emerging participatory culture (Burgess and Green 2009; Jenkins 2006; Harvey 2004). The school shooters in Columbine (1999) and Virginia Tech (2007) had already been active in using media for mass self-communication before committing their crimes (Kellner 2008). Another example can be found in the field of terrorism. The videos of Osama Bin Laden circulating in the global media can be described as an example of how web-based media are used for mass self-communication, as a terrorist strategy to create fear and anxiety in the parts of society that find themselves threatened. 9/11 offers another case in point. The attacks were planned so that the world media in New York had enough time to organize themselves around the crime scene in order to start circulating live material of the second plane crashing into the towers (e.g. Zelizer and Allan 2008; Altheide 2002).

Contexts for Circulation

There were many reasons why the Jokela and Kauhajoki school shootings became the object of such intense media coverage in the Finnish news media during the first two days after the shootings. Firstly, Finland had never before witnessed violent youth crime on that scale. The school as a crime scene in Finland was unexpected, as was the manner in which the school as an institution was attacked. It seemed that the Jokela and Kauhajoki school shooters were ordinary school boys who 'suddenly' turned out to be mass murderers capable of conducting their crimes in a particularly cruel manner. The total number of dead was twenty, including the killers. The victims were classmates, other pupils and school personnel. Also, it was shocking news for many in Finland that the shootings took place in rural areas of the country, considered to be notably secure and protected environments to live in.

Secondly, there was an explicit cultural manuscript that the shootings were copied from, namely the previous massacres in Columbine (1999), Erfurt (2002) and Virginia Tech (2007). The shootings were thus immediately interpreted as part of a larger, international phenomenon that had now reached Finland (see Newman et al. 2004; Burns and Crawford 1999; Muschert and Carr 2006; Muschert 2007; Kellner 2008; Sumiala and Tikka 2010). Thirdly, the fact that the killers were skillful and active users of new media technologies caused major anxiety among the Finnish public. The killers had violated the myth of new media technology, a utopia bringing prosperity and success to Finnish society. As competent users of the Internet and new media technology, the young shooters chose to use their skills not to serve society but to try to destroy it. The Jokela and Kauhajoki cases made it explicit that the potential dangers attached to new media technology might not be located 'outside' society (such as foreign, adult influences) but inside society – as society had been hatching a monster within. So, it was not surprising that the news value of the school shootings was immediately considered high in both the Finnish and the international news media. What is perhaps less expected is the prominent role given to the shooters' images in the media coverage of these crimes.

School Shooters as Amateur Video Makers

As Pekka-Eric Auvinen, the Jokela shooter, noted in his diary, he started to plan the shooting by the latest in March 2007, six months before he realized his plan. Around that time, he registered with various online communities under the usernames Sturmgeist and NaturalSelector89. The shooter voiced his political and ideological opinions in the IRC-Gallery's Eric Harris & Dylan Klebold chat community named after the shooters in the Columbine school massacre and posted various home-made videos on YouTube. Right before setting out to the school on 7 November 2007 the shooter uploaded a video titled *Jokela High School Massacre* on YouTube and included a link to a package containing extra material. He also posted the message 'Today history is made' in the IRC-Gallery. After sending these messages he set out to the school to begin his shooting rampage (KRP 2008).

The online history of the Kauhajoki shooter shows that Matti Saari used, for example, the usernames Wumpscut86 and Mr. Saari. He had registered with the IRC-Gallery in 2004, and with YouTube six months before the massacre. In the course of 2008 the images of the young man smiling at the camera changed into profile photos taken at a shooting range and eventually into a video where Saari points a gun at the camera. The shooter posted the first aggressive photos hinting at the shooting on the IRC-Gallery one month before the massacre. Not much later, Saari uploaded a picture of his weapon on the IRC-Gallery, titled 'Pity for majority?'. Less than a week before the massacre the Kauhajoki shooter again added two more gunman photos of himself to his gallery. During the last month Saari had uploaded altogether four shooting videos on YouTube. The videos show the man firing his weapon at a location that looks like a shooting range. On the day of the shooting, 23 September 2008, the Kauhajoki shooter logged into the IRC-Gallery for the last time and posted three more photos in which he points his weapon straight at the camera. Only half an hour before Saari started shooting he included a link to his 'Massacre in Kauhajoki' file package which contained the videos *You will die next, Goodbye* and *Me and my Walther* as well as an aerial shot of the school centre and photos of him aiming the weapon at the viewer (KRP 2009).

In order to analyse the making and circulation of the Jokela and Kauhajoki killer images one needs to discuss their special nature as amateur images. To begin with, the images were mainly self-portraits and can be characterized as highly aggressive in terms of their content and form. This imagery idealizes men with guns, portraying killers as heroes. The prominent emotional tone of the images is misanthropy. Images of guns and men shooting

Figure 7.1: The Kauhajoki school shooter downloaded number of videos on his websites in which he fantasized about the shooting.

in the woods or at shooting ranges are accompanied with aggressive music, black and red colour effects and violent slogans cried out by the killers.

As active producers and users of social media both killers can be characterized as enthusiastic 'mass self-communicators' and 'prosumers', members of the new emerging media culture that emphasizes participation, circulation and a blurring of the categories of production and reception. Both the Jokela and the Kauhajoki shooters were actively involved in the IRC-Gallery and YouTube. In both cases the shooters had uploaded dozens of videos on their websites in which they fantasized about the shooting. But in contrast to the conventional understanding of participatory culture in which participation is seen as a form of emancipation and a resource for a new type of democratization of media culture, the Finnish school shooters used social media to destroy others through shameless self-proclamation relying on visual communication. In this sense the shooters can be characterized as representatives of what we could call 'the dark side' of this new culture.

How Did the Killer Images Circulate?

In order for the killer images to contribute to the construction of the moral hierarchy of visual representation they had to be publicized not only in the social media but also, most importantly, in the national news media. The publication was carried out through intensive circulation of the killer images in the crime news of all the major news organizations whether print, electronic or online. The first news reports from Kauhajoki came from YLE and *Ilta-Sanomat* on their websites. The *Iltalehti* online tabloid first published Saari's killer images about 45 minutes after he had already shot himself but was still alive. At this time Saari's face was not recognizable in the images, as it was covered with a black box. The tabloid headline read *Is He the Shooter?* Later in the afternoon all the three online newspapers, *Helsingin Sanomat*, *Iltalehti* and *Ilta-Sanomat*, published images of Saari shooting and aiming his gun at the camera as well as images of his face originally published in the IRC-Gallery. The operators of IRC-Gallery and YouTube started to remove Saari's material less than an hour after the tragedy had begun in Kauhajoki. But when googling 'Kauhajoki' later in the same day one could still find at least 15 of his videos (or at least bits and pieces of the clips) on YouTube.

The newscasts from all the four national news channels showed Saari's own images as part of their broadcast. The differences were mainly in the nuances and volumes. The two channels of the public service broadcasting company, YLE, were more cautious to show Saari's visual material, whereas the commercial channels, MTV3 and Channel Four Finland, used more time and a larger number of images, both still and moving, to represent the killer with his own material. By the end of the day the Kauhajoki killer had not only become the most prominent figure of the shootings nationwide, but also internationally. The next day only strengthened the effect. The two tabloids, *Iltalehti* and *Ilta-Sanomat*, came out with extra issues that used Saari's visual material across several spreads. Especially interesting is *Iltalehti*'s spread featuring front pages from online news sites worldwide: Spiegel Online, Mail Online, CNN.com, BBC news, El Pais.com, Expressen and Aftonbladet, which all but one had Saari's image on the frontline.

In the case of the Jokela School shooting, the first report was published on the website of *Helsingin Sanomat*. The next to report the shooting was the *Ilta-Sanomat* tabloid. The Jokela killer's images were downloaded from the Internet and distributed widely in all the main news media. One of the prominent images on the first day of news was the video clip that featured the Jokela High School, the place where the crime was committed. The other clip was a self-portrait of the killer, the black figure of a shooter aiming his gun at the viewer. In the image Auvinen wore a T-shirt with the text 'Humanity is overrated'; next, the video turns blood red, showing Auvinen with a gun again. The third widely distributed video featured the perpetrator shooting an apple in the woods and then waiving at the camera with a smile on his face. The print media published still images of the video clips and made active reference to their own online sites, where there were more images to be seen. An impression of the importance of the events was created with extra newscasts both on YLE and on the

Figure 7.2: 'The world in shock'. Finnish newspaper *Iltalehti* featured front pages from international online news sites with Kauhajoki school-shooter's self-portraits.

commercial TV channels. As an outcome of this excessive circulation, both killers became visualized as dangerous, violent and outrageous murderers who were capable of using their skills to manifest their hateful intentions and then to carry them out in a cruel manner.

Framing the Killers

The fact that the killers were apt to make their videos and send them into wide media circulation, and the fact that professional news organizations were willing to offer a professional platform for their images, reflects larger media cultural changes in the structures of circulation in crime news (see also Chyi and McCombs 2004). The evil frame offered by the killers suited well the frame of the crime reporting. Mäkipää and Mörä (2009: 207–21) argue that one of the characteristics of present-day crime reporting, especially in a case of homicide, is that the perpetrator is prominently portrayed as the deviant other, the ultimate immoral. It is the irrationality and immorality of the perpetrator that is held to have caused the crime. It is not unusual that the evilness of the perpetrator is then contrasted with the idealized, pure victim (see also Greer 2004). Interestingly enough, in the Jokela and Kauhajoki cases there was a conspicuous invisibility of the idealized victim in the mainstream crime news. The only victim that to some extent could be considered idealized was the Jokela headmaster, Helena Kalmi, who died. She was the sole victim who was given greater visibility: a face, a name and a story. Some stories were published about the death of the Jokela school nurse, whereas the other people who had lost their lives in Jokela largely remained absent in the news media during the days of intense news circulation. Instead, the visual image of the victim was constructed around some teenage schoolgirls who had escaped from the school and survived the massacre. Young, blonde Katarina Alanko became the icon of a survivor. Videos and still images in which she was fleeing from the school with fear in her eyes were circulating intensely in the mainstream media during the first days of the coverage. She was interviewed on national TV news channels and her pictures covered both tabloids on the next day. In the Kauhajoki case none of the victims became visually known. The names of the victims were published about half a year later, but this did not cause any major media attention.

Moreover, the mainstream media invited authorities such as psychologists, teachers, doctors and social scientists to comment on the news coverage of the events. Some of the specialists offered fairly critical comments on the way in which the news media had treated the killers, giving them such an enormous amount of visibility. But again, when looking at what was actually circulating in the news during the initial days, the critique did not have a visible impact. Furthermore, it was underlined by many of the media professionals interviewed later that people had a right to know what kind of a person the killer was. From that perspective, the killers' images offered rich visual evidence for their actions and motives and made the evil frame offered by both the killers and the news media even more convincing (Raittila et al. 2008, 2009).

The main ethical concern in the mainstream media was centred on the issue of whether or not to publish the name of the shooter (YLE TV News was the last major news organization to publish the name in both cases). In the following weeks the ethical debate, again in Jokela, turned more towards the issue of the treatment of the underage witnesses who had escaped unhurt from the school. This became an issue, as many of the young Jokela survivors felt that they had been abused by the media and journalists who had constantly bombarded them with interview requests and cameras (Juntunen 2009; Raittila et al. 2008).

Consequently, the overall picture of the circulation – what was shown and given visibility – in the mainstream Finnish news media during the first days after the shootings was that of the killers. This is how the mainstream news media incorporated the killers into major actors on the crime scene. It is also important to acknowledge that it was not any individual news medium that was mainly or solely responsible for creating the bias favouring the killers in the reporting. The killers became the most visible actors in the mainstream news media, not because of any single news medium, but because the same images were constantly circulating over and over again in all the mainstream Finnish news media during the first days of news coverage. Eventually, powerful international media (CNN, BBC World) contributed to the expansion of the circulation and made it global. Different national and international television companies began to air videos, photos and texts consisting of the killer material. In the news race new associations were made. The Jokela and Kauhajoki killer images gained new significance as they were related to each other as well as to previous school shootings in the United States and Germany. The killer images of the Kauhajoki shooter were quickly connected on the Internet to material on the Jokela school shooter, and mirrored against it. The chilling images of the Jokela shooter, in turn, were compared to the gun-wielding photos of the shooter at Virginia Tech. The images were circulated alongside one another. Especially powerful became images in which the shooters were all pointing their guns at the viewer. And this is hardly a thing of the past. A fairly recent example of the circulation effect can be found in the news reporting on the school shooting in Winnenden, Germany, on 11 March 2009. The Jokela and Kauhajoki cases were immediately referenced in the coverage of the Winnenden shooting (Sumiala and Tikka 2010).

The analysis of the incorporation of the Jokela and Kauhajoki killer images into national news media shows that the killer images became 'the image' of these news events via circulation by a range of news organizations. The direction of the circulation of the killer images was from the social media to the online versions of the national news media, and then to electronic and print form. From the perspective of actors, the movement of circulation was from the killers to the mainstream news producers.

When trying to understand the logic of incorporation of killer images in crime news it is necessary to look at three elements of the contemporary news culture: tabloidization, technologization and truthiness (Zelizer 2009). The first element concerns the increased competition among news houses shaped by commercialization and tabloidization. The shift from deadline journalism into online journalism has forced newsrooms to engage in an ongoing news race and constant updating (Raittila et al. 2008, 2009; Juntunen 2009). During the first hours of reporting on Jokela and Kauhajoki there was not very much visual or textual material available to provide new news about the crimes. This scarcity in the newsrooms was contrasted with the rich, visually dramatic material offered by the killers – free and available to all media. The second element, linked with the first one, concerns technology, in such terms as mobility, digitalization and distance. Killer images on the Internet travelled much faster than people with cameras. The issue of physical distance made a difference especially in Kauhajoki. The town is located far away from Helsinki, the capital and the centre of the largest media and news organizations. Only the best-resourced news organizations were able to send journalists and photographers to the scene with helicopters and planes, the others had to sit in a car or train for hours to get to Kauhajoki. The critical moment was already past when they finally arrived (Raittila et al. 2009). Thirdly, from the perspective of truthiness, there was an existing 'evil frame' preferred by the news media that suited well the 'authentic' frame and material offered by the killers. The killer images provided for a strong reality effect, and they offered visual evidence for the killers' motives and an explanation for their cruel acts. In short, the killer images visualized a story of the killers as outrageously violent perpetrators, evil and immoral creatures who favoured severe misanthropy which perfectly suited the media frame that already existed in newsrooms.

Media Ethics on Circulation

Following Mark Allen Peterson (2005) we can argue that it is consistent with the very logic of circulation that the news media provide links and grounds by which people can imagine 'the absolute other' and thus participate in the mediated construction of the moral hierarchy of visual representation. The way in which the Jokela and Kauhajoki killer images were incorporated into professional news work should therefore not be regarded as an innocent, let alone inconsequential, media cultural phenomenon. There are ethical and moral dimensions included in it. By offering such massive visibility, the mainstream news media included killer images in Sekula's (1986) 'shadow archives' of contemporary media society, making the killers visible on a scale and in a manner not even imaginable for previous generations. Through the massive circulation of the killers' self-portraits, the shooters were transformed into people who were 'not-like-us' and who were 'in society, but not of it', as formulated by Greer (2004: 111). This, I argue, provided the audience with the possibility to achieve at least for a moment a sense of identity; belonging and community through visually excluding the shooters from the society (see also Greer 2004: 117).

But there is a dilemma in this type of exclusion that is performed in such an excessive manner. The killers as the 'absolute other' were brought into the centre in a style that made the exclusion highly ambiguous and paradoxical. The killers were portrayed as 'not-like-us' but not by diminishing their centrality. Instead, the shooters were transformed in the news media into superior individuals, well above ordinary people and powerful enough to orchestrate the news event even from behind the boundaries of death. The invisibility of the 'idealized victim' in crime news – a reference point for positive identification according to Greer's (2004) terminology – only underlined the pivotal role given to the killers and their images. Consequently, in mainstream Finnish crime news the Jokela and Kauhajoki killer images can be argued to have contributed to creating a moral hierarchy that, instead of working to diminish the power of the killers and raise the moral standard against the perpetrators, twisted the binary code and made the killers 'celebrities of the dark' in a way only possible in the era of excessive media circulation.

References

Altheide, D. (2002), *Creating Fear: News and the Construction of Crisis*, New York: Aldine de Gruyter.

Burgess, J. and Green, J. (2009), *YouTube. Online Video and Participatory Culture*, Cambridge, UK: Polity.

Burns, R. and Crawford, C. (1999), 'School Shootings, the Media, and Public Fear: Ingredients for Moral Panic', *Crime, Law, and Social Change*, 32: 2, pp. 147–68.

Carrabine, E. (2009), *Crime, Culture and the Media*, Cambridge: Polity Press.

Castells, M. (2009), *Communication Power*, New York: Oxford University Press.

Chyi, H. and McCombs, M. (2004), 'Media Salience and the Process of Framing: Coverage of the Columbine Shootings', *Journalism and Mass Communication Quarterly*, 81: 1, pp. 22–35.

Greer, C. (2004), 'Crime, Media and Community: Grief and Virtual Engagement in Late Modernity', in J. Ferrell, K. Hayward, W. Morrison and M. Presdee (eds), *Cultural Criminology Unleashed*, London: The Glass House Press, pp. 109–20.

Hancock, L. and Matthews, R. (2001), 'Crime, Community Safety and Toleration', in R. Mathews and J. Pitts (eds), *Crime, Disorder and Community Safety*, London: Routledge, pp. 98–119.

Jenkins, H. (2006), *Converge Culture: Where Old and New Media Collide*, New York: New York University Press.

Juntunen, L. (2009), 'Kiireen ja kilpailun haasteet journalistiselle etiikalle', in E. Väliverronen (ed.), *Journalismi murroksessa* ('Journalism in Transition'), Helsinki: Gaudeamus, pp. 171–92.

Kellner, D. (2008), *Guys and Guns Amok: Domestic Terrorism and School Shootings from the Oklahoma City Bombing to the Virginia Tech Massacre*, Boulder & London: Paradigm Publishers.

KRP (2008), Final report on the investigation of the Jokela school massacre, released by the Finnish National Bureau of Investigation (KRP) on 17 April 2008.

KRP (2009), Final report on the investigation of the Kauhajoki school massacre, released by the Finnish National Bureau of Investigation (KRP) on 11 June 2009.

Lee, B. and LiPuma, E. (2002), 'Cultures of Circulation: The Imaginations of Modernity', *Public Culture*, 14: 1, pp. 191–214.

Lury, C. (1998), *Prosthetic Culture: Photography, Memory and Identity*, London and New York: Routledge.

Mäkipää, L. and Mörä, T. (2009), 'Henkirikos yhdistää', in E. Väliverronen (ed.), *Journalismi murroksessa* ('Journalism in Transition'), Helsinki: Gaudeamus, pp. 207–21.

Muschert, G. (2007), 'Research in School Shootings', *Sociology Compass*, 1: 1, pp. 60–80.

Muschert, G. and Carr, D. (2006), 'Media Salience and Frame Changing Across Events: Coverage of Nine School Shootings', *Journalism & Mass Communication Quarterly*, 83: 4, pp. 747–66.

Newman, C., Fox, C., Harding, D., Mehta, J. and Roth, W. (2004), *Rampage: The Social Roots of School Shootings*, New York: Basic Books.

Peterson, M. (2005), *Anthropology & Mass Communication: Media and Myth in the New Millenium*, New York: Berghahn Books.

Raittila, P. et al. (2008), *Jokelan koulusurmat mediassa* ('Jokela School-Shooting in the Media'), Journalism Research and Development Centre/Department of Journalism and Mass Communication, Series A 105/2008, Tampere: University of Tampere.

Raittila, P. et al. (2009), *Kauhajoen koulusurmat mediassa* ('Kauhajoki School-Shooting in the Media'), Journalism Research and Development Centre/Department of Journalism and Mass Communication, Series A 111/2009,Tampere: University of Tampere.

Seaton, J. (2005), *Carnage and the Media: The Making and Breaking of News about Violence*, London: Allen Lane.

Sekula, A. (1986), 'The Body and the Archive', *October*, 39, pp. 3–64.

Spitulnik, D. (1997), 'The Social Circulation on Media Discourse and the Mediation of Communities', *Journal of Linguistic Anthropology*, 6: 2, pp. 161–87.

Sumiala, J. (2008), 'Circulation', in D. Morgan (ed.), *Keywords in Religion, Media, and Culture*, London: Routledge, pp. 44–55.

Sumiala, J. and Tikka, M. (2010), '"Web First" to Death: The Media Logic of the School Shootings in the Era of Uncertainty', *Nordicom Review*, 31: 2, pp. 17–29. .

Wardle, C. (2007), 'Monsters and Angels: Visual Press Coverage of Child Murders in the USA and UK, 1930–2000', *Journalism*, 8: 3, pp. 263–84.

Zelizer, B. (ed.) (2009), *The Changing Faces of Journalism: Tabloidization, Technology and Truthiness*, London: Routledge.

Zelizer, B. and Allan, S. (eds) (2008), *Journalism after September 11*, London: Routledge.

Chapter 8

From Columbine to Kauhajoki: Amateur Videos as Acts of Terror

Marguerite Moritz

In today's world of instant and global communication, planning a high visibility criminal act increasingly involves a media strategy to publicize, politicize and often memorialize the event. Whether it be a hostage scene, a filmed execution, a terror attack or a school shooting, hostile acts captured on home videos are gaining visibility over national and international news networks. Blondheim and Liebes (2003: 275) argue that 'we are increasingly witness to anti-normative acts, that rather than shy away from publicity, are manufactured precisely for that purpose'. Natural disasters are random and arbitrary, but as they note, man-made traumas involve a 'mastermind launching the drama', one who likely does so with 'the *modus operandi* of journalists in mind'.

In the case of recent school shootings, young killers have created home videos expressly to gain news media attention. While offering documentary evidence as well as potential insights into the motivation and intent of the actors involved, these messages can by their very existence elevate the newsworthiness of the event itself, iconize those responsible for it and encourage others with like-minded aspirations to carry out similar acts. Moreover, they allow the killers themselves to shape their own public images as well as advance their self-aggrandizing narratives and exert at least a measure of control over news accounts of their crimes. A macabre form of participatory journalism, these first person accounts from the grave do not raise the typical questions of authenticity for journalists but instead generate concerns over aesthetics, ethics and editorial control. Indeed, videos produced with hostile intent open a new aspect of the debate over non-professional content, one in which journalists struggle to reconcile their resistance to relinquishing authority with their desire to offer a full accounting of the documentary record available from a high-visibility criminal act.

This chapter takes Finland, the site of school shootings in 2007 and again in 2008, as a case in point. It is based on interviews with 17 journalists, all of whom played prominent roles in the coverage of the shootings and in the subsequent debates over the appropriate role of media in reporting such sensitive crimes. My intention and interest in conducting the interviews was to understand how contemporary journalism deals with photographic materials produced with hostile intent. Perhaps not surprisingly, much critical commentary in this area focuses on the American model, which for decades has influenced news reporting standards, first for television and then for the web. By investigating journalistic work in a Nordic country with strong public service broadcasting and free press traditions, my aim was to look for approaches that may be applicable to the US system where public confidence stands at a two decade low (Pew 2009).

American journalists and news organizations often naturalize their choices and present them as somehow inevitable. The Finnish coverage demonstrates that journalists have a wide array of reportorial strategies and indeed the same kind of event may be packaged differently in different social, political, cultural and temporal contexts. However, the Finnish cases also illustrate how video technologies have facilitated the global circulation of visual and textual crime narratives, Columbine in 1999 and Virginia Tech in 2007 being the pertinent examples here. Shooters Pekka Eric Auvinen in 2007 and Matti Saari in 2008 both made specific references to Columbine in their writings (Sumiala 2009; Sumiala and Hakala 2010). Dylan Klebold and Eric Harris were their 'idols'. Like Seung Hui Cho at Virginia Tech, the Finnish shooters both recorded videotapes of themselves with their weapons. They also posted them to the Internet before carrying out their attacks, thus facilitating if not assuring the level of media response that the US cases had generated. The videos produced in all four cases have strong intertextual links, suggesting that each exerted influence on the ones that followed. The US cases also prompted the first debates over editorial treatment of amateur videos that may themselves be seen as acts of terror.

The Columbine Template

In 1999, when Klebold and Harris carried out a massacre at their school in Littleton, Colorado, injuring 21 and killing 15, including themselves, live broadcasts from the field began less than an hour after the incident began. Some 750 news organizations from scores of countries sent 5000 journalists and support staff to report on the event (Moritz 2003). Widely considered a seminal case for US news organizations (Coleman 2004; Cullen 2009; Moritz 2003), the shootings generated 96 hours of local and national television programming in the first week of reporting, much of it re-transmitted via satellite across international channels. These graphic, dramatic, live action images coalesced into a collective memory captured in the single word, Columbine.

Bandura (2001) describes how this media environment, in which video plays a central role, impacts individuals and communities at great distance from the original event: 'The accelerated growth of video delivery technologies' expands the range of behaviors to which members of a society are exposed on a daily basis. New ideas, values, behavior patterns and social practices are now being rapidly diffused worldwide by symbolic modeling in ways that foster a globally distributed consciousness' (p. 271). It was precisely in this way that Columbine became a familiar shorthand for various kinds of school violence and killers Klebold and Harris acquired iconic status among alienated youth around the world.

Preti (2008: 544) uses the term 'suicide with hostile intent' to describe school shootings which typically end with the killer or killers taking their own lives. In hostile suicides, killers have a 'desire that other people understand their reasons', and the messages they leave behind provide the justification for their actions. In today's media-saturated environment, those messages are now meant to reach beyond family and friends to a much wider audience and thus explain to the world at large how they were provoked and how others deserve the real blame. In addition to their handwritten notes, Klebold and Harris left what police called the basement tapes, video diaries they recorded themselves that reveal their plans to blow up the school as well as their generalized rage. Although YouTube did not come on line until 2005, video cameras had become common in both public and private settings by the late 1990s. Klebold and Harris used them for school projects. Along with the basement tapes, a classroom video project, footage from surveillance cameras at the school all emerged as part of the visual record (Kowalski 2010). US journalists competed heavily to obtain and use these amateur images for their own reporting, but from the start they were problematic. The surveillance video from the school cafeteria, for example, captures Klebold and Harris in the midst of their killing spree. Wearing T-shirts, cargo pants, leather boots and flak vests, automatic rifles strapped to their bodies and hanging casually at their sides, baseball caps on backwards, they are a picture of machismo and nonchalance that could have come from a Hollywood movie. One news outlet reported receiving 300–500 e-mails a day from viewers protesting the use of the surveillance camera images in news reports (Moritz 2003).

Cullen (2009: 335) describes the emphasis on 'cinematic elements' in the wardrobe, staging and other details of the Columbine attack, noting that the basement tapes, journals, maps and blueprints of the plan were all supposed to have been mailed to television stations in Denver. In fact, the basement tapes, which were recorded with cameras belonging to Columbine High School, remain closely held by local authorities. Although they have never been shown to the public (Kowalski 2010) their content was summarized in a 1999 *Time* cover story. In the videos, which *Time* (Gibbs et al. 1999) describes as 'almost unbearable to watch', Klebold and Harris reportedly detail the maltreatment they suffered at the hands of classmates, 'stuck-up' kids and family members. The image chosen for the *Time* cover, inscribed with the time code of 11:57:20, was extracted from the cafeteria surveillance video. Black and red, the colours of death and blood, were chosen for the background field and lettering. Hitting newsstands right before the Christmas holiday, the *Time* cover story drew widespread public criticism for being exploitive and sensational.

The Cho Manifesto

Seung Hui Cho, the Virginia Tech University student who killed 32 people in his 2007 attack, interrupted his shooting spree to mail his homemade videos to the offices of NBC News in New York (Bergstein 2007; Bauerlein and Steel 2007). Cho's recorded voice describes a lifetime of being mistreated and misunderstood. In the classic manner of suicide with hostile intent that Preti (2008) describes, he places blame for his murders on those who mistreated him. The video captures an intensely hostile, angry, unbalanced young person, brandishing knives and guns as he looks into the camera and in a leaden voice spews profanities and hatred to an audience he clearly wished to address. Here for the first time, the video manifesto of a school shooter was broadcast on a major American network and subsequently re-played across the country and the world.

At the time it received the Cho package, NBC News argued that it had a journalistic obligation to air it. But even within its own ranks there was disagreement over that decision. *Today* anchor Matt Lauer told his morning show audience that 'there are some big differences of opinion right within this news division as to whether we should be airing this stuff at all, whether we're taking the right course of action' (Carter 2007). NBC (2007) issued a public statement defending its decision, saying the video 'provides some answers to the critical question, "Why did this man carry out these awful murders?"' The president of NBC News attempted damage control by appearing on a number of news and talk shows, but viewer reaction was almost universally negative. *Washington Post* media critic Howard Kurtz (2007) said the Cho video 'sparked an outcry from friends and relatives of the 32 victims, online commentators and radio hosts from both ends of the political spectrum'.

The Canadian Broadcasting Corporation (CBC) was the one broadcaster that decided against airing any of the Cho videos stating that its journalistic merit was outweighed by the potential harm the video might do. What is noteworthy about the CBC case is that a prior school shooting in Canada at Dawson College in 2006 had alerted the public broadcaster to audience sensitivities. Editor-in-chief Tony Burman (2007) had written two open letters to viewers in connection with the Dawson events asking, 'Are the media partly to blame for student killings?' Most viewers – highly critical of media's performance – said yes. When the Virginia Tech story broke the following year, Burman directed that CBC coverage would focus on the victims of the crime and not on the killer. As to the Cho video, Burman opted to prohibit any use of it on any CBC platform, fearful that it would spark copycat killings. Burman's concern was soon to be realized. More than three dozen school shootings have taken place since the massacre at Virginia Tech, two of the most deadly taking place in Finland.

Strategies for Reporting the Finnish Shootings

In the highly literate and socially conscious Finnish society, the sense of communal grief over the 2007 and 2008 shootings that together left 18 people, most of them young students, murdered was profound – a national trauma. So too was the sensitivity to media coverage of the events. Finnish reporters were criticized for being overly aggressive and insensitive to the plight of the victims. Rumours that journalists were misrepresenting themselves to gain access to traumatized students were widespread (Sumiala and Hakala 2010). News agencies were repeatedly taken to task for glorifying the shooters by featuring their video images and referencing their websites. Ultimately, Finnish journalists said they had to question their own standards and practices in light of these public critiques. Just how heavily audience reactions weigh on news management decisions is difficult to determine, but it seems clear that in Finland, reporters and editors were sensitive to criticisms they received in 2007 and attempted to find less offensive strategies when they covered the 2008 case.

In interviews with journalists, all of whom played prominent roles in the coverage of the shootings and in the subsequent debates over the appropriate role of media in reporting such sensitive crimes, the question of how to represent the shooter was the most vexing. Journalists who worked in the field as well as editors responsible for signing off on overall content, expressed deep concern over being manipulated by the killers into glorifying their acts by showing their videos on line, on television or in single frame captures used as still photos. Sumiala and Hakala (2010) show that 'it was only after the mainstream media had confirmed the news' that the school shooting reports 'began to disseminate on a new level confirming the mediatization effect'. Reetta Meriläinen, editor-in-chief of *Helsingin Sanomat*, the largest and most influential newspaper in Finland, recognized that mainstream media played an essential yet unavoidable role in publicizing the crimes:

> Web publicity is not enough for them. They want to see their face on TV and the front pages of papers. Net publicity is limited. They are looking for mass media and we who are working in mass media are satisfying their need. So what to do when you are part of the problem?
>
> (Meriläinen 2010)

Reporter Marcus Lillkvist covered the 2008 shooting for *Hufvudstadsbladet*, the major Swedish language newspaper in Finland. Lillkvist said he easily located the videos Saari had posted simply by searching 'Kauhajoki massacre' on Google:

> He pumped us with so much information when there was a vacuum of information, resulting in thousands and thousands of viewers on our website reading about this guy when police said nothing. It gives him just what he wants and we did it.
>
> (Lillkvist 2010)

Coleman (2004) notes that researchers have for at least three decades identified links between heavy media coverage and copycat crimes. In the case of school shootings, they appear in clusters and, he argues, detailed accounts of how shooters prepared their weapons, scouted their locations and targeted their victims provide models that others then follow. In fact, Finnish journalists saw such striking similarities between the 2007 Jokela shooting and the 2008 Kauhajoki crime that they were forced to ask:

> Would Kauhajoki ever have happened had there not been a Jokela shooting? There were too many similarities. The way he [Saari] posted the message, making his own videos with the gun. We [at MTV3] had a heavy discussion after Jokela and we made a very strict decision. If we have this again, we do not post the link. We do a journalistic story about the material.
>
> (Sipilä 2010)

Television news outlets had to determine how to use the shooter videos in their live reporting which is obviously dependent on moving images. News manager at public broadcasting's YLE said the material generated 'big discussions [...].We didn't want to give him the publicity. That is what the shooter wants' (Ahonen 2010). Marjo Ahonen was in her first day on the job when the Kauhajoki story broke. Despite claims that YLE has its own high standards ('we have the public service ethic and it protects us'), she acknowledged that 'there is huge pressure in terms of what other media does'. In the end, YLE opted to use the Kauhajoki shooter video on its TV broadcasts, but 'not to show his face. [...] we tried not to show the close pictures of his face' (ibid.). The YLE website carried stories about Saari's Internet postings, but did not link to his web pages. The school shooting cases demonstrate the unresolved nature of the debate over appropriate handling of shooter materials. Less than a year earlier, during the Jokela coverage, YLE had made just the opposite decision, publishing a link to the shooter videos on the YLE website, but prohibiting use of the video on its news broadcasts.

The commercial broadcaster MTV3 used the shooter videos in 2007 and in 2008 on the first day of coverage, acknowledging that 'it was pretty rough'. But 'after day one it was taken out. It was decided we don't use it after the first day' (Sipilä 2010). In fact, many viewers complain that television stations needlessly replay sensational images – the crumbling Twin Towers and the Cho home video being two prominent US examples. Crime reporter Jarkko Sipilä who covered both shootings for MTV3 said there was never any interest in using graphic images from the scene. He did, however, argue that the web material left by the shooters was a crucial part of reporting the story, 'to show that is was pre-meditated, well planned and not just done by someone who happened to shoot a gun' (Sipilä 2010).

Perhaps the greatest pressure in covering the story was felt by online editors where the news cycle spins ever faster. 'More and more, you must have new material even though they are still investigating. Even when we don't have anything, still we need to have something,' explained YLE online editor Timo Huovinen (Huovinen 2010). At the same time, ethical questions relating to shooter-generated materials remain unresolved, as seen in the comment of Heikki Lammi, the managing editor of the YLE online news: 'Should we make a link to pages of the shooter? Should we publish the video? He wants to be a hero and releasing everything and telling everything, you somehow create (a hero)' (Lammi 2010).

As a practical matter, newspaper journalists had to decide whether to put an image of the shooter in the printed paper and if so, what image should be chosen, what page should it run on and how prominently should it be displayed. Editors all reported that the decisions made in 2008 were subject to extensive deliberations precisely because the media had received such widespread criticism for its work on the Jokela shootings less than a year earlier. Rather than use an image from Matti Saari's video, *Helsingin Sanomat* instead put his innocent looking school photo on page one. Managing editor Reetta Räty (2010) recalls talking about the image 'over and over' before making the decision to publish it on the front page 'even though we knew we would get the critics'. To this day, Meriläinen, the chief editor of the

Figure 8.1: The biggest Finnish daily newspaper *Helsingin Sanomat* decided against publishing an image from Kauhajoki school-shooter's hostile videos on its front page and instead opted for his school photo. Permission to reproduce granted by *Helsingin Sanomat*.

paper, says she is uncertain about the choice that was made, even though it was her idea to use the school photo: 'I don't know if it was the right decision. People who criticized us said we are making him a hero and creating a positive halo around him. We just wanted to show that he looks very normal, a good looking, neat guy' (Meriläinen 2010).

Meriläinen noted that the second shooting was more troubling than the first one, as it could not be seen anymore as something completely exceptional. With the 2008 case taking place less than a year after the Jokela event, that theory or hope was shattered, undermining 'my security and that of many other Finns too'. In addition to putting Saari's school photo on the front page, she took the unusual step of having her own picture on the page two with her editorial which raised deeper questions about violence in Finnish society:

We have a violent history and I was asking [...] why can't we solve our problems in another way, a less bloody way and what is this dark side which we have in Finland. The other big question was whether media is part of the problem. If it is so that these guys are looking for some minutes of being a hero, if they are looking for publicity and this short time to be a famous person, it is not possible without media. So in a way we are always a part (of it).

The editor Lars Rosenblad of the *Vasabladet* in Western Finland chose a different approach to the front-page coverage of the 2008 shootings. There was no image of Matti Saari, nor did one appear in *Vasabladet* until page five, and even then it was very small scale. In fact the most prominent feature of page one was its heavy use of large, stacked headlines accompanied by one small image, taken from behind, showing the back of a student being helped from the crime scene. In all, the front page carried four separate stories about the event, each with prominent headlines and sub-headlines. Editor Lars Rosenblad said the emphasis on text over photos was the paper's way of recognizing reader concerns that the media 'not make them heroes'. The paper's front page 'reflects what we learned. One year later, we found another way'. Images of Saari that *Vasabladet* published were kept small precisely because 'we already knew that these kinds of people want to be famous' (Rosenblad 2010).

Hufvudstadsbladet opted to blow up an image of Matti Saari brandishing his gun and run it across two inside pages. Despite numerous reader complaints, news editor Matts Lindqvist does not regret his decision, but acknowledges that the size of the image was a mistake. For him, the image itself was justified by the magnitude of the crime and the interest it generated across Finland. 'We want to show what kind of person the murderer is, how he prepared. I would print the picture smaller, but it would be there' (Lindqvist 2010).

The interviews reveal journalists looking for nuanced ways of being all things to all people, expressing restraint in response to public criticism yet remaining competitive on their reporting. *Hufvudstadsbladet* did not post shooter video on its website, nor did *Vasabladet* which also chose to prohibit web commentaries from readers. 'We did not allow them because of speculations and rumors' (Rosenblad 2010). *Helsingin Sanomat's* managing editor said their use of the material was highly fluid: 'We are making those distinctions between what to publish and what to hold all the time. And we are watching (the competition) all the time – the TV, YouTube, Twitter and Facebook, all that' (Räty 2010).

Journalists said decisions made during the Kauhajoki coverage would not necessarily apply in the future: 'It is understandable to react and dangerous to overreact' (Lillkvist 2010). They noted that no new rules were adopted by them collectively and that in the aftermath of Jokela, many statements were made regarding the public's right to know and the right of young people to speak. Far from providing some kind of template that will be used should another such crime occur in the future, the Kauhajoki coverage was a particular response to a particular moment, said Vasabladet photojournalist Gunnar Backman (Backman 2010). As the editor-in-chief of *Helsingin Sanomat* expressed it, '[E]very case is so different and that is [...] one of the intellectually challenging things. You cannot repeat. You have to find case by case the right thing to do' (Meriläinen 2010). Ultimately, journalists said they had to attempt their best efforts at being thorough, accurate, competitive and sensitive to crimes that had to be reported. Whether they succeeded is a question they themselves cannot completely answer.

Shooter videos, which achieve their relevance only in the aftermath of a gruesome crime, clearly undermine the collective sense of social normalcy. Schools, after all, are imagined as safe, secure places of innocence and affirmation. When young people themselves turn their own classrooms into bloody battlefields and their own classmates into human targets, the emotional stability of a community or a nation is placed under considerable stress. In these moments, audiences may be simultaneously drawn to and repelled by news coverage while journalists are left to explain the shattering event. Among the key questions they must confront are who committed this crime and why. The video diaries offer some answers to those questions, a first person accounting of the killer by the killer. Nonetheless, allowing school shooters to circulate heroic self-portraits in which their alienation is valorized and their depression and psychological ills are masked is no doubt difficult for audiences to see at a moment of communal crisis.

In terms of representing school shooters, the point of common agreement among Finnish journalists is that news images and texts should not make heroes out of villains. How that is achieved on a practical level is another matter, but blown up images on front page showing the shooter with a gun, or the heavy, repetitive use of video prepared by the shooter have been repeatedly criticized by readers and viewers. Like most images in the news, those of and by school shooters are embedded in crime narratives that receive extensive coverage. The images of Auvinen or Saari brandishing guns instantly connect to their actions. Not only had they murdered fellow students, their words and images were there to remind viewers of just how deliberate they were in doing so.

Journalists say they are careful not to air raw, unedited shooter video on their news programmes or link to it on their websites. Framing devices such as captions, electronic graphics and titles and narrated commentaries that introduce edited video segments and audio overrides that bleep obscenities are all commonly imposed. No bloody or graphic scenes that would violate mainstream news standards adhered to in Finland are permitted. But audiences still expressed a sense of outrage at these images, no matter how carefully they are controlled. As Finnish journalists discovered, even ordinary, seemingly harmless and inherently inoffensive school photos of killers elicit heated audience reactions.

The power of these images is derived from the context in which they emerge and is explained in the associative logic of the visual. In terms of manifest content, that which exists on the surface level, an image may be utterly inoffensive, school photos being a case in point. Yet on the level of latent content, even a yearbook photo is now inextricably linked to a brutal crime and thus associated with all the terror that crime invokes. Representing a killer by showing a photo in which he appears to be, in the words of one editor, 'very normal, a good looking, neat guy' can thus register as a cruel irony with readers.

The target practice video made by Matti Saari offers another example. In it he is shown discharging a weapon. The Finnish police officer who saw this video the day before the

Kauhajoki shooting took no action to revoke Saari's licensed gun. A Finnish court subsequently reviewed the video and ruled that the officer had acted appropriately; there is nothing in the surface content of the video that is criminal or even frightening. It is only when the scene is considered in the context of the school shootings that it takes on a different and very dark meaning.

Conclusion

The debates between news professionals and the public over school shooting coverage may be irreconcilable. Just as journalists have many strategies for reporting on such events, audiences have many demands – including no coverage at all. Competition between the public's right to know, the killer's desire for public affirmation and the myriad choices of images, topics, and framing all must be weighed by journalists along with public commentary, sociocultural norms and a host of other factors. In this complex mix it is likely that professional choices will never satisfy all critics. The important issue is rather that the debates take place, citizens argue their cases and journalists listen and carefully evaluate those arguments as one important factor in their deliberations.

Obviously, communication with major media outlets is much easier for readers and viewers in the Internet era. At the same time, once video materials are posted on the web, they are very likely to remain there permanently. Today, images of school shooters are easily re-circulated in both their original and altered forms. As MTV3's crime reporter Hanna Ruokangas described:

> So many followers, Columbine fans, you would not believe. People of all ages, fans with tribute videos to both Columbine killers and also for the Jokela and Kauhajoki killers. There are websites who keep track of body counts. The fan videos are quite disgusting [...] They talk about these murderers so lovingly and lovingly is the correct word.

As noted, much of the valorization of school shooters began with Columbine. US coverage was extensive and arguably excessive and the narrative of the killers as outcasts struck a responsive chord with other alienated young people. Cho as well as both of the school shooters in Finland specifically referenced Klebold and Harris in their web postings. Ruokangas (2010) said that from the Finnish perspective, the Columbine killers were compelling because they were 'both white, they came from normal families, not inner city ghettos and (because of) the role they took against the beautiful, successful people'. In addition, the Columbine events were distributed globally and led television newscasts in Europe and many other parts of the world. The story later generated a documentary film, Michael Moore's *Bowling for Columbine* (2002), that itself gained considerable cultural currency, winning the Academy Award for Best Documentary as well as a special prize at the Cannes Film Festival. Events at Columbine have since been the subject of scores of articles, books, films and websites now comprising an extensive and readily available cache of materials which may add to the Columbine mythology and inspire other, similar crimes.

The Finnish school shooting cases suggest that reader and viewer concerns do have an impact. When there is a common public opinion condemning a particular practice, as with the coverage at Virginia Tech and later that year at Jokela, journalists are forced to examine their choices and perhaps just as importantly to acknowledge that they do have a variety of options in their choice of placement and repetition of images. Another key point is that regardless of what specific choices journalists make, today's practitioners must be able to articulate to an increasingly active and vocal audience why they make the choices that they do. This applies to editors and news managers as well as to reporters in the field who have the most direct contact with members of the public. Similarly, audiences should realize that their own concerns carry more weight when they are argued clearly and logically. And there is much evidence (Simpson and Cote 2000; Preti 2008) to support the claim that media coverage in school shootings does matter and can in fact save lives.

References

Ahonen, M. (2010), Interview, 2 June.

Backman, G. (2010), Interview, 9 June.

Bandura, A. (2001), 'Social Cognitive Theory of Mass Communications', in J. Bryant and D. Zillman (eds.), *Media Effects: Advances in Theory and Research*, Hillsdale, NJ: Lawrence Erlbaum.

Bauerlein, V. and Steel, E. (2007), 'How the Web Helped Identify Virginia Tech Victims: Networking Site Gave Student Newspaper Head Start on Names', *Wall Street Journal*, 19 April, p. 16.

Bergstein, B. (2007), 'Virginia Tech Tragedy: Internet Keywords Boosted On-line Visits', *Seattle Post Intelligencer* 18 April, 2007, http://www.seattlepi.com/business/312208_vatechkeywords19.html?dpfrom=thead. Accessed 29 September 2010.

Blondheim, M. and Liebes, T. (2003), 'From Disaster Marathon to Media Event: Live Television's Performance on September 11, 2001, and September 11, 2002', in A. M. Noll (ed.), *Crisis Communication: Lessons from September 11th*, Lanham, MD: Rowman and Littlefield, pp. 185–98

Burman, T. (2007), 'A Story of Victims and Issues, Not Only the Killer', CBC News, http://www.cbc.ca/news/about/burman/letters/2007/04/a_story_of_victims_and_issues.html. Accessed 31 October 2010.

Carter, B. (2007), 'NBC Defends Its Use of Materials Sent by the Killer', *New York Times*, 20 April 2007, http://www.nytimes.com/2007/04/20/us/20nbc.html. Accessed 29 September 2010.

Coleman, L. (2004), *The Copycat Effect: How the Media and Popular Culture Trigger the Mayhem in Tomorrow's Headlines*, New York: Simon and Schuster.

Cullen, D. (2009), *Columbine*, New York: Twelve.

Gibbs, N., Roche, T., Goldstein, A., Harrington, M. and Woodbury, R. (1999), 'The Columbine Tapes', *Time*, 20 December 1999, http://www.time.com/time/magazine/article/0,9171,992873,00.html. Accessed 31 October 2010.

Huovinen, T. (2010), Interview, 12 June.

Kowalski, B. (2010), Interview, 9 April.

Kurtz, H. (2007), 'The Media, The Killer & The Video', *The Washington Post*, 20 April 2007, http://www.washingtonpost.com/wp-dyn/content/blog/2007/04/20/BL2007042000504.html. Accessed 31 October 2001.

Lammi, H. (2010), Interview, 2 June.

Lillkvist, M. (2010), Interview, 3 June.

Lindqvist, M. (2010), Interview, 3 June.

Meriläinen, R. (2010), Interview, 31 May.

Moritz, M. (2003), '7, in L. Gross, J.S. Katz and J. Ruby. (eds.), *Image Ethics in the Digital Age*, Minneapolis: University of Minnesota Press, pp. 71–93.

NBC (2007), 'Statement from NBC News on the Decision to Air the Video and Photographs from the Virginia Tech Gunman', http://www.11alive.com/news/article_news.aspx?storyid=95667. Accessed 31 October 2010.

Pew (2009), 'Public Evaluations of the News Media: Press Accuracy Rating Hits Two Decade Low', Washington, D.C.: Pew Research Center for the People and the Press, http://peoplepress.org/report/543/. Accessed 31 Oct 2010.

Preti, A. (2008), 'School Shooting As a Culturally Enforced Way of Expressing Suicidal Hostile Intention', *Journal of the American Academy of Psychiatry and the Law*, 36: 4, pp. 544–50.

Räty, R. (2010), Interview, 31 May.

Rosenblad, L. (2010), Interview, 9 June.

Ruokangas, H. (2010), Interview, 3 June.

Simpson, R. and Cote, W. (2006), *Covering Violence: A Guide to Ethical Reporting About Victims and Trauma*, New York: Columbia University Press.

Sipilä, J. (2010), Interview, 3 June.

Sumiala, J. (2009), 'Networked Diasporas: Circulating Imaginaries of Violence', *The Romanian Review of Journalism and Communication*, IV: 4, pp. 75–80.

Sumiala, J. and Hakala, S. (2010), 'Crisis: Mediatization of Disaster in the Nordic Media Sphere', in þ. Broddason, U. Kivikuru, B. Tufte, L. Weibull and H. Østbye (eds), *The Nordic Countries and the World: Perspectives from Research on Media and Communication*, Göteborg: Nordicom, pp. 361–78.

Part III

Circulations

Chapter 9

Visual Blowback: Soldier Photography and the War in Iraq

Liam Kennedy

The rapid developments in digital media technologies, contemporaneous with the wars in Afghanistan and Iraq, have facilitated the explosion of imagery documenting violent international conflict and the real time experiences of warfare normally beyond the gaze of the media and of their audiences. The now infamous imagery of abuses at Abu Ghraib was produced by participants and bystanders, not conventional journalists, and circumvented established forms of news production and dissemination. Hugely important as Abu Ghraib is as an instance of the documenting of abuse and of the biopolitical power of the United States at war, though, it is but one example of the visual 'blowback' from Iraq as imagery of the making and conduct of warfare is produced and disseminated by varied individuals and groups. This includes the imagery produced by civilians in the war zones and by serving US soldiers, who have diverse reasons for documenting their experience and disseminating that imagery globally.

This 'amateur' imagery is disruptive of the conventional flows of news and has become a major issue of concern for both military and media elites. For the military, the primary concern is over operational security though there are many related concerns about access to information and freedom of speech. For the media, it is disturbing as it circumvents their traditional channels and frames of production and representation, and even threatens the professional standing of journalists (perhaps especially of photojournalists). To be sure, the explosion of vernacular imagery of international conflict does not in itself subvert the understandings of war and foreign policy so powerfully framed by military and media elites. There is an ongoing struggle over the framings and interpretations of such imagery, with both the military and the media working to neuter the inherent challenges of citizen journalism by incorporating it into established frames of presentation. However, there can be no doubt that the advent of digital photography, of cameraphones and of photoblogging has altered the dynamics between image-makers, the medium and the audience.

Within this larger picture I want to focus on one example of the production and dissemination of vernacular imagery in Afghanistan and Iraq that has not received as much critical attention as the Abu Ghraib imagery, that of serving US soldiers who are photographing their experiences and posting them on the Internet. Soldiers are doing this in large numbers, some within dedicated web clusters, others in a more ad hoc fashion, and they are creating something new in the process. These images have a distinctive visual language, blending the genres of institutional, touristic and war photography into a new type of soldier photography. This form of visual communication – in real time and communal – is new in the representation of warfare; in earlier wars soldiers took photographs, but these were not immediately shared in the way websites can disseminate images globally. Digital cameras, cameraphones and photoblogs are the media that have proved visually commensurate to the war in Iraq, and the soldiers using them are truly 'embedded' photographers. This digital generation of soldiers exists in a new relationship to their experience of war; they are now potential witnesses and sources within the documentation of events, not just the imaged actors – a blurring of roles that reflects the correlations of revolutions in military and media affairs.

The digitalization of war imagery has introduced a fascinating uncertainty into the documentation of warfare that is exacerbated by the disintegration of discrete categories and genres of visual information in the digital age. There is an ongoing blurring of the boundaries between news and entertainment, between media and public diplomacy, between professional and amateur journalism and between modes and genres of photographic representation. This blurring of boundaries characterizes the instability of contemporary visual fields and also renders the visualization of the United States at war a potentially volatile representation. It also troubles common assumptions about the role of photography as a discrete medium of representation in relation to conflict and warfare. Documentary news photography and photojournalism have long invested in the idea of 'bearing witness' in war and conflict contexts. Today, the proliferation of amateur imagery of such contexts presses us to rethink the role of photography as a form of documentary witness to our shared humanity or inhumanity. Next, I will examine some of the functions of soldier photography, analyse genres and conventions at work in them and consider some of the implications of the opening of real-time windows on the American soldier at war.

Blogs of War

American soldiers have diverse motivations for producing imagery of their experiences in Afghanistan and Iraq and there are several platforms for the dissemination of the photographs. The most common functions of the imagery are to communicate with family member and friends in the United States and to provide alternative imagery of the war zone to that being produced by mainstream media. For some, the focus is on everyday life on the base; for others, it is to produce imagery that challenges viewers to see the 'real' war. Most want to share their personal stories and perspectives and they frequently register a sense of compulsion, fuelled in some part by the technology, to record their experiences and in particular the everyday happenings around them. This compulsion is also a response to the popular American culture they still interact with and in which the recording of personal diaries is a common practice, facilitated by digital technologies.

Soldiers send a great deal of imagery to family and friends via e-mail or burned to CDs. Much of this, as with soldier imagery of earlier wars, remains invisible, contained within family networks and memories. However, a great deal of the imagery is shared more publicly, especially through blogging formats. Blogs function as an interactive media of communication that operate in real-time and create potential for new relationships between soldiers and the home front, both its private and public spheres. While pro-military and pro-war perspectives are common and strongly asserted as a collective identity in the milblogging world, there are soldiers using blogs to express alternative views, some overtly political, others questioning the culture of military life. Several blogs have provided moving narratives about their author's post-traumatic stress disorder. However, the great majority of soldier bloggers eschew overt commentary on the conduct or effects of the war. Following the diary format, they tend to focus on their everyday thoughts and experiences, and these too are dispatches from the war zones.

Photographs provide something more than visual illustrations of textual diaries or other blogging commentaries. In many instances they are not accompanied by text but posted on photoblogs designed for online presentation of visual diaries. This visualization of war experiences adds another dimension to the blogging soldier phenomenon, providing a form of documentation and expression that has a deep 'reality-effect' in its impact and the assumptions made by those who make and respond to the imagery. It is in the presentation of images that the authenticity of the soldier's perspective is underscored, the 'reality' of their experience lending a sense of veracity to their representations of that experience. The 'real war' is signified either in the graphic depictions of violent confrontations or, more candidly and compellingly, in the mundane habitats and actions of everyday soldier life.

For the same reason, it is photographic imagery that has caused the most unease within the military. The abuses in Abu Ghraib were textually documented and known in this form to human rights organizations and the American military and political leaders before the digital photographs appeared in the public realm. It was the images that ignited an outcry and continue to haunt the architects and supporters of the war (see Levi-Strauss 2004). An early example of this unease about soldiers posting visual material on the Internet was evident in the military censuring of Jason Hartley, a National Guardsman whose blog, titled 'Just Another Soldier', included many photographs of his experiences on tour and at base. Hartley posted several graphic images, including one of troops setting fire to a dead dog, which he described as 'a common place to hide explosives'. He also posted images that represented his acerbic perspective on military culture, including an image depicting himself and a comrade sitting on toilets with their pants down, 'performing synchronized bowel movements' (Hartley 2009). The image that finally activated official censure was one of a man detained at the scene of a blast in 2004. Hartley was asked by his commander to remove the blog but surreptitiously continued and was eventually discovered and punished with a fine and demotion. He was told he had violated the Geneva Convention by posting pictures of detainees on the Internet. Today, the image of the detainee remains on his blog site but with the word 'GENEVA' printed in bold across the top half of the man's face.

While there are examples of soldiers posting material that has commanders raising concerns about operational security, the great majority of imagery is focused on everyday experiences of the war zone, some violent but most of it focused on the day-to-day activities of their lives. Sean Dustman, a Navy hospital corpsman, runs a popular photoblog titled

'Doc in the Box'. He posts large numbers of images regularly and acts as photographer for his unit, with families of his comrades leaving comments on his site thanking him for the images of loved ones. Dustman comments on his role: 'I've always been a shutterbug, and it grew to the point that my guys always wanted copies of my pictures. It was easier posting them online than giving out individual pictures or e-mailing them. Three-hundred-eighty marines – too much work for one person to handle without it being a full-time job. So here I am, the unit's unofficial photographer' (Herbert 2004). Sites like Dustman's, or that run by Debby Prieve of the 101st Airborne who has constructed an extensive photo gallery over the past five years, follow the format of milblogging sites generally, while focusing on visual documentation. The communicative functions of their images are primarily those of bearing witness and providing visual documentation of the lives of a military community to extended families. While much of this is upbeat it can also focus on grief and death and provide a symbolic site for mourning. A common example is the imagery of memorials to dead comrades, and particularly the ritual of placing the dead soldier's rifle in their boots, with their helmet and dog tags on top of the rifle. As these sites grow – both as individual sites and as a loose communicative network of similar sites, shared both in the war zones and domestically – they are becoming significant archives, electronic sites of collective memory that are a new feature in the history of the documentation of soldiers at war.

Many other soldiers post images of their experiences on the Internet in a less formal or regular way. Popular photoblogging sites such as flickr and fotopages have many thousands of images posted by serving soldiers (just as soldiers are sending video imagery of their experiences to sites such as YouTube and My Space). The communicative functions of these images vary greatly. Again, we see many image banks devoted to pictures of friends and colleagues that are primarily intended to be shared with units and families, but also images depicting humorous or absurd moments in unit life, or emotional or violent moments that the photographer felt motivated to share with a larger audience. Few would seem to fit the conventional frames of visual journalism, yet the urge to document and to disseminate the material is strongly expressed by those posting the images.

'Debbie Does Saddam's Palace'

In the 'amateur' imagery being produced by serving soldiers much of the content is mundane and everyday depictions of their lives, yet these images suggestively trace the values and perspectives of the American soldier at war. These are traced not only in the overt content of the imagery but also in its compositions and generic frames and references; that is, the photographs show not only what the soldiers see but how they look at the world around them, what they felt curious about, what they valued, what they found significant. Much of what they photograph is simply unavailable to the professional news photographer, either because they would lack the access or simply not value the perspective. The mundane nature of the imagery resides in part in the rigours and rhythms of everyday soldiery – whether on patrols checking for roadside bombs, or relaxing in barracks. It is also an aesthetic effect of its framing and production, as the documentary impetus is shaped by snapshot compositions and styling. Yet it is this very amateurism that heightens the reality effects – of immediacy and authenticity – already so powerfully signified by the sense of looking inside an otherwise closed subculture.

Certain visual tropes and categories of photograph are apparent. A tourist frame is very common, with images depicting smiling soldiers posing in the desert, or in front of ancient monuments, or murals, or statues. There are also many images devoted to natural landscapes – desert sunsets are a favourite – and to animals (mostly camels and lizards) and insects. In the photographs in which soldiers pose for the camera they adopt conventional postures of tourist photography, but there is some incongruity in their wearing full military uniforms and carrying weapons. This tourist frame is closely linked to 'trophy pictures' that depict soldiers in proximity of buildings or belongings associated with Saddam Hussein or his family. There are many such images, including soldiers in sports cars said to belong to

Figure 9.1: 'Debbie Does Saddam's Palace'. Copyright – Debbie Prieve. Source: Website 'Pictures from the 101st Airborne', http://www.pbase.com/sms/101st_airborne.

Hussein's sons, posing in opulent palaces belonging to the family, or swimming in palace pools.

Touristic imagery has such a widespread presence in the Iraq-based soldier photography that it is suggestive of a strong sense of estrangement from the culture. The work of the camera signifies and offsets this in two related ways: as touristic interest in landmark sites and scenes and as the more imperial gaze of a victorious, occupying force. We see the restrictions placed on the American soldiers' lives through the spatial compositions in the imagery, and we also see the limitations in their perspectives on cultural difference. On patrols, the distance from and distrust of local people is often very clear from the camera position and angles. Often, this is due to the care required during a sweep for roadside bombs or house searches but it is apparent that the distance is often an overt visual objectification of 'others' as enemy or unknowable subjects. Cultural difference and respect (or lack of) is often signified visually. In a photograph taken by Petty Officer Brian Aho, we see a group of young Iraqi women walking towards the camera and passing a lone National Guardsman walking in the opposite direction. They do not look at each other. The photographer comments, 'We didn't approach [local women], we didn't talk to them. We weren't supposed to look at them. We weren't supposed to take many photographs of them either' (Friedman 2006: 125). At such points the camera becomes both an anthropological instrument and an indicator of imperial curiosity.

A great volume of imagery shared online by serving soldiers is removed even further from Iraqi culture, focused on life at the barracks or bases occupied by the soldiers. We see them playing electronic games, watching DVDs, or playing cards, bathing, or shaving or cutting each other's hair, playing ballgames or napping in their bedrooms or makeshift cots. Much of the activity seems designed to offset boredom. McKinney observes, '[Y]ou could argue boredom was the hardest thing to deal with over there. You just try to find something to do. Telling stories, watching movies, even doing laundry. Dirty-water laundry, which probably made your clothes dirtier. But still, anything to keep your mind occupied' (Friedman 2006: 160). While this imagery does not say anything directly about the war in Iraq, it does function as a documentary representation of more private aspects of the soldiers' lives and their interpersonal relations and of the ways in which they 'domesticate' certain spaces. Within the barracks there are many signifiers of their efforts to create more private spaces, especially in their sleeping areas which are often surrounded by pinned-up images from American popular and pornographic cultures.

Humour is a key feature of the barracks and base imagery – again, suggesting the need to offset boredom – and it takes many forms. There are some images linked to public figures and the politics of the war, such as the photograph of a bobblehead of George W. Bush on a Humvee, while another depicts two soldiers holding up a sign in late 2004 reading 'Fuck Michael Moore, Go George Bush'. Also common is frat-style humour, with soldiers pictured sitting on toilets, or using military paraphernalia as humorous props. There is a notable interest in play and performance within these more humorous scenarios – performing for the camera as much as for unit colleagues. This is evident in the many images depicting

Halloween and other festivals, with soldiers invariably dressed in makeshift costumes – many of these events are filmed as well as photographed and often set to music. It is also evident in imagery of sporting play, of impromptu football and basketball games and wrestling matches. In all of these and other ways the soldiers are alleviating boredom, releasing stress and confirming their camaraderie. They are also playing out rituals of military and especially male military culture.

Pornographies of Vision

Within that culture, of course, there are subcultural netherworlds that are only rarely documented visually, but that too is changing due to digital image-making. There can be no doubt that the most controversial imagery produced by soldier photographers is the more graphic representations of their violent war experiences. This takes several forms. Most of the battle imagery is distant from enemy bodies, depicting bombs going off or the aftermath of a bomb or firefight. Usually, these are images passed by public affairs officers and soldiers are aware more graphic material would be censored. However, there are also many examples of more graphic imagery appearing on the Internet. A common example is images of dead bodies (presumed Iraqi, possibly insurgent, though this is not always made clear) shot from the middle distance, or with the body filling the frame, or of close-ups of wounds and fragments of bodies. The more gruesome close-ups do not enter mainstream media platforms. Rather, they are posted within small communal networks among soldiers and if posted online appear in sites dedicated to the presentation of such imagery. It is difficult to tell how widespread the practices of taking and posting the more graphic imagery is as it is rarely attributed and the need to circumvent various censors creates considerable confusion about the sources and volume of the imagery.

Pornographic codes often become explicit in the production and dissemination of this gruesome imagery. There are now websites devoted to pornographic images relating to the Iraq War and the American military presence there; many stock visual scenarios are enacted in these image repertoires, many of them violent. Perhaps more disturbing and more indicative of the impact of digital media on the representation of war are the images US soldiers are posting of dead and mutilated Iraqi bodies. The most famous example is a website titled 'Now That's Fucked Up' (now removed from the Internet), which offered US troops in Iraq and Afghanistan free access to its menu of amateur porn in return for their photos of death and violence in war. There were many photos posted on the site, many of them close up photographs of dead bodies that had been torn apart by weaponry. The webmaster of the site claimed that 30,000 US soldiers used the site and defended it as a 'community' site representing the 'soldier's slant' on war: 'This is directly from the soldiers' point of view. They can take a digital camera and take a picture and send it to me, and that's the most raw you can get it. I like to see it from their point of view, and I think it's newsworthy' (Glaser 2005). The connections between war, violence and porn notwithstanding, I think the webmaster may be right and that these soldiers turned to the web in an attempt to make sense of what they were doing in Iraq – and so, the photographs function as desperate, deadly articulation of their fears and desires. This is to suggest the photographs register the 'optical unconscious' of American policies in Iraq, refiguring 'unknown knowns' of American culture, what Slavoj Zizek (2005) defines as 'the disavowed beliefs, suppositions and obscene practices we pretend not to know about, even though they form the background of our public values'(see also Kennedy 2008).

A case could be made that the soldiers' repetitive creation and use of violent images are symptoms of an affective reliving of traumatic war experience, serving at once to authenticate and cancel out a hurtful reality (Andén-Papadopoulos 2009). At the very least, we should consider here the underlying question of this chapter: what is the function of photography in representing and mediating soldiers' experiences, however extreme or exceptional these may be? The simple answer is this: the documentary impulse, the drive to document, to take a picture in order to authenticate what you are experiencing. The more complex, paradoxical answer is that the soldiers took photographs in order not to see. The paradox of this photographic act is echoed throughout the imagery and commentary by US soldiers on the Now that's Fucked Up site. But the most significant evidence of this function of photography among US soldiers in Iraq is in the detailed testimonies of soldiers at Abu Ghraib prison who took the infamous images of abuse. These testimonies have become available due to the work of Errol Morris and Philip Gourevitch – Morris' film and Gourevitch's book, both titled *Standard Operating Procedure* – drawing on hundreds of hours of interviews conducted by Morris.

In both texts the motivations of the soldiers conducting and photographing the abuse are explored. Gourevitch focuses particularly on Specialist Sabrina Harmon of the 372nd Military Police company who took many of the most famous images. He notes with some sympathy her alarm at what she witnessed and her stated aim to document it with a vague idea of exposing wrong, but he shows that 'she managed gradually to subtract herself from the scenes she sketched', to reposition herself 'as an outsider at Abu Ghraib, an observer and recorder [...]. In this way she preserved her sense of innocence [...] to Harman, taking pictures was a way of deflecting her own humiliation in the transaction – by taking ownership of her position as a spectator' (Gourevitch and Morris 2008: 104).

I am wary of conflating the imagery of Abu Ghraib abuse with the atrocity images on the Now That's Fucked Up site, but there are certain commonalities that are inescapable. Firstly, in both instances the act of photography functions to both authenticate and distance the reality of what is imaged. Secondly, in both instances, the images illuminate aspects of American military culture that are officially disavowed and only rarely documented. The more obscene practices of the military at war, accentuated by conditions of stress and trauma, remain largely hidden. Thirdly, in both instances, the motivations of the US soldiers have been widely interpreted as individual or collective pathologies, so delimiting further investigation of what is at issue. The role of photography is significant in both instances, for what it both reveals and conceals about the 'reality' of American soldiers at war. The images produced are deeply disturbing depictions of what is disavowed within American military culture yet haunt it in sublimated forms of physical and psychological violence. Here, perhaps, reside some of the deepest 'reality-effects' of soldier culture – as a lived system of values and assumptions, and as a representation – as well as the paradox of a visual mode of representation that registers the authenticity of the human in the most dehumanizing imagery imaginable.

While the explicit abuse and violence of the images from Abu Ghraib and those posted on Now That's Fucked Up set them apart from the mainstream of soldier photography, they are also closely linked to this mainstream. The detachment – the empty gaze – evident in the violent imagery is also present in much of the more mundane imagery produced by American soldiers in Iraq. The tourist frame that we considered earlier recurs as a motif of this detachment – much of Harman's photo imagery of Iraq prior to her move to Abu Ghraib is made up of tourist-style images. This is not to suggest that the wish to document conceals perverse, violent desires among all soldiers who use a camera. Rather, it signals the continuity of the occupier's gaze as an abstracted signifier of their imperial presence in Iraq.

Many soldiers comment on this sense of detachment. Javal Davis, one of the soldiers at Abu Ghraib during the abuse though not active in it, comments:

> Everyone in theatre had a digital camera. Everyone was taking pictures of everything, from detainees to death. Like in Vietnam where guys were taking pictures of the dead guy with a cigarette in his mouth. Like, 'Hey, Mom, look.' It sounds sick, but over there that was commonplace, it was nothing. The mind-set over there, I'd say, would be numb. I mean, when you're surrounded by death and carnage and violence twenty-four hours a day, seven days a week, it absorbs you […] .You could watch someone running down the street burning on fire, as long as it's not an American soldier, it's, 'Somebody needs to put that guy out.'
>
> (Gourevitch and Morris 2008: 56)

Davis' references to the Vietnam War suggest a continuity of experience and response by American soldiers in theatre, a numbing of ethical sensibilities as a consequence of their experiences in that theatre. However, I think the imagery produced by American soldiers in Iraq exceeds this (historical) explanation due to both the nature of the conflict and the technologies representing it. In this particular theatre, at this juncture in America's imperial history, the role of photography points up the changed conditions and perceptions of warfare for a digitized soldiery.

'A Dull Violence'

Not surprisingly, a number of soldiers have used photography to reflect upon some of their questions about their role in Afghanistan or Iraq and the effects of the wars on both soldiers and indigenous communities. Often, they foreground their roles as witnesses to disturbing realities and raise questions about their responsibilities, including responsibility for what they are looking at.

Jason Hartley in his blog, 'Just Another Soldier', occasionally provides tentative thoughts about the violent action of his colleagues. Following the killing of a civilian Iraqi family by US forces, who mistook them for insurgents, Hartley reflects on his inchoate feelings about such killings:

> As I try to fathom what it must feel like to be a poverty-stricken eight-year-old girl and experience the epic pain of your family suddenly and violently killed in front of you, I have to pause and ask myself, Now what am I doing here again? [...] . I've been stewing over this dead family things for couple of weeks now. I've been painstakingly mulling over in my mind the things these insurgents do and the things we, the US Army do and the unintutitive peculiarity of how the *drive* to be violent seems to precede the *purpose* to be violent and how rampant it is to meaninglessly develop one's identity through injury, but frankly I don't feel I've figured it all out well enough yet to even cludge together a coherent line of thought.
>
> (Hartley 2009)

Along with his commentary Hartley posts a photograph of one of the dead civilians. It is discretely composed, showing a bloodied torso lying beside what appears to be the door of a vehicle. The head of the body is not visible, possibly due to respect for the dead individual but also possibly due to security regulations. Although he does not comment on the image, it appears to supplement his desire to act as witness to an event he was not present at. He notes that he 'didn't see any of this first-hand' and adds 'I wish I had been there, to bear witness I suppose. So tell me, why would I wish for this?' (Hartley 2009). Hartley's commentary is a troubled and troubling reflection on the compulsion to visually document such experiences as a form of 'bearing witness'.

Some of the images being posted by serving soldiers have a more manifest journalistic quality and intent. There are a number of soldier photographers who have set out to create their own visual dispatches from the war front and supplement, if not challenge, mainstream reporting. One of the best of these is Jay Romano, who has extensively documented his tours in Iraq since 2005 and posted many of the results on flickr. By carefully editing for online posting only several hundred of the 18,000 images he claims to have taken, Romano has produced several sets of imagery that establish thematic and stylistic traits that become recognizable looking across his work. A prominent and consistent theme in his photographs is imagery of improvised explosive device (IED) explosions, which he often captures in the middle distance during the fullness of a blast. The images are remarkably crisp and composed given the immediacy of the event and that they are usually shot from inside an armoured vehicle. On his adeptness at capturing these explosions on camera, he comments: 'When it comes to balancing the soldiering and photographing, the act of looking and seeing has helped both. I can only say this because of the results. In comparison with my peers, I can locate 300% more IEDs. Why? It's because I'm looking for images, not that I have a gift or am working with the insurgency as some of the guys tell me' (Romano 2009). This compulsion to look for images (rather than to snapshot what randomly occurs) sets his work apart from many soldier photographers and lends it both depth and insight. The work is not political but it is more engaged with the contexts of the war on the ground than most.

Romano is a little unusual among soldier photographers in that he had already had training as a photojournalist before going to Iraq. He acknowledges that there can be tension between his military role and his journalistic sensibility but asserts his primary allegiance to the army and dryly notes 'with journalists being as rare as a unit function sponsored by Budweiser [...] how can I not take on the burden of documentation' (Romano 2009). The quality of his imagery stands out from much soldier photography due to the quality of the equipment he uses but also due to his skills in composition and other techniques. As noted, much of his imagery is of scenes viewed from moving military vehicles. This can lead to blurred or banal imagery by many soldier photographers but Romano is able to produce clearly focused shots that capture remarkable street scenes and the expressions on the faces of Iraqis nearby. The distance that is so much a feature of this imagery is maintained but also becomes a stylistic device in Romano's work (with conscious references to the genre of street photography), so that he uses it to signify the ways in which being a soldier frames particular experience of the war zone and encounters with indigenous peoples.

Posting images of his last tour in Iraq, Romano selected one image for particular emphasis as symbolic of the distance between the Americans and the Iraqis. It depicts a young street sweeper staring at the photographer. Of this image he remarks:

I will always remember the countless blank stares received from the people we were supposed to be helping, supporting and fighting for [...]. If this was my life, my world [...] the indifference makes sense. For a pseudo-American civilian life I've now found myself in, these stares have left me guilty. There's a certain detachment many of us 'over there' have spoken about during our time over there. And it is true if you look at how

Figure 9.2: 'Purgatory Road'. Mosul, Iraq 2008. Copyright – Jay Romano. Source: Website: http://www.flickr.com/photos/70355737@N00/

we have evolved our war fighting. I come home and see where this indifference and detachment has come from.

(Romano 2009)

Such reflections denote a critical self-consciousness about his dual roles as soldier and photographer, and also about the relations between colonizer and colonized. In this image, the blank stare of the sweeper obliquely mirrors the empty gaze of the occupying forces, emphasizing the indifference and detachment of the latter. Notably, Romano associates this detachment with new forms of warfare and the sense of distance they instil in both warfront soldiers and homefront citizens. Another image by Romano powerfully, if quietly, reflects upon this sense of distance. It depicts his desk in the corner of a dimly lit tent in his station in Iraq. On the desk is his open laptop, which displays a pornographic image of a naked woman. Romano's short statement posted with the image reads: 'My new home, simple yet utilitarian. All madness usually begins and ends right here'. A poster on the flickr site leaves a comment: 'Strong picture, it could be a metonymy of the soldier's condition. The dim light, the rough set-up, the empty chair, the obscene desktop wallpaper, all these elements produce an atmosphere of dull violence, in complete contrast of your description of the place as a "home" […]'. Romano responds:

It's an interesting place to say the least. Much of my time here it feels as if the war is so far away […]. A lot of what has happened in the last seven months seems to start coming out of the closet so to speak. I think with a lot of time on my hands more images like this will start surfacing […]. I like your description on how it is a 'dull violence'. I never really thought about it but that's how it feels. You know it's there but it's just not actually happening.

(Romano 2009)

This is a suggestive exchange, indicating not only a soldier's sense of distance from 'the war', but also the collapse of distance between the warfront and the homefront. It also suggests that this image references what is commonly disavowed in representations of American military culture. What it depicts is not only a metonymy of the soldier's condition in Iraq but a primal site for the screening of soldiers' fears and desires – what is 'surfacing' in and through such images is the optical unconscious of US policy in Iraq.

Conclusion

Ultimately, the historical significance of soldier photography may reside less in the controversial or revelatory images (though some of these will undoubtedly take on iconic status) but in the mundane images, in the documentation of the environments, activities and feelings of American soldiery at war, especially in more ordinary moments. These images constitute a chronicle of what American soldiers desired and feared, of what they avowed and disavowed, of 'the things they carried' (O'Brien 1990). This material is slowly building into what will become one of the most complete archival records of the experience of war. We have yet to learn to see it and to understand it.

For now, this photography offers compelling, real-time perspectives on the American soldier at war that suggestively supplement other forms of visual knowledge about the conflicts in Iraq and Afghanistan and indicate the effects of such 'amateur' documentation on our understanding of war today. In particular, the compulsion to visually document war experiences – vividly illustrated above – suggests a new invigoration of the documentary impulse to bear witness to otherness, an impulse long shaped by colonial and postcolonial conditions of power and knowledge. Assumptions about the reciprocity of attachments and identifications in documentary image-making – focused on the idea and image of the human – still have great force in media reportage and in broader western depictions of war, conflict and human rights abuses (especially in organization of narratives of humanitarianism) but they are losing the power to explain what we are looking at. In some part, it is the failure of this way of seeing that is encoded in the imagery from Iraq and Afghanistan – a failure that is exacerbated not so much by these wars as by the conditions of 'perpetual war' that underlie and drive these particular imperial adventures. What we see in Romano's image of his 'home' in Iraq is the mise-en-scène of the war in that country as the epicentre of a perpetual war, where the boundaries between soldier and civilian, between actor and observer, between home and war and between here and there have collapsed. This perpetual war has dislocated the ethical registers of temporal and spatial distance that structured and promulgated particular ways of seeing and understanding America's international relations. Today, like the soldiers taking these photographs, we live in the perpetual present of a war that exists in real time and for which we have as yet no adequate ethical gauge of our human affiliations. Amateur soldier photography mimics this lack, reminding us of the limits of our knowledge formations and ethical imaginations.

The US military is attempting to contain the uncertainties that the digitalization of war imagery has introduced into the documentation of warfare. There is an ongoing effort by the military to exploit the public relations potential of soldier blogging; they know that the troops can function as effective, credible advocates for the operations in Iraq and elsewhere. Major Elizabeth Robins, a leading Public Affairs officer, notes: 'The primary reason to support milblogs is that they reveal the human face of the army' (Robins 2007). A similar reasoning shapes the approach of military public affairs to soldiers' use of photography and video imagery. In 2007 The Multi-National Force in Iraq set up a channel on YouTube (see http://www.youtube.com/MNFIRAQ). According to a statement on the site, it has been created 'to give viewers around the world a "boots on the ground" perspective of Operation Iraqi Freedom from those who are fighting it'. On flickr, there are regular postings by 'soldiermediacenter' (see http://www.flickr.com/photos/soldiersmediacenter) which posts thousands of military photographs 'drawn from a variety of Defense department sources. These photos capture the essence of our Soldiers, living the Warrior Ethos and answering the call to Duty'. In each instance, the emphasis is on the soldier's perspective as the real, the authentic, the credible. The reality-effects of the image are a potent currency in media and public relations terms.

These initiatives are an element of the US military's evolving communications approach to the war. They recognize that the soldier bloggers and image-makers can function as a form of soft power, humanizing the activity of the United States at war. They are also learning that by providing the soldiers with more and more access and information they can bypass the mainstream media and disseminate positive messages and images about the conduct and course of the war. This is not a smooth process though as it goes against the instincts of military strategists and the organizational culture of the military. As a former public affairs officer at the Pentagon puts it: 'How do you balance an organization that's bent on command and control with a medium that inherently has none? It's the million dollar question' (Glaser 2007). The search for an answer is now seen as imperative within powerful sectors of the military. It is at one with the recognition that the making and representing of war in the digital age are so closely entwined as to be inseparable, and the 'image wars' of the twenty-first century must be fought within and across multiple media platforms and publics.

References

Andén-Papadopoulos, K. (2009), 'Body Horror on the Internet: US Soldiers Recording the War in Iraq and Afghanistan', *Media, Culture & Society*, 31: 6, pp. 921–38.

Friedman, D. (ed.) (2006), *This Is Our War: Servicemen's Photographs of Life in Iraq*, New York: Artisan.

Glaser, M. (2005), 'Porn Site Offers Soldiers Free Access in Exchange for Photos of Dead Iraqis', *Online Journalism Review*, 20, www.ojr.org/ojr/stories/050920glaser. Accessed 20 November 2010.

Glaser, M. (2007), 'Milbloggers Upset With Restrictions, But Won't Stop Blogging', Mediashift, 23 May 2007, http://www.pbs.org/mediashift/2007/05/digging_deepermilbloggers_upse.html. Accessed 15 November 2010.

Gourevitch, P. and Morris, E. (2008), *Standard Operating Procedure*, London: Picador.

Hartley, J. (2009), Just Another Soldier, http://blog.justanothersoldier.com/. Accessed 25 November 2010.

Hebert, J. (2004), 'The Front Line Online', *The San Diego Union Tribune*, 18 July, http://www.signonsandiego.com/uniontrib/20040718/news_blogcpy.html. Accessed 21 September 2010.

Kennedy, L. (2008), 'Securing Vision: Photography and US Foreign Policy', *Media, Culture & Society*, 30: 3, pp. 279–94.

Levi-Strauss, D. (2004), *Abu Ghraib: The Politics of Torture*, New York: North Atlantic Books.

O'Brien, T. (1990), *The Things They Carried*, New York: Houghton, Mifflin, Harcourt.

Robins, E. L. (2007), 'Muddy Boots IO: The Rise of Soldier Blogs', *Military Review*, September-October 2007, http://www.au.af.mil/au/awc/awcgate/milreview/robbins.pdf. Accessed 21 June 2010.

Romano, J. (2009), http://www.flickr.com/photos/70355737@N00/. Accessed 9 August 2010.

Zizek, S. (2005), 'The Empty Wheelbarrow', *The Guardian*, 20 February, p. 22.

Chapter 10

In Amateurs We Trust: Readers Assessing Non-Professional News Photographs

Liina Puustinen and Janne Seppänen

The current flow of amateur photographs to the pages of newspapers challenges the visual monopoly of professional photojournalism and poses many questions. What is the future of professional photojournalism? How to edit non-professional pictures and verify that they are taken according to the codes of reliable photojournalism? And, finally, do readers trust images taken by non-professionals?

Journalists themselves strongly hold that it is important to preserve and maintain readers' trust in news photographs, whether they are taken by amateurs or professionals. In order to achieve this, media houses have launched different kinds of codes of conduct to limit the digital editing (Mäenpää and Seppänen 2010). However, nobody really know whether readers trust news images in the first place, and if they do, what the real substance of this faith, reliance or confidence is. In this chapter we ask the following question: what kinds of trust do readers afford to amateur news photographs?

We conducted 30 qualitative individual interviews with readers of print and online newspapers. To affix the interview situation to concrete media content, the respondents were exposed to examples of published amateur news images. In semi-structured interviews, the informants discussed their trust in news images from various angles. They were also directly asked what kinds of trust they afford to amateur pictures.

We read the interviews and distinguished the most relevant ways – Goffmanian frames – to discuss the informants' notion of trust. At the same time, we tried to understand these articulations in the light of pertinent theoretical insights, especially those provided by the sociologist Niklas Luhmann (1988). From this base, we have discerned four frames of trust: *silent trust*, *measured trust*, *contextual trust* and *doubt*.

These frames penetrate the whole interview material horizontally, which means that the individual respondent may use different frames as the interview proceeds. Hence, she or he is not fixed in a clear-cut 'de-coding' position (cf. Hall 1996). On the contrary, the articulation of trust is a dynamic process which is constantly renegotiated. Hence, we argue, the question of trust cannot be covered with binary yes/no answers but it needs to be seen as a multidimensional – sometimes contradictory – social and psychic process.

Amateur Photographs in News

Amateur news photography is a clear example of how media companies encourage people to take part in the content creation of journalism. For the companies, the participation provides a means to advance a loyal, intimate and trustworthy relationship with the audiences. Honest conversation and passionate collaboration are seen to instil respect and trust in the relationship between both parties (e.g. Bowman and Willis 2003: 53; Hermida and Thurman 2008).

However, there are also more down-to-earth reasons to allow citizens' content to enter into the realm of professional journalism. The all-pervasive presence of personal cameraphones has expanded the recordable visibility of the whole society, and the competition *forces* the news media to use first-hand amateur pictures from the news scenes. In previous studies, journalists and editors have been interviewed to find out how and why amateur photographs and videos are used in the established news in online, broadcast and print context (Pantti and Bakker 2009). However, audiences' views on amateur news images have not been studied in depth. In Finland, Janne Matikainen (2009) conducted a survey where the respondents were asked whether they considered veracious the amateur images and videos published in online and print press. According to the survey, 54% of the respondents disagreed, 34% felt neutral and only 14% agreed with the statement (pp. 83–84.) The results give only a suggestive answer because the concept of trust itself remains poorly elaborated and operationalized when using simple, rating scale variables. Karin Wahl-Jorgensen, Andrew Williams and Claire Wardle's (2010) study on audiences' views on user-generated content (UGC), conducted with an extensive survey of the users on BBC's news website and a series of audience focus groups, partly resonates with our study (see their chapter in this book). The study focuses on why and how audiences value news-based UGC (still images, footage and eyewitness accounts), which are perceived as authentic, immediate and 'real'. The results touch upon the question of trust by implying that the inclusion of amateur material decreases the lack of public trust in the institution of journalism.

Trust itself is a concept that has been a subject of ample debate among social scientists in the last 20 years. In order to understand our interviewees' multidimensional discourses of trust, we need to explore its social dynamics.

Trust, Society and Media

Anthony Giddens (1990), Adam Seligman (1997) and Pierre Rosanvallon (2008), among others, have written about the role of trust in today's society. Giddens uses the term 'abstract systems' to describe expertise-based late-modern social institutions involved, for example, with health care and maintenance of the technical infrastructure of society. The whole existence of society and the reproduction of social order are dependent on citizens' capability to trust in the basic institutions of a society. Social upheavals may take place if the trust is undermined considerably (Giddens 1990: 83). Media can be seen as a one abstract system among others whose importance has actually increased within the mediatization (see Couldry 2008) of the other social institutions and the whole society. For example, the trustworthiness of a big company heavily depends on its public image.

Anthony Coleman and his fellow researchers also emphasize the importance of trust in today's society (Coleman, Anthony and Morrison 2009). They draw upon Rosanvallon's thinking and define three vital functions for trust in the context of news media: first, trust serves as an 'institutional economizer' that decreases the need for procedures of verification and proof. 'We need to be able to rely upon the reputation of the reporter without having to check and recheck every single account that is given to us' (ibid.: 4). Secondly, news media look after the connection between the representative government and the ordinary citizen: 'The ways in which news are produced, circulated and made sense of are intimately linked to the enactment of citizenship in confident, timid or withdrawn fashions' (ibid.). Thirdly, trust enables interaction with others (strangers) in a predictable manner: there are some basic rules and norms of conduct which base – more or less explicitly – on a mutual agreement. This means, in the context of journalism, that the readers of newspapers, for example, have certain expectations that journalists will deliver them correct information on the world. There is a kind of silent agreement between readers and news journalists, whom the readers normally do not know personally.

If the media and especially news organizations establish a part of society's abstract systems and governmental democracy, the trustworthiness of the media is an essential part of the legitimacy of the social system as a whole. However, there is ample evidence that the public's trust in (news) media is in decline (e.g. Vanacker and Belmas 2009; Harwood 2004; Tsfati and Cappella 2003). In recent years the capacity of the news media to reflect social reality and also take part in it has also been a subject of debate (Coleman, Anthony and Morrison 2009: 4). In most cases, the trust in news media has been studied under the label of media credibility or accuracy (Bentele 2008; Tsfati 2008). As we have already mentioned, these surveys do not recognize the flexibility of trust, or that its evolving disposition is affected by personal, situational, cultural, social and historical factors.

From our point of view, Niklas Luhmann's distinction between confidence and trust is useful. Both notions refer to expectations that may lapse into disappointments. Confidence is a silent and, in a sense, passive stance: 'You are confident that your expectations will not be disappointed: that politicians will try to avoid war, that cars will not break down or suddenly leave the street and hit you on your Sunday afternoon walk' (Luhmann1988: 97). People cannot live without forming expectations to contingent events and they tend to neglect, more or less, the possibility of disappointment. Trust, on the other hand, requires a previous engagement on your part and presupposes a situation of risk. If you do not consider alternatives, you are in a situation of confidence. If you choose one action in preference to others in spite of the possibility of being disappointed by the action of others, the situation can be defined as one of trust (ibid.: 97–98).

It is also obvious that the semiotic qualities of the photographic image affect how the question of trust is expressed in the interviews. As a sign – or as a combination of different signs – the unique attribute of photographic representation is indexicality. Charles Sanders Peirce (1960: 137) defined the indexical sign: 'If the Sign be an Index, we may think of it as a fragment torn away from the Object, the two in their existence being one whole or a part of such whole'. Peirce summarized his conception:

> Photographs, especially instantaneous photographs, are very instructive, because we know that they are in certain respects exactly like the objects they represent. But this resemblance is due to the photographs having been produced under such circumstances that they were physically forced to correspond point by point to nature. In that aspect, then, they belong to the second class of signs, those by physical connection.
>
> (Cit. in Doane 2007: 134)

Hence, the indexicality of the photographic image means that it has been a material part ('fragment torn away', 'physical connection') of the object it represents. This semiotic quality equips the photographic image with an exceptionally strong evidentiary potential, which could be used in different social practices. In a sense, the photograph works like a piece of circumstantial evidence (e.g. fingerprints), which is inevitably physically connected to the presence at the crime scene. This indexicality of the photographic image is an essential part of the photographic commonsense and a base for the trustworthiness of photographs. However, indexicality seldom is consciously expressed as such. It is part of our tacit expectations concerning the nature of the photographic image.

The indexical power of the photographic image has proved to be very useful in the service of different documentary practices – including journalism – from the mid-1800s onwards. Indexicality goes hand in hand with the eyewitnessing function of journalism (Zelizer 2007) and, hence, serves to authenticate the news story as such. It is the material evidence of 'having been there' at the actual scene of events as they took place.

From this point of view, it is understandable how strongly media houses react against the infringements on indexicality in the news context. Photojournalists have been fired after they have taken liberties to digitally manipulate their pictures in an inappropriate manner and, hence, violated the indexicality of the news photograph. Such infringements have undermined the trustworthiness of news photographs and media houses as well. As a consequence, news agencies and media houses have adopted different kinds of codes of conduct for photo editing to limit the threat caused by 'digital darkrooms' (Mäenpää and Seppänen 2010).

Study

This chapter covers a part of a larger study on audiences' trust in news images. We conducted 30 qualitative interviews with readers of print and online newspapers in Finland in 2009. The interviewees' age range is 15–65: there were equal numbers of men and women. The average length of an interview was 45 minutes. All the interviews have been recorded, transcribed and analysed with the qualitative tool of Atlas/ti. The informants were posed questions from various angles about their trust in news images. They were asked directly what kind of trust they afford to news images, and they were also shown examples of news photos to evoke more discussion. This is related to the method of photo elicitation, which renders the topic of the interview present and tangible (Rose 2007: 240-45). In these interviews the role of the news photo was even more important, as the reception, the viewing situation, was also the object of research. The topic discussed via photographs was the photographic image and the medium itself in the context of trust.

The interviewees were exposed to random examples of amateur news images in print and online newspapers. One of the pictures was from the print version of *Metro*, which is a free newspaper distributed in public transportation locations and on the streets. The image shows a car accident, which was taken at the moment when a person was falling out of the car. The other image was taken from *Kaleva.fi* which is the online version of a local newspaper in the north–west part of Finland. Also that picture was an illustration of a car accident showing cars demolished in wintery weather conditions. Some images shown in the interviews were chosen from the newspapers of the very same day of the interview. Both tabloid papers and quality newspapers were represented. However, we were not interested in analysing the images as such. The images served as examples of amateur photographs, and they were chosen only to elicit discussion on the phenomenon of citizen news photographing. Consequently, the interviewees were asked: What do you think about this new phenomenon of amateur news photography? Is there a difference in the trustworthiness of a news image taken by an amateur as compared to a professional? The interviews were analysed by a close reading method, dividing them first into emerging themes and then looking for how the informants talk about trust in amateur images.

For a closer analysis of the audience's trust articulations we used frame analysis, drawing from Erving Goffman (1974). The frames can be defined as culturally shared ways of structuring perceptions, understanding and talking about various issues and situations. Through framing, a person makes an interpretation and definition of the situation. People make observations of signs or cues through which they – both consciously and unconsciously – choose the frame of interpretation (pp. 25–27). The units of frame analysis can be various situations of social interaction. Our analysis will focus on the frames expressed in interview speech. In other words, we analyse the interview speech as text, as a written transcript, and therefore we will not consider the other situational factors.

Our findings on the frames of trust are closely related to Luhmann's (1988) ideas of confidence and trust. Yet, on the basis of the frame analysis of the interviews, we have named these as silent trust and measured trust. Moreover we found the process of trust more complicated and discerned two more frames which we call contextual trust and doubt. These frames are strongly present throughout our study and reflect the speech of our informants. Hence, our theoretical orientation has not dictated our reading of the interviews.

The frames of trust are not, of course, clear-cut categories, but they are often overlapping. The speaker might start speaking in a certain frame, then, quite rapidly move on to another. Moreover, we are aware that our analysis is also a way of framing the research object, the

Figure 10.1: Reader's picture in free newspaper *Metro* Helsinki, 27 May 2009 ('A car landed upside down after collision'). This image was shown to the interviewees as an example of amateur news photographs in Finnish newspapers. Permission to reproduce granted by Metro Helsinki newspaper.

interview speech. It needs to be kept in mind that the questions of the interviewer impose a certain frame to which the informants reply. In the following we will move on to analyse how the dynamics of the frames of trust are established when the informants talk about the amateur images.

Silent Trust – The Common Presupposition

Luhmann defines confidence as silent, unreflective and passive stance which is the baseline for relating to different issues and to other people. People cannot live without forming expectations on contingent events and they tend to neglect the possibility of disappointment

(Luhmann 1988: 97). Related to the idea of confidence the frame of silent trust is the dominant way in which the Finnish interviewees respond to news images in general. This happens when the interviewees discuss the news images: they describe what they see in the photo, they analyse the characters' poses, the colours or shades in the picture, they take guesses about what has happened in the situation of the photograph or talk about the background of the news story. But they do not talk about their relationship of trust regarding the news image. Hence, in most cases, they do not question the veracity of the photograph and they do not talk about their trust in the image before the interviewer asks them about it. Sometimes they bring up the question of trust because they have learned from the previous photo example that this is something they are asked about.

In the frame of silent trust, our interviewees very often talked about the incidents depicted in the photograph as if the image itself were an open window to the external reality. Also in case of the amateur news photographs, the informants described the elements and contexts of the image. They made guesses about what had happened before the car accidents, and why the photographer had been there right at the moment when it all happened. They talked about the image as if it were an indexical photographic evidence on what had happened. 'This seems like someone has really been on the spot', says one of the informants (male, 23 years). This raises the value of immediacy, as proof for having confidence in the image.

The emotions evoked by the image serve as evidence of its authenticity and immediacy, according to the informants. Often when the speaker follows the emotions aroused by the image, s/he silently accepts the veracity of the picture. For example, the informants talked about their feelings of grief and worry over the victims of the car accident depicted in the news image. This is exemplified in the following quotes:

Well, it is actually quite sad. Someone has apparently had very bad luck, I could imagine. This is some kind of everyday realism, which luckily I myself confront very seldom, but this is one possible outcome.

(Male, 40 years)

The topmost thought on my mind is that I hope all the people have survived.

(Female, 38 years)

The absence of the question of trust in the interview speech can be interpreted as a frame of silent trust. Of course, one could argue, silence does not guarantee trust. People can feel distrust without expressing it verbally. Therefore our analysis can only extend to what people *say* about their trust in news images. But it is also important to consider what they choose not to mention: what remains outside the chosen frame. Briefly, we define the frame of silent trust as an absence of doubt and an absence of a verbal recognition of the veracity of the news photograph or its context.

Measured Trust – Awareness of a Risk

To fully grasp and analyse the cultural frames of trust, there must be some talk about the issue. Therefore, the interviewer often had to ask questions to evoke discussion. Hence, our study simulated the process where silent and more or less self-evident confidence is gradually transformed into measured trust and expressed accordingly.

For Luhmann (1988: 97), trust requires a situation of risk: 'You may or may not buy a used car which turns out to be a "lemon"'. In contrast to silent confidence, he uses the word trust to refer to a reflective and active stance. We call this frame of measured trust when the person is making measures or evaluations about the possibility of trusting in something or someone. The possibility for disappointment is understood and pondered in one way or another. In this case, the situation of risk means that if the viewer decides to trust the news image s/he articulates the possibility of a risk of being deluded. For instance, there is a possibility that the image has been made to look authentic, but it could turn out to be digitally altered. The viewer's trust in the news medium and in the functioning of society, then, is at stake. If newspapers distort the news events, how do we get to know what is 'really' happening out there? Yet in choosing the frame of measured trust, we evaluate the situation and decide to take a risk, we trust in what we see and hear and act accordingly.

A majority of the respondents say that they have a trusting relationship to most news images and it does not make a difference if they are produced by professional or amateur photographers, or published in print or online papers. In the frame of measured trust the informants talk about their trust in news images, reflecting on their own feelings and saying they believe in the veracity of the image. They can, however, also evaluate the images from a critical distance and still express a relationship of measured trust.

The most common arguments expressed for the trustworthiness of amateur images are their authenticity and immediacy (see also Williams et al. in this book). The interviewees often percieved the poor quality of an image as a token of its authenticity. It proves that it is really taken by an amateur photographer who does not know how to shoot good photos. The composition is not optimal and very likely the photograph has been taken with a mobile phone camera. Also, the amateur is not expected to have the opportunities, abilities or software to do any image processing. This is illustrated in the following excerpt where the interviewee is looking at the news photo in the *Metro* newspaper:

> I think they could be more trustworthy in the sense that you can see that they are taken with a mobile phone. I don't think that this photographer has had the possibility to do any kind of manipulation. I think that someone has just happened to be on the spot, taken the photo and sent it in. I guess when you see an image you just believe it very easily. Very seldom would I doubt an image, that it would be fake, even when it's taken by an amateur.
>
> (Female, 38 years)

The informants speak of the amateur as an innocent and objective passerby who does not have any preconceptions of the event. She or he just happens to be there; many people carry mobile phones with them and can easily snap a photo on the spot. This is to prove that the photo is immediate. The respondent quoted above affirms the indexical quality of and her measured trust in the images in general by saying: 'I guess when you see an image you just believe it very easily'. In the next citation we are looking at another amateur news photo from the scene of a car accident (Image 1). The informant answers to the question on whether an amateur's news images are as trustworthy as a professional's images:

> They could be even more trustworthy. When a person happens to show up in a place and takes such a picture, I could think that a normal person – I mean, not a professional photographer – takes a photo and does not go to do any retouching. That s/he would just send it to the news desk as such. This is how I imagine it happens. [...] A person just snaps a photo and sends it in, and that's it. I would trust people's own pictures even more. This must be an authentic car accident. It certainly is.
>
> (Female, 38 years)

Comparing the Contextual Elements as Basis of Trust

The contextual frame of trust exemplifies trust as a relationship and a complicated process which is constantly negotiated and contested. In the frame of contextual trust the interviewees evaluate and compare the various elements of the image, the paper, media and the whole society in general. A trusting relationship with the news image is constructed through the intertextual context. This is illustrated in the interviews when the informants compare a news image to another news image or to an advertisement, film or art image. The news images of different papers and different media are also compared. In general, trust arises from the authority of the news media. When the informants speak about the trustworthiness of various media they evaluate the national newspaper as the most trustworthy and the tabloids as the least trustworthy. However, it is interesting that the question of the quality of the tabloid media does not arise when talking about non-professional images, even when both the amateur news image examples happened to be from tabloid newspapers. This emphasizes the high investment of trust in amateur images.

The question of comparing amateur images with images produced by professional photographers already presupposes a frame of contextual trust. Most of the informants would also respond in the frame of contextual trust that they regard amateur images equally trustworthy as images produced by professional photographers.

One of the informants states that she has done some photographing herself, and says that one can also make photographs appear authentic through bad quality. She is expressing the frame of contextual trust by comparing the photo to her earlier experience of news photos. She says that it is possible that newspaper photographers stage seemingly authentic images.

Yet she speaks in the frame of contextual trust, placing value on the high trustworthiness of the reader's images:

> I've come across bluffing with an unfocused image. But I don't know if I would suspect at all that this kind of a reader's image could be manipulated. I could even take it to be more trustworthy than a technically high-quality newspaper image. Yes, I would. When one knows that the car in a formula race has crashed against the bank five minutes ago one knows nobody can possibly have had the time to stage it.
>
> (Female, 53 years)

In the contextual frame of trust the informants talk about the differences between the preconceptions or attitudes that amateur and professional photographer may have. The informants show their media literacy when talking about the process of photographing and editorial selection of news images. They say that professionals choose a certain point of view for their photographs and, in doing so, they discard other points of view. In contrast, the informants suppose that amateurs do not think or select certain angles: 'They just take the picture as they see it in front of them, and in that sense they can be a bit more trustworthy' (male, 46 years).

Professional photographers are seen as being more skillful in processing the image, while ordinary people are not as equipped. Moreover the professional is seen as more skillful in choosing the angle and thereby s/he is capable of encoding certain preferred readings into the image. This undermines the immediacy and authenticity of the professional's photograph in the informant's view. They also say that the professional has the skill to process a photo unnoticeably:

> I would think that when a layperson takes a photo, she/he takes it as it is. You don't manipulate or stage it. Not everyone is like those image processing hackers who know how to do it. And then sell the photo, it seems very unlikely. The professionals can, they have the skill, to choose the angles.
>
> (Male, 62 years)

The amateur is seen as someone who has just happened to pass by coincidentally, while the professional photographer has been given the assignment and briefing to be on the spot. The informants say that for this reason the professionals may have presumptions connected to their profession, and this directs their way of perceiving what has happened and how it should be photographed. In this sense, also, professional pictures are not considered to be as objective and immediate as amateur images:

> They may have a preset attitude to what they want to do there on the spot, because they have that work experience and some kind of a routine. And so at the moment of taking the picture the photographer has intentionally decided, this is the kind of picture I want.
>
> (Male, 41 years)

In comparing the work of amateur and professional photographers, the informants only rarely afford more trust to professional photographers in their comments. We can find a few comments defending the proficiency of professional photographers. The informants say that professionals might be able to get pictures of higher quality which could better convey the news message and ambience of an event. One interviewee says: 'A professional can bring the emotions out better than just some random guy. The professionals aim to look for some deeper causes behind the events' (female, 23 years). The interviewees note that the professionals may be able to process the images better than ordinary people, but they are also supervised and controlled by the news desk where they work. One of the informants says that amateur images are not suitable as main images for news stories. He says that it would be 'Ok to have another complementary picture from another angle which is taken by the amateur, but not as the single photo' (male, 35 years). This contextual comparison of news images produced by professional and amateur photographers already overlaps with the frame of doubt, as the respondent suspects the authority of the amateur image.

The Erosion of Trust

Most of the time, the informants speak about the amateur images in terms of affording them various frames of trust. But sometimes there are also explicit and spontaneous expressions of doubt. On the basis of observations produced by the cues in the images, the informants also seem to regard them in a somewhat uncanny or controversial light. Two main objects of doubt can be identified in the study. Firstly, the informants talk about their doubt related to the content of the image, or the choice of images and their purposefulness. Secondly, they speak doubtfully rergarding the veracity of the image, i.e whether it might have been digitally altered after the photograph was shot. In the framing of doubt there are several arguments. The interviewees raise the ethical dilemma of payment. They question the practice that amateurs receive payment for sending photos to news rooms. Another main cause of doubt is surveillance. The interviewees express their worry that voyeurism in various forms will increase as papers spur people on to send in pictures.

In the frame of doubt the reader's image is regarded with reservation and even open distrust. Some interviewees say they have doubts about all news images and it does not make any difference whether they have been taken by professional or amateur photographers. They say that in both categories there can be both honest photographers and those who process the images. 'This has gone all wild, anything can be retouched. This image could be one of those famous cut and paste Photoshop things as well', says an informant (female, 48 years).

The ethics of photojournalism features prominently in the respondents' talk. They note that today amateurs also may have the capabilities and suitable software for digital image processing. This is illustrated in the following quote:

It is so hard to say, I don't trust the ordinary readers either and don't think they would always be truthful either. The truth is in their eyes, of course. And it is possible that some people manipulate images and then send them to the paper, but I don't think it is very common. Or why not, since there are so many of those computer freaks, they can do whatever they like.

(Female, 61 years)

The informant continues to deliberate whether amateurs follow similar ethics as professionals. She defends the professionals for their proficiency and says that they have high ethical standards. She also suggests that amateur news photo shooting might decrease work opportunities for the professionals: 'The amateurs might eat up their bread'. Another informant poses another ethical question: he is doubtful about how effectively the news desk is able to control the amateur photos and whether the amateurs are held accountable for their photos. In the following extract we are looking at a reader's photo of a car accident in which the name of the photographer is indicated in very small writing in the right corner of the photograph, but the informant does not notice it:

This is a reader's image. And it does not say who the reader who shot the picture is. S/he is not accountable for the picture. But a professional photographer is accountable for what s/he shoots and what s/he does with it. Here I think this image is on Metro's account, and they would not notice it if the photographer had manipulated the image. Therefore I think professionals' images are more trustworthy, because this kind of a private photographer has no responsibility. I would think that some names should be stated if a photo like that is taken, or if you get money for it.

(Male, 23 years)

The papers do have different policies about identifying the source of a particular user-generated image. The responsibility of the veracity of the photo rests on the publisher. Journalists and editors-in-chief assure that the amateur images are checked and go through a similar editorial process of verification as any other media content (Pantti and Bakker 2009: 10). In our interviews, in the first image example the name of the amateur photographer was not indicated and in the second one it was barely visible, yet this does not serve as evidence that the images were not vetted.

As it is shown at the end of the previous quote, the motives and ethics of the amateur are sometimes questioned. It is suspected that some people send in photos only in expectation of a reward from the paper. One of the informants said that she is worried about a scenario where people happen to pass by accident scenes and the first thing they do is start shooting photos instead of helping the ones in need. The next interviewee continues the same line of thought by expressing a concern that people may start looking for situations that they could photograph and, moreover, they could even stage accidents or events in order to receive a reward for a photo in the paper:

[I]t is questionable because they are paid for that, and this is a double-edged issue. Some might think, oh yes, now we've found a suitable gold mine, let's shoot a pic. So they are thinking already when taking the picture that they can cash in this way, and the picture is valuable as such. They don't even need to manipulate it. And also, the more common this phenomenon becomes the more people want to take advantage of it. And soon people will come up with the idea that hey, let's stage some situations so that we can get some money. This way the trustworthiness erodes.

(Male, 41 years)

Another argument for doubting readers' images was the question of citizen surveillance. This means that the papers are encouraging people to watch over each other and take photos. Surveillance is also an ethical question and it can be seen both in positive and negative terms. One informant points out how it is important for citizens to watch over authorities' actions, presenting an example of a situation where bouncers beat up a man thrown out of a bar and a passerby captured this on mobile phone video. On the other hand the surveillance is seen as threatening when citizens are urged to keep an eye on each others' doings. The informants speak about growing control and the Orwellian Big Brother phenomenon:

It has its good and bad sides that people send these pictures. It creates this 'Big Brother is watching' effect. There may not be video cameras everywhere, but there's always someone with a cell phone camera, which increases the control.

(Female, 38 years)

Conclusion

In general, our respondents articulate amateur news images as equally trustworthy or even more trustworthy than photos taken by professional photographers. In only a few comments professional photos were considered more trustworthy. The interviewees afford a significant degree of tacit trust and measured trust to news images in general, too. As it is based on only 30 qualitative interviews, the result cannot be generalized more widely. However, it is evident that the result reflects prevailing and essential aspects of readers' articulations of amateur news photographs.

The talk about amateur images evolves mostly within the frames of silent trust, measured trust and contextual trust. The respondents' main argument for the trustworthiness of reader's images is that they provide immediate and authentic testimony to that the photographer has been on the spot (Zelizer 2005, cf. Williams et al. in this book). The focus group respondents of Williams' and his colleagues' study place value on audience content, which is seen as immediate, fresh and authentic. Moreover, it is considered emotionally engaging and democratizing.

Immediacy and authenticity is one possible context for articulating the complex phenomenon of photographic indexicality. When the respondents engage in the articulation, the normally tacit and unspoken indexical quality of the photograph is put into the discourse' (Foucault 1990: 11). It becomes the material evidence of 'having-been-there' where the actual news scene has taken place. The indexical quality – whether articulated or not – is a common, shared denominator of every photographic image. It is also an attribute which renders the photograph beyond the amateur/professional distinction and helps newsrooms to accept amateur photographs without considerable doubt. For the amateur photojournalist, indexicality serves as a ticket to the realm of professional journalism. The medium is a message, indeed!

However, even if the amateurs may have their contents published in mainstream media, they do not have any command over the journalistic work process itself. The tasks of selecting, framing and final digital editing are still in the hands of the professionals. Amateurs are, literally, content providers. The fact sets certain limits to the expectations that amateur images would provide a non-conventional view, an 'outlaw vision' (see Pantti and Bakker 2009: 2).

In the frame of contextual trust the respondents evaluated the amateur news photographs in relation to professional photos. First, some respondents insisted that professionals always choose a certain point of view to their photographs, whereas amateurs 'just take pictures' without giving very much consideration to the meanings of the image. Secondly, some of the respondents emphasized the coincidental nature of amateur images, in contrast to the assignment and briefing of professional photojournalists. Thirdly, some of the interviewees also brought up the lack of professional skills as a distinctive feature of amateurs. The question of trust is entangled with these differences in a very subtle and complicated manner. In general, the respondents express trust in the established media organizations because they are professional, expert-led institutions. However, at the level of journalistic practices, this professionalism is articulated differently. Amateur news photographs are trustworthy just because they lack certain professional qualities, such as pre-planning, assignment, briefing and skilled image editing. Spontaneity, coincidental snapshot quality and unskilled photography practice are articulated to support the trustworthiness of amateur images.

The interesting point in the respondents' discussion is that they did not articulate the medium as a contextual factor which could have some effects on the trustworthiness of amateur images. When the respondents discussed – in the frame of contextual trust – the trustworthiness of different media, they ranked the national newspaper as the most trustworthy and the tabloids as less trustworthy. However, respondents did not ponder on the question in relation to our example photographs, some of which happened to be from tabloids. The silence around the issue does not mean that it does not have any relevance to the trustworthiness of amateur photographs. However, according to our interpretation, the silence could be one more indication of the indexical power of the photographic image. The respondents looked at the photographs as indexical pictures, not as photographs published in a specific medium.

The amateur images also evoke doubt and distrust to some degree. The expressions of doubt are articulated often through the questions of ethics, responsibility and surveillance. The respondents expressed a worry over the increase of citizen surveillance where people are conditioned to watch over each other. The interviewed audience members, then, do not see the aspect of surveillance as an empowering dynamic, like some contemporary scholars do, but merely as oppression. In contrast, scholars have written about citizen surveillance in terms of bringing transparency to the workings of the state, businesses and organizations and making them operate in a more responsible way (e.g. Häyhtiö and Rinne 2008). Amateur images may serve as evidence to reveal, for example, misuses of public property or misconducts of authorities.

In our study, in the context of amateur news images, there was much talk about the authenticity and immediacy of the image, which was based on the non-professional quality and origin of the photographs. This was also recognized in Coleman et al.'s (2009) study where some focus group participants seemed to be asking for 'untreated' news: 'They claim to want to remove the intermediary role of storytellers and opinion shapers, leaving the public to produce its own news narratives' (pp. 10–11). However, Coleman and his fellow researchers were doubtful about how many of their informants really were ready to 'go to the trouble of shifting through and deciphering the entire news feed' (ibid.). The theme of authenticity also reflects a more profound cultural condition in which authenticity works as a part of late modern life politics (Giddens 1992), where people are looking for original, authentic experiences and lifestyles. Hence, the trust in reader's photographs resembles the trust people have in locally produced food or local grocery stores, which are closer, more intimate and trustworthy.

References

Bentele, G. (2008), 'Trust of Publics', in W. Donsbach (ed.), *The International Encyclopaedia of Communication*, Oxford, UK and Malden: Blackwell-Wiley, pp. 5180–84.

Bowman, S. and Willis, C. (2003), *We Media: How Audiences are Shaping the Future of News and Information*. The Media Center at the American Press Institute, Thinking paper, http://www.hypergene.net/wemedia/download/we_media.pdf. Accessed 21 August 2010.

Coleman, S., Anthony, S. and Morrison, D. E. (2009), *Public Trust in the News: A Constructivist Study of the Social Life of the News*, Oxford: Reuters Institute for the Study of Journalism.

Couldry, N. (2008), 'Mediatization or Mediation? Alternative Understandings of the Emergent Space of Digital Storytelling', *New Media Society*, 10: 3, pp. 373–91.

Doane, M. A. (2007), 'The Indexical and the Concept of Medium Specificity', *Differences*, 18: 1, pp. 128–52.

Foucault, M. (1990), *Power/Knowledge: Selected Interviews and Other Writings 1972–1977* (ed. G. Colin), New York: Pantheon Books.

Harwood, R. C. (2004), 'In Search of Authenticity: Public Trust and the News Media', *National Civic Review*, 93: 3, pp. 11–15.

Giddens, A. (1990), *The Consequenses of Modernity*, Cambridge: Polity Press.

Giddens, A. (1992), *The Transformation of Intimacy: Sexuality, Love and Eroticism in Modern Societies*, Cambridge: Polity Press.

Goffman, E. (1974), *Frame Analysis: An Essay on the Organization of Experience*, New York: Harper & Row.

Hall, S. (1996), 'Encoding/Decoding', in P. Morris and S. Thornton (eds), *Media Studies: A Reader*, New York: New York University Press, pp. 51-61

Häyhtiö, T. and Rinne, J. (2008), 'Seeking the Citizenry on the Internet – Emerging Virtual Creativity', In T. Häyhtiö and J. Rinne (eds), *Net Working/Networking: Citizen Initiated Internet Politics*, Tampere: Tampere University Press, pp. 11–38.

Hermida, A. and Thurman, N. (2008), 'A Clash of Cultures: The Integration of User Generated Content within Professional Journalistic Frameworks at British Newspaper Websites', *Journalism Practice*, 2: 3, pp. 343–55.

Luhmann, N. (1988), 'Familiarity, Confidence, Trust: Problems and Alternatives', in D. Gambetta (ed.), *Trust: Making and Breaking Cooperative Relations*, Oxford: Blackwell, pp. 94–107.

Matikainen, J. (2009), *Sosiaalisen ja perinteisen median rajalla* ('At the Border of Social Media and Traditional Media'), Department of Communication, Research Reports 3/2009, Helsinki: University of Helsinki.

Mäenpää, J. and Seppänen, J. (2010), 'Imaginary Darkroom. Digital Photo Editing as a Strategic Ritual', *Journalism Practice*, 4: 4, pp. 454–75.

Pantti, M. and Bakker, P. (2009), 'Misfortunes, Sunsets and Memories: Non-professional Images in Dutch News Media', *International Journal of Cultural Studies*, 12: 5, pp. 471–89.

Peirce, C. S. (1960), *Collected Papers of Charles Sanders Peirce*, Vol. 2, Cambridge: Belknap Press of Harvard University Press.

Seligman, A. (1997), *The Problem of Trust*, Princeton: Princeton University Press.

Rosanvallon, P. (2008), *Counter–Democracy: Politics in an Age of Distrust* (trans. A. Goldhammer), New York: Cambridge University Press.

Rose, G. (2007), *Visual Methodologies: An Introduction to the Interpretation of Visual Materials*, second edition, London: Sage.

Tsfati, Y. (2008), 'Journalists, Credibility of', in W. Donsbach (ed.), *The International Encyclopedia of Communication*, Oxford, UK and Malden: Blackwell Publishing.

Tsfati, Y. and Cappella, J. (2003), 'Do People Watch What They Do Not Trust? Exploring the Association between News Media Scepticism and Exposure', *Communication Research*, 30: 5, pp. 504–29.

Vanacker, B. and Belmas, G. (2009), 'Trust and the Economics of News', *Journal of Mass Media Ethics*, 24: 2–3, pp. 110–26.

Wahl-Jorgensen, K., Williams, A. and Wardle, C. (2010), 'Audience Views on User-Generated Content: Exploring the Value of News from the Bottom Up', *Northern Lights*, 8: 1, pp. 177–94.

Zelizer, B. (2005), 'Journalism through the Camera's Eye', in S. Allan (ed.), *Journalism: Critical Issues*, New York: Open University Press.

Zelizer, B. (2007), 'On "Having Been There": "Eyewitnessing" as a Journalistic Key Word', *Critical Studies in Media Communication*, 24: 5, pp. 408–28.

Chapter 11

'More Real and Less Packaged': Audience Discourses on Amateur News Content and Their Effects on Journalism Practice

Andy Williams, Karin Wahl-Jorgensen and Claire Wardle

News organizations increasingly view audience-produced material as a vital resource. It allows them to give the impression of democratizing journalism and strengthening the public sphere. More pragmatically it also offers a valuable way of securing stronger 'brand loyalty' (Jenkins 2006: 254; Vujnovic et al. 2010: 287); it gives them access to new and possibly newsworthy material; and it can subsidize the news by providing cheap content (Deuze and Marjoribanks 2009). Researchers have investigated the production practices and journalistic cultures surrounding audience material but have paid less attention to the audiences who produce and consume the content. This chapter seeks to fill this gap in knowledge, at least partially, by drawing on a representative survey of the UK population and a series of focus groups designed to understand whether or not, and for what reasons, audiences value the use of amateur audio-visual material in mainstream news coverage.

We find that audiences very much like news-based audio-visual material produced by amateurs, and although not many have actually contributed before, large numbers see themselves as potential 'citizen reporters'. One of the major reasons for these high levels of audience approval for the inclusion of amateur content lies in the fact it is perceived to be authentic, more 'real' and less 'packaged' than news produced solely by journalists. Much of this sense of realism and authenticity also derives from the often emotive and emotional nature of citizens' contributions to the news. We then begin to discuss some of the broad ideological implications of these emergent audience discourses on amateur content. Our findings suggest that in some respects this way of understanding active audiences' contributions to participatory media forms can have a democratizing effect by challenging traditional hierarchies between producers and consumers of news. However, such discourse about the added realism afforded by the incorporation of amateur content can also limit the scope of citizen participation in news production. It allows journalists the opportunity to recuperate the participatory potential of audience content as one of the strategic rituals of newswork and to cement their power as designated producers of knowledge about society.

The rise of what mainstream journalists usually call user-generated content (UGC) is often described by commentators and practitioners as part of a larger set of trends significantly changing journalism by disrupting traditional relationships between reporters and audiences (e.g. Deuze, Bruns and Neuberger 2007). This should also be viewed in the light of a longer historical trajectory of news organizations seeking to connect with audiences, often explicitly cast in terms of participatory and egalitarian ideals. Most famously, the public journalism movement, which started in the United States in the 1980s, was linked to concerns about the health of public life and citizen engagement, and sought to rethink the relationship between journalists and the people on the basis of increased dialogue and participation. But critics often pointed out the limited participatory potential of these activities. For example, Heikkilä and Kunelius (1996) commented that in order to truly realize the ideal of an active public, 'people would [have to] be active in the process of producing journalism' (p. 91).

It is still unclear whether the rise of UGC has led to a profound transformation of journalism practices and, by extension, significantly democratized audience participation in newswork or created stronger links between journalists and active citizens in public life. Some practitioners and academics have suggested that UGC can and ought to transform journalism practices (e.g. Horrocks 2008), arguing that the increasing centrality of UGC has redefined aspects of the relationship between journalists and audiences (Beyer et al. 2007) and changed newsroom hierarchies (Erdal 2009). Elsewhere, however, research has struck a more cautious note in observing the enduring nature of conventional journalistic practices and hierarchies (e.g. Singer 2009; Singer and Ashman 2009; Williams, Wardle and Wahl-Jorgensen 2010). For instance, Jane Singer has written about how mainstream media have 'normalised' participatory formats until they become subsumed within 'traditional journalistic norms and practices' (2005: 173). As Henrik Örnebring (2008) elaborates in his study the ways in which tabloids enable UGC, much participation tends to be limited to consumer-oriented sections and features, leaving little space for more substantive contributions. Here we address these issues in relation to amateur audio-visual content with a particular emphasis on how it is talked about by audiences, a category which is frequently neglected within journalism studies (cf. Madianou 2009) and in research on new media technologies, which tends towards a heavy emphasis on news production rather than reception.

Study

The material discussed here is drawn from a large multi-method Knowledge Exchange research project funded by the UK Arts and Humanities Research Council (AHRC) and the BBC on the BBC's use of UGC. Carried out in 2007–08, it is based primarily on the findings of a representative survey of the UK population designed to gather data on attitudes to UGC in the mainstream news media, and a series of focus groups with strategically chosen sets of people representing a range of key demographics in terms of class, age and levels of socio-political activism, selected to be broadly in line with the makeup of the UK population overall. It also draws in part on interviews conducted during a multi-sited ethnographic observation carried out at ten BBC newsrooms.

Our survey, which employed quota sampling, was designed by the Cardiff research team and carried out by Ipsos MORI between 29th November and 7th December 2007. A total of 944 adults over the age of 16 were interviewed in their own homes. The data were weighted to the known British population profile, with 184 sample points across Britain. Ten focus group interviews were completed with people who were not active contributors of news content, and two with people who were active in different ways. Groups consisted of between four and ten participants, and a total of 100 people attended discussions overall. Discussions were designed to explore: whether or not and why participants value different kinds of audience content in news output across platforms; whether they might participate in the future; possible motivations for and barriers against participation; perceptions of those who do participate; and comparisons of attitudes to different forms of public participation in the news.

Finally, our newsroom observations were designed on the basis of awareness of the complexity caused by the sheer size of the BBC as the largest broadcaster in the world. We conducted multi-sited newsroom observations with a team of five Cardiff University academics spending a total of 38 days in different newsrooms at the BBC at the Network, regional, and local level and across platforms of news delivery. Access to newsrooms was facilitated by the fact the BBC co-funded our work along with AHRC in the United Kingdom. Researchers spent time at the following locations: BBC Devon Plymouth (ten days); BBC Wales Cardiff (five days); BBC Sheffield (ten days); BBC Leeds (three days); the UGC Hub (six days); *BBC Breakfast* (one day); *News 24* (one day); World Service *Newshour* and *World Have Your Say* (one day); and the BBC College of Journalism 'Have They Got News For Us?' course at BBC Wales, Cardiff (one day). The journalists we cite in this chapter were interviewed during observations at BBC regional television newsrooms.

Realism, Emotion, and the Democratizing Effects of Amateur Content

Our survey results show that a large majority of people think it is 'a good thing that news organisations are using material sent in by the public now more than they used to'. Almost two-thirds of those polled agreed (72%), and only 5% disagreed. When we asked whether people think it is a good thing that 'the public have a bigger role in the production of the news than previously' six out of ten people agreed. By comparison the numbers of those who disagree are tiny; only one in ten people said they disagree that public involvement in news production is a good thing. We also sought to determine whether people would be prepared to act as 'citizen reporters', and send in material to news organizations when presented with the opportunity. We composed a hypothetical scenario for survey respondents in order to determine what proportion of the public would be likely to contact the media when faced with a newsworthy event. Respondents were asked to imagine they were on a quiet road near a town centre when a large fire and explosion breaks out in a nearby factory. The example was based around a real 'UGC story' encountered during our ethnographic observation of BBC news online journalists in Leeds. It was decided not to present survey respondents with a story of national or international significance, such as a terrorist attack because we were more interested in determining people's likely responses to less high-profile, yet nonetheless visually arresting, incidents in order to limit possible social desirability bias in responses. Our results show that almost one in ten members of the public would contact the media when faced with such an incident. And 4% of the people would tip off the media when faced with such a fire, and 6% would video or photograph the scene and send the results to a news organization. We also found that 8% would photograph or video the blaze for their own use and not contact the news media.

The grounds for this widespread appreciation of the use of eyewitness photographic and audio-video material in BBC news were examined in our focus group interviews. The reasons given are complex but in large part revolve around notions of realism and authenticity along with associated notions of expertise. One of the primary reasons BBC news audiences like such material is because it is seen as 'more real and less packaged' than news produced solely by reporters. This perception of increased realism is closely linked to the idea that such news is more immediate (allowing early coverage before news teams can be on the scene), and that it adds drama and human emotion to a cultural form which is often understood to be dry and distanced from 'ordinary people'. Most of sessions were marked by the prominent and repeated presence of discourses around the realism of eyewitness content. One group which epitomized this attitude was a collection of over-65-year olds from a Cardiff day centre, and another was a group of young students. When shown examples of eyewitness photographs and video from the national and regional television news the following exchanges ensued:

Glenys:	That's real life that is.
	[...]
Researcher:	Are you saying that because people are sending in their own news like that
	[...]
Glenys:	It's more real.
Rosina:	Yeah. That's it, yeah. (FG 4)
Becca:	But isn't it like, getting, at different interesting take on the news? Getting real people to give their views, rather than just getting a journalist's point of view, you get members of the public's point of view. Which is kind of like, who the people watching it are. Just your average Tommy Bloggs on the street.
Freema:	And I think it adds a little bit of authenticity to it. Rather than it being a person who is placed there, it's the people who're already there.
Chris:	It makes it, like, more real. (FG 2)

The creation of realistic, authentic, narratives, images and characters is central to factual programming (Thornborrow 2001). In Annette Hill's (2005: 176) study of reality television viewers, she found that audiences looked for '"moments of authenticity" when the performance breaks down and people are "true" to themselves' (see also Aslama and Pantti 2006). Work on broadcast talk has described 'authentic' forms of public discourse as ones in which 'traces of performance are effaced or suppressed' (Montgomery 2001: 98). The more fresh and spontaneous an appearance is considered, the more 'truthful', or real, it seems. Moreover, many of our respondents implied the emotional depth of personalized storytelling has a normative element insofar as it incites empathy and compassion and allows us to see the world through they eyes of 'ordinary people'. This is often contrasted with the professional and distanced approach of the journalist.

It is telling that participants compare the information they get from trained journalists unfavourably with the footage filmed by what one pensioner termed an 'ordinary person like me'. It was common to hear audience content being favourably compared with news solely produced by journalists. The fact that content came from the perspective of ordinary people made many feel that it was a significant advantage and made for a far more 'realistic' representation of events than they would have normally got. When faced with amateur images of severe flooding in the United Kingdom, two Women's Institute members expressed a comparable sentiment:

Esther:	I mean, that poor lady with her furniture [...] her video told more than [...]
Rose:	Yes, yes, yes, yes, yes. That's right.
Bertha:	That was reality.
Researcher:	Reality?
Bertha:	Yes, that's the way it is. That is the word. Reality. It really hits you. (FG 6)

This comparison of realistic, authentic footage from the public with distanced, staged news from professional journalists was taken further by a student focus group participant who claims that amateur footage allows the audience access to a more unmediated version of events than the news as it has traditionally been conveyed:

Bobby:	It almost seems more authentic in a way than, sort of, prearranged, with a presenter standing in front of a camera. Because it seems like that was the immediate reaction before the news crews got there. [...] I know there was a lot of this kind of thing around the 7/7 bombings and in a way, for me that was, I thought that was the best kind of coverage because there you were getting the perspective of someone who was very [...] if not directly involved with, then almost immediately involved with all the destruction that went on. And in a way that is a better way of conveying news I think, than having a really mediated and official, sort of, news report. (FG 1)

This assumption of realism has serious implications for the public's perceptions of the trustworthiness of the news. Far from fearing that increased use of amateur content might lead to lapses in the accuracy of reporting (as many journalists do), audience members value the (often multiple) alternative perspectives on unfolding events afforded by increased use of eyewitness material. The implication here is that the inclusion of amateur material mitigates a lack of public trust in the institution of journalism. There is clearly a feeling that if something has been filmed, photographed or reported on by a member of the public this makes it somehow more believable. Such perspectives, which value the credibility of 'ordinary people' over the slickness of the 'experts' – in this case, trained journalists – mirror the comments of television talk show audiences studied by Livingstone and Lunt (1994) in their classic work on the genre. They found that such shows subvert mainstream culture's reliance on expert knowledge. In the context of these shows, the personal stories of ordinary individuals and their victories and problems told in everyday language are deemed more authentic, legitimate and valuable than the abstracted discourse of experts. Expert testimony is rejected because it is seen as 'unreal', cold, disembodied and distant.

Audience members also tend to value the immediacy afforded to news items which incorporate eyewitness user-generated material, a factor which is bound up with an increased sense of the 'realism' of a piece. One group of students was impressed by how UGC can provide fast access to breaking news which gives an 'insider' feel that eyewitness material affords the viewer. They value how audience content gives an alternative, and more dramatic, insight on events normally covered by professional crews who may not have witnessed a news event occurring and unfolding:

David: Instant access, it's faster than getting a crew down there.

Susan: It can be quite dramatic too, if you were a reporter you would probably be outside the event, so being able to see first-hand inside is good and adds value to the news item.

[…]

Tim: I like the way it gives the opportunity for us to see what actually happened, rather than rather more boring footage of two hours after the main event when the news crews actually arrive. I mean […] the drama of the event makes it more interesting than just someone speaking the events to the viewer. (FG 11)

This emphasis on the increased drama of news which incorporates amateur material also often included reference to the emotional impact of viewing news events from the perspective of those affected, or those who are direct witnesses. One participant was particularly impressed with a piece of mobile phone footage sent in by a school pupil to the *Look North* regional television news which depicted her school bus slowly filling up with water during the floods of summer 2007:

Flo: It's more dramatic, you know, I think. Like the bus video was really good. When you hear all the screaming, you sort of felt a bit, […] you did feel like it was a big deal with these people that were going through it. (FG 2)

Such approval emerged especially strongly during the different groups' discussions of a piece of home video footage taken by a Sheffield woman whose house had been flooded. In the package the woman films the waterlogged ground floor of her house, and also captures a torrent of water flowing down her street as she films from her upstairs window. A group of Lions Club members summed this up:

Gilbert: It really does hit you when you see people's homes being [...] you know? It
           brings it home what the flooding was all about actually.
           [...]
Faith: I thought the woman's distress, though, stops you in your tracks really.
Gilbert: She was about to break down wasn't she?
Faith: It was quite upsetting, I thought. (FG 10)

Another group discussed in depth the empathy invited by news packages which include audience footage of extraordinary events. Again, they contrast the poignancy of this footage with the cold detachment, they imagine, a professional journalist would bring to the coverage of the same story:

June: Well I think that a professional person couldn't feel like that woman,
           because it's her home, so she's giving a more accurate [...] she's bringing it
           home to you more than if it was a professional person in her house.
Juliet: That's really important actually, I never thought of it like that. The person
           behind the camera is feeling all of those things, and you are seeing it literally
           through her eyes [] what's important to them, like.
June: It's her stuff. [...] it's hers, and she's worked and saved, and it's a place where
           she lives. And if a professional man was in there he could feel upset for the
           woman but it wouldn't come across like that.

Figure 11.1: Amateur footage of a flood-damaged home aired on BBC regional television news programme *Look North*, summer 2007. Permission to reproduce granted by BBC Look North.

Figure 11.2: An eyewitness records severe flooding from her bedroom window, broadcast on BBC regional television news programme *Look North*, summer 2007. Permission to reproduce granted by BBC Look North.

Christopher: It's not as emotive by any stretch of the imagination if it's professional footage.

[...]

June: It's a job to him isn't it? He's there to get the news over. (FG 8)

In contemporary public debate, the authority of the 'deep personal' experience often trumps that of specialized professional or political knowledge of the facts surrounding an issue, because the personal angle is seen as more authentic, more real. Such judgements often assume that people can only speak truthfully about matters of personal experience (e.g. Livingstone and Lunt 1994). In the context of a variety of participatory genres, such assessments form the basis for a valorization of the perspectives of 'ordinary people' and a dismissal of experts and figures of authority (including journalists), who are seen as less truthful. For although the media are the key source of our collective truths, there is also a widely held belief that access to media power corrupts individuals and groups, making their contributions *less* truthful. As such, the valuing of 'realistic' and authentic audience content can be seen as a democratic and normatively driven impulse which assumes that 'good' content has less to do with conventional journalistic values and production practices, and more to do with its ability to generate compassion in the viewer.

Figure 11.3: Local resident Mike Easdown was on hand to take this photograph of the Gatecrasher nightclub fire in Sheffield in 2007. It was later published on the BBC Local Sheffield and South Yorkshire website. Permission to reproduce granted by BBC Nations and Regions and Mike Easdown.

But the democratic and democratizing impulse implied by this way of understanding the role of the audience is limited in its scope. This implicit challenge to the power of journalists as privileged truth-tellers cannot be understood solely as a boon to the participatory potential of media audiences. In characterizing the use of audience images as they do, audiences might also be seen to curtail the depth of their engagement with the journalistic production process, limit the nature of their contributions to the news and (somewhat paradoxically) strengthen the power of journalists. In order to unpick and explain this problem we must explore an important epistemological difference between what focus group participants described as the increased 'reality' of news which includes audience images and what scholars have called the 'reality effect' of such content (Pantti and Bakker 2009: 472, Barthes 1986: 141). To do this we must also examine how this way of understanding the role of the audience in news work is situated in relation to journalistic ideologies of news production.

The Limits of Democratization: The 'Reality Effect' and Journalism Practice

Roland Barthes introduces the concept of the 'reality effect' in an essay about the thick description of seemingly inconsequential details in French classic realist fiction. Despite appearances, the novelistic attention to mundane detail characteristic of such fiction does not bring us any closer to reality itself, he argues; instead it acts to obscure the constructed nature of social reality presented by the nineteenth-century novel. This cultural form uses verisimilitude to present itself as a mirror of contemporary reality, but this is a conceptual trick, a 'referential illusion' (1986: 147). The novels are not simple and true representations of reality, but complex constellations of discourses inextricably linked to their historical moments of textual production and the relations of power that form their conditions of existence. Why did the classic realist novel operate in this way? Barthes claims that such textual practice naturalizes and obscures the role of ideology in the construction of the novel by offering instead the illusion of unmediated access to reality. Such verisimilitude allows the novel to efface its 'constructed' nature and hide the fact that it is, in fact, a man-made interpretation of the world which produces and circulates very specific outlooks and values (relating to, for example, nation, gender and class).

Twenty-first-century journalism, like the nineteenth-century novel, is a realist cultural form which generates the effects of reality rather than straightforward representations of reality itself (Graddol 1994: 140). A number of influential studies into news content have shown that news does not (indeed, cannot) offer a neutral presentation of events. It is instead a discursive mediation of real events. As Stuart Hall puts it in his seminal essay on ideology in the news, the media does not hold up a mirror to the world, it 'encodes' or constructs reality:

Reality exists outside language, but it is constantly mediated by and through language: and what we can know and say has to be produced in and through discourse. [...]

Naturalism and 'realism' – the apparent fidelity of the representation to the thing or concept represented – is the result [...] of a discursive practice.

(Hall 1980: 169)

Writing from a different sociological and theoretical tradition, Gaye Tuchman characterizes the social construction of reality by the news in an analogous way to Hall. When one hears the words 'once upon a time', she suggests, we know that what we are about to hear is a fairy story; likewise, '"Egyptian planes bombed and strafed a Libyan airbase today" is the obvious start of a news story' (Tuchman 1978: 5). She continues:

'Once upon a time' announces that what follows is myth and pretence, a flight of cultural fancy. The news lead proclaims that what follows is factual and hard-nosed, a veridical account of events in the world. But, ultimately, both the fairy tale and the news account are stories. [...] Jack Kennedy and Jack of beanstalk fame are both cultural myths, although one lived and the other did not. Drawing on cultural conventions, members of Western societies impose distinctions between stories about the two men that obscure their shared features of public character and social construction.

(Tuchman 1978: 5–6)

Like classic realist fiction, news is a cultural construct, and like Barthes' Flaubertian novel it also attempts to mask this fact. News seeks to legitimize itself as a mirror on the world: a provider of unrestricted access to reality. It does this largely with reference to the concept of objectivity and with recourse to the journalistic practices designed to ensure it is objective. But journalistic objectivity, far from guaranteeing access to real events, operates as a defensive 'strategic ritual' to guard against accusations of bias (Tuchman 1972), an ideological alibi similar in effect to the kind of thick description and verisimilitude identified by Barthes. Objectivity can act to 'obscure truth instead of revealing it', writes Tuchman (1978: 179). She shows how the journalistic routines which reporters point to as a guarantor of objectivity and professional disinterest (mainly to do with selecting newsworthy events and outsourcing the definition and description of such events to news sources) do not adequately fulfil this role. In fact, they often serve to protect the privileged position of journalists as producers of knowledge, limit the scope of what can and should be described as news and perpetuate existing power structures within the media and wider society. The strategic ritual of objectivity constructs very limited subject positions for producers, news audiences and news sources, all of which can be seen to maintain existing social power relations. The lofty detached realism of the 'objective' journalist takes the form of an 'authoritative account of the state of the world' addressed to a passive audience of consumers rather than an active audience of political participants (Hallin 1985: 140). Likewise the (largely powerful and official) news sources used by journalists to maintain the illusion of objectivity benefit from opportunities to set the news agenda and shape the news which gets published or broadcast. Far from being neutral, then, the routines of news production 'impose a frame for defining and constructing social reality', and they also 'block inquiry by preventing an analytic understanding through which social actors can work to understand their own fate' (Tuchman 1978: 180).

The rise of UGC has no doubt contributed to a certain erosion of the power of the mainstream newsworker, and in limited ways it has put pressure on some of the journalistic routines identified by Tuchman and others. But as stated above, recent research into how reporters use audience material suggests that these changes have not substantially altered key elements of journalism practice and journalistic ideologies. The norms and routines of newswork are extremely durable, and the 'audience revolution' has not significantly changed them at the BBC. As we have argued elsewhere the BBC's institutional approach to eliciting, processing, and broadcasting audience material means that members of the public who submit content are usually treated much more like conventional news sources than collaborating participants in acts of journalism (Williams, Wardle and Wahl-Jorgensen 2010). The audience discourse on the 'realism' of UGC we identify here can in many respects be seen to prop up, as well as challenge, conventional power relations between audiences and journalists. To suggest that images or video from the public can make the news more 'realistic', as many of our focus group participants do, perpetuates the ideology that the news can objectively represent real events as they actually are or were. It implies an uncritical understanding of journalism as 'an enterprise geared to representing an observer-independent reality' (Poerksen 2010: 297) and it limits the role of the audience member in this enterprise to that of a realist adjunct, an accidental witness supplying newsworthy content.

This can be illustrated with reference to the way journalists, rather than audiences, talk about the use of amateur audio-visual content. Like Pantti and Bakker in their study of journalistic discourse on amateur images we found that journalists value the 'perceived authenticity' that amateur images can lend the news. However, they explain that when reporters talk about authenticity they primarily refer to the 'intrinsic *aesthetic* quality of amateur images' and how their often grainy and unfocussed nature merely *signifies* rather than *guarantees* access to the real (2009: 482–83, our emphasis). Many of the BBC journalists we interviewed spoke in analogous terms. A regional television journalist for the Look North regional news bulletin told us how it did not matter that UGC was often of inferior technical quality because the lack of quality was compensated for by the 'feel for the reality of what's going on' (Williams 7 September 2007). Another broadcast journalist was even more explicit about his use of amateur content to enliven conventional news reports and construct the *impression* of authenticity. Firstly, he spoke disparagingly of some of the conventional tools used by journalists when constructing a television news package:

> You can get a really crisp shot of a local councillor sat behind his desk pretending to write a document, when quite obviously he must know that the camera is there. It can be really sharp picture quality, and the audio quality can be superb, but it's bollocks. It just doesn't look real. It's obviously us pretending and sticking to a device that we have used for years.

And for me it's just televisual death. It doesn't mean anything. [...] The traditional way of doing TV news stories, where you have set-up shots, where you have a *vox pop*, where you have a presenter in shot doing his thing, we do those every day over and over again.

(Williams 10 September 2007 interview)

Since the rise of audience content, however, another tool has become available to the journalist. UGC, he continues, 'is different, and it has impact'. Importantly, he does not suggest that audience images actually bring us any closer to real events than his catalogue of pre-existing journalistic techniques. On the contrary, he acknowledges that in time, and if it is used too often, amateur content might itself also become formulaic and stale: 'There might be a time when I'm sitting here saying exactly the same stuff about UGC. That it's tired and boring, and doesn't get to the heart of a story. But right now it's fresh and it looks real, and it gives you insight and emotion' (Williams 10 September 2007 Interview). Our data suggests a subtle but crucial difference between how audiences and journalists characterize the added authenticity afforded by the use of amateur content. Audiences largely talk in unsophisticated terms about how amateur material brings them closer to the 'reality' of events. Journalists, however, align themselves with the more distanced and knowing discourse of 'reality effects'. This acknowledgement of the ways UGC can be used tactically as an instrument in the toolbox of realist news reportage is important because it allows journalists to protect their privileged status as producers of knowledge in the face of unprecedented levels of participation from audiences.

Another limit to the participatory potential of the public to collaborate with journalists in producing the news is signalled by the appreciation we found in audience discourse for the emotional and emotive nature of amateur content. Their celebration of audience content is premised on a relatively circumscribed understanding of how 'ordinary people' can most usefully and meaningfully contribute to the news. Focus group participants clearly appreciate the ability of amateur images to mobilize an emotional public and generate compassion on the basis of perceived authenticity. They also downplay the significance of conventional, detached and distanced journalistic modes of address. On the one hand, this perception clearly challenges some of journalism's normative and practical hierarchies, calling for more inclusion of the personal experiences of the public in news discourse. On the other hand, however, it can also be seen to support and further entrench such hierarchies. The implication is that audiences are welcome to participate as news sources some of the time, but only in limited ways. As we have observed elsewhere our audience research findings suggest a clear difference between the value the public attach to emotive amateur audio-visual content in the news and the esteem in which they hold those who submit opinion-based comment material (Wahl-Jorgensen, Williams and Wardle 2010). Put simply, the public appreciate *emotional* amateur audio-visual content based on first-hand experience of events, but denigrate the importance of audience members who contribute to participatory news forums designed for *rational* debate. Such implicit normative ideals around the importance of emotion and compassion can be seen to structure a peculiarly depoliticized vision of audience participation. This way of understanding the role of the audience relegates the citizen journalist to that of an even more circumscribed bit-part in the realist lexicon of news reportage; that of provider of supplementary emotional and emotive rather than rational and political material.

Conclusion

Our research shows that audiences value the use of amateur audio-visual material in the news for a variety of different reasons, but principal among them is the added realism it can afford. A key factor in contributing to this sense of authenticity is the emotional engagement invited by seeing news events through the eyes of lay populace, and not exclusively through the detached frames conventionally provided by professional newsworkers. This way of understanding the role of amateur audio-visual content can be seen to contribute to the democratization of journalism by stressing the value of introducing material from a wider range of sources than have traditionally been habitually used. It also shows how audience perspectives may provide novel normative frameworks for understanding the value of participatory forms and genres of news. As well as this critical democratizing function, however, this way of conceiving the role of such amateur content can be seen to cement many of the power relations which have traditionally underpinned journalism practice. Indeed, rather than seriously bolstering the role of citizens in producing the news, these ways of understanding the (limited) role of the audience allow journalists to recuperate the participatory potential of the audience in the processes of journalistic production. This can be understood further with reference to the seemingly minor, but actually crucial, differences between the discourses on realism and authenticity employed by journalists and audience members.

Amateur content is desirable to journalists largely because they can use it tactically to construct and tell their stories in new and arresting ways. The use of such content has become a strategic ritual which bolsters the role of news journalism as a realist cultural form. In large part this serves to maintain the power of professional journalists as sanctioned producers of knowledge about society. The potentially democratizing interventions of citizens into the processes of journalism can then be recuperated into an only slightly modified set of journalistic routines and practices. The emphasis on the emotional value of audience material further limits the potential for citizens to participate more meaningfully in this process of knowledge production as they are assigned the circumscribed role of accidental witness, realist adjunct and/or the provider of emotive or emotional, more than rational or political, responses to events. In turn, this strengthens newsroom hierarchies and allows journalists to continue privileging authoritative and elite voices as news sources. Thinking about amateur content in this way ultimately allows journalists to harvest desirable images and footage whilst at the same time limiting and annexing the role of the audience, securing the importance of the journalist, and bolstering the power of official news sources.

References

Aslama, M. and Pantti, M. (2006), 'Talking Alone: Reality TV, Emotions and Authenticity', *European Journal of Cultural Studies*, 9: 2, pp. 167–84.

Barthes, R. (1986), *The Rustle of Language* (trans. R. Howard), Oxford: Blackwell.

Beyer, Y., Enli G.S., Maasø, A. and Ytreberg, E. (2007), 'Small Talk Makes a Big Difference: Recent Developments in Interactive, SMS-Based Television', *Television & New Media*, 8: 3, pp. 213–34.

Deuze, M. and Marjoribanks, T. (2009), 'Newswork', *Journalism* 10: 5, pp. 555-61.

Deuze, M., Bruns, A. and Neuberger, C. (2007), 'Preparing for an Age of Participatory News', *Journalism Practice*, 1: 3, pp. 322–38.

Erdal, I. (2009), 'Cross-Media (Re)Production Cultures', *Convergence*, 15: 2, pp. 215–31.

Graddol, D (1994), 'The Visual Accomplishment of Factuality', in D. Graddol and O. Lloyd-Barrett (eds), *Media Texts: Authors and Readers*, Clevedon: Multilingual Matters, pp 136–59.

Hall, S. (1980), 'Encoding/Decoding', in M. G. Durham and D. Kellner (eds.), *Media and Cultural Studies: Keywords*, Malden: Blackwell, pp. 166-76.

Hallin, D. (1985), 'The American News Media: A Critical Theory Perspective', in J. Forester (ed.), *Critical Theory and Public Life*, Boston: MIT Press.

Heikkilä, H. and Kunelius, R. (1996), 'Public Journalism and its Problems', *Javnost*, 3: 3, pp. 81–95.

Hill, A. (2005), *Reality TV: Audiences and Popular Factual Television.* London: Routledge.

Horrocks, Peter (2008), 'The End of Fortress Journalism', in BBC College of Journalism, *Future of Journalism Conference*, London, UK, 7–8 December, BBC: London.

Jenkins, H. (2006), *Convergence Culture: Where Old and New Media Collide*, New York: NYU Press.

Livingstone, S. and Lunt, P. (1994), *Talk on Television: Audience Participation and Public Debate*, New York: Routledge.

Madianou, M. (2009), 'Audience Reception and News in Everyday Life', in K. Wahl-Jorgensen and T. Hanitzsch (eds), *Handbook of Journalism Studies*, New York: Routledge, pp. 325–57.

Montgomery, M. (2001), 'Defining "Authentic Talk"', *Discourse Studies*, 3: 4, pp. 397–405.

Örnebring, Henrik (2008), 'The Consumer as Producer – of What? User-Generated Tabloid Content in The Sun (UK) and Aftonbladet (Sweden)', *Journalism Studies*, 9: 5, pp. 771–85.

Pantti, M. and Bakker, P. (2009), 'Misfortunes, Memories and Sunsets: Non-professional Images in Dutch News Media', *International Journal of Cultural Studies*, 12: 5, pp. 47189.

Poerksen, B. (2008), 'Theory Review: The Ideal and the Myth of Objectivity', *Journalism Studies*, 9: 2, pp. 295–304.

Singer, J. (2005), 'The Political J-Blogger: "Normalizing" a New Media Form To Fit Old Norms and Practices', *Journalism*, 6: 2, pp. 173–98.

Singer, J. (2009), 'Separation Within a Shared Space: Perceived Effects of User-Generated Content on Newsroom Norms, Values and Routines', in Cardiff University School of Journalism, Media and Cultural Studies, *Future of Journalism Conference*, Cardiff, Wales, 9–10 September, Cardiff University: Cardiff.

Singer, J. and Ashman, I. (2009), '"Comment is Free, But Facts are Sacred": User-Generated Content and Ethical Constructs at the *Guardian*', *Journal of Mass Media Ethics*, 24: 1, pp. 3–21.

Thornborrow, J. (2001), 'Authenticating Talk: Building Public Identities in Audience Participation Broadcasting', *Discourse Studies*, 3: 4, pp. 459–79.

Tuchman, G. (1972), 'Objectivity as Strategic Ritual', *American Journal of Sociology*, 77, pp. 660–79.

Tuchman, G. (1978), *Making News*, New York: Free Press.

Vujnovic, M., Singer, J., Paulussen, P., Heinonen, A., Reich, Z., Quandt, T., Hermida, A. and Domingo, D. (2010), 'Exploring the Political Economic Factors of Participatory Journalism', *Journalism Practice*, 4: 3, pp. 285–95.

Wahl-Jorgensen, K., Williams, A. and Wardle, C. (2010), 'Audience Views on User-Generated Content: Exploring the Value of News from the Bottom Up', *Northern Lights*, 8:1, pp. 177-94.

Williams, A. (2007), Interview, 7 September. (The interviewee wished to remain anonymous).

Williams, A. (2007), Interview, 10 September. (The interviewee wished to remain anonymous).

Williams, A., Wardle, C. and Wahl-Jorgensen, K. (2010), 'Have They Got News for Us? Audience Revolution or Business as Usual at the BBC?', *Journalism Practice*, iFirst: http://www.informaworld.com/smpp/content~content=a921303452~db=all~jumptype=rss. Accessed 4 September 2010.

Contributors

Stuart Allan is Professor of Journalism in the Media School, Bournemouth University. He is the author or editor of fifteen books, including *Digital War Reporting* (co-authored with D. Matheson, 2009), *Citizen Journalism: Global Perspectives* (co-edited with E. Thorsen, 2009), *The Routledge Companion to News and Journalism* (2010) and *Journalism After September 11* (co-edited with B. Zelizer, second edition, 2011). He is currently researching and writing about citizen photojournalism.

Kari Andén-Papadopoulos is Associate Professor at the Department of Journalism, Media and Communication, Stockholm University. Visual culture, news and images in times of crisis and war are her fields of specialization. She has published extensively on the ethics, aesthetics and politics of photojournalism and amateur visual practices related to traumatic news events, such as 9/11 and the Iraq war. She is the author of the forthcoming book *Global Image Wars: Geopolitics and Post-9/11 Visual Culture*.

Karin Becker is Professor of Media and Communication Studies at Stockholm University. Her research examines cultural histories and contemporary contexts of visual media practices, focusing on the press, museum collections and private settings, and critical applications of visual media in ethnographic studies. She serves on the steering committee of the Nordic network of visual studies, an affiliate of the International Visual Sociology Association, and has engaged in studies of visual aesthetic practices in public space collaborating with artists and researchers. She currently leads the research project Changing Places, examining global and local events as mediated through screens – both public and private – in public space. Her co-authored books include *Picturing Politics: Visual and Textual Formations of Modernity in the Swedish Press* (2000) and *Consuming Media* (2007).

Liam Kennedy is Director of the Clinton Institute for American Studies at University College Dublin. He is the author of *Susan Sontag* (1995) and *Race and Urban Space in the American City* (2000) and editor of several books and numerous articles on US culture, media and foreign affairs. He is currently researching a book on photography and US foreign policy. He directs an IRCHSS-funded project titled 'Photography and International Conflict' (www. ucd.ie/photoconflict).

Marguerite Moritz is Professor and UNESCO Chair in International Journalism Education at the University of Colorado, and a former news and documentary producer for NBC. She has served on the board of governors of the National TV Academy, Heartland Chapter, and was a founding member of GLAAD's National Research Advisory Board and a founding board member of the Bent Lens film festival. Her research looks at professional codes and practices in contemporary news and entertainment media. Her analysis of television news imagery surrounding the September 11th attacks appears in *Representing Realities: Essays on American Literature, Art and Culture* (2003). In 2005, she received a National Science Foundation grant to conduct research on media coverage of Hurricane Katrina. Her article 'Covering the News Come Hell and High Water: Journalists in a Disaster' appears in *Learning from Catastrophe* (2006). She wrote, produced and directed the documentary film *Covering Columbine* that examines ethical issues in the coverage of the high school shooting.

Mette Mortensen is Assistant Professor at the Department of Media, Recognition and Communication at the University of Copenhagen. Her book *Kampen om ansigtet. Fotografi og identifikation* (Facial Politics. Photography and identification) is forthcoming in 2011, and she is the co-editor of *Pas. Identitet, kultur og grænser* (Passports: Identity, Culture, and Borders) (2004) and *Geometry of the Face* (2003). She has written numerous articles on photography, war and the media and digital activism.

Ray Niekamp is Assistant Professor in the School of Journalism and Mass Communication at Texas State University-San Marcos. He holds a Ph.D. in Mass Communications from Penn State University. Prior to university teaching, Niekamp worked in television news and developed an interest in the effect new technology has on the news gathering and news presentation process. His current research focuses on the use of new media in broadcast journalism.

Mervi Pantti is Associate Professor at the Department of Social Research, Media and Communication Studies, University of Helsinki. Her research interests include mediated emotions, disaster reporting and participatory journalistic practices, amateur images in particular. Her publications include the forthcoming book *Disasters and the Media* (co-authored with S. Cottle and K. Wahl-Jorgensen, 2011), as well as articles in journals such as *International Journal of Cultural Studies*, *Javnost/the Public*, *European Journal of Communication* and *Media, Culture & Society*.

Liina Puustinen is Research Fellow at the Department of Political and Economic Studies at the University of Helsinki. She has written books and articles on constructions of consumerhood in advertising institutions and audiences' trust in news images. Currently she is working on historical change of the consumer representations in Finnish journalism and advertising. She is editor of the Finnish *Journal of Media and Communication*.

Janne Seppänen is Professor of visual journalism at the School of Communication, Media and Theatre, University of Tampere. His main research areas are visual culture and journalism. He has published five books and over fifty articles. He has also worked as a project leader in many research projects. He is the author of *The Power of the Gaze: An introduction to Visual Literacy* (2006).

Helle Sjøvaag is a Ph.D. candidate at the Department of Information Science and Media Studies at the University of Bergen. Her dissertation investigates the function of journalistic ideology in the context of digitalization. Central to the work is a combination of journalism sociology, social contract theory, media policy perspectives and media economic theory.

Johanna Sumiala is Adjunct Professor at the Department of Social Research, Media and Communication Studies, University of Helsinki. Her main interests are death and media, visual culture, ritual and violence. She is the author of numerous articles and co-editor of books *Implications of the Sacred* (2006) and *Images and Communities* (2007). Her book *Media Rituals: An Introduction to Media Anthropology* was published in Finnish in 2010.

Karin Wahl-Jorgensen is a Reader at Cardiff University's School of Journalism, Media and Cultural Studies. She is the author and editor of numerous books including *Journalists and the Public* (2007) and *Citizens or Consumers?* (2005), and is currently co-writing a book called *Disasters and the Media* (2011).

Claire Wardle is a digital media consultant, trainer and researcher, specializing in journalism, social media and UGC. She currently works with the BBC College of Journalism. She previously worked at the Cardiff School of Journalism, Media and Cultural Studies.

Andy Williams is a Lecturer at Cardiff University's School of Journalism, Media and Cultural Studies. His research interests are media convergence and the rise of user-generated content and the role of PR in the UK media, particularly in science, health and environment news.